Sarmiento's

Travels in the United States

in 1847

Sarmiento's *Travels in the United States in 1847*

TRANSLATION AND INTRODUCTORY ESSAY BY

MICHAEL AARON ROCKLAND

PRINCETON UNIVERSITY PRESS

PRINCETON, NEW JERSEY

1970

L.C. Card No.: 70-113009

I.S.B.N.: 0-691-04602-6

Publication of this book has been aided by the
Rutgers University Research Council
and the Argentine Embassy in Washington.

This book has been composed in
Linotype Baskerville

Printed in the United States of America
by Princeton University Press
Princeton, New Jersey

Second Printing, 1971

For David, Jeffrey, and Keren

Contents

List of Illustrations

Following page 34

Acknowledgments

In the course of this work I have become indebted to many persons and institutions for advice, information, and facilities. I owe the deepest gratitude to the late Alberto Palcos, an Argentine historian who was devoted to bringing about an awareness of and interest in Sarmiento in the United States. He provided much of the inspiration for my translation and essay. Dr. Palcos died in 1965 while participating in the ceremonies at the University of La Plata commemorating the anniversary of Sarmiento's death.

Other Argentines who were especially helpful to me include Dr. Amaranto Abeledo, the historian; Dr. Luis Alfonso, Secretary General of the Academia Argentina de Letras; the late Eugenio Hendler, editor of *Comentario* magazine; the Señoritas Julia and Raquel Ottolenghi, both distinguished Sarmientistas; Dr. Bernardo Lopez Sanabria, Director of the Museo Sarmiento in Buenos Aires; Dr. Daniel Santos, Secretary General of the Biblioteca Nacional; Señor Francisco Fallon, Secretary of the Archivo General de la Nación; Dr. Cesar Guerrero, Director of the Museo Sarmiento in San Juan; and Señora Gertrude Besler Leeds, daughter of one of the American schoolteachers brought to Argentina by Sarmiento.

In addition to the institutions mentioned in association with some of the above gentlemen, I was aided in my research by the Museo Mitre in Buenos Aires; the Biblioteca de Maestros of the Consejo Superior de Educación in Buenos Aires; the library of *La prensa* and the archives of *La nación*, both prominent Buenos Aires newspapers; and the Biblioteca Nacional in Santiago,

Chile, the city where Sarmiento lived during his periods of exile.

I am indebted to many Americans for their advice and encouragement. The late Alice Houston Luiggi, with whom I corresponded from Argentina and whom I visited in New York just prior to her death, was particularly helpful in guiding me to possible repositories of Sarmiento-Mary Mann correspondence. Madaline Nichols was kind enough to send me a copy of her valuable little book on Sarmiento and to make possible my introduction to several Argentines important to my research. Merle Simmons of the University of Indiana gave me several excellent ideas. Milton and Bessie Rockland helped with a particular aspect of my research. But I am particularly indebted to Bernard Bowron and Mary Turpie of the University of Minnesota American Studies Program, who spent many painstaking hours going over my various drafts and corresponding with me about my work while I was living abroad. I would also like to say a word of thanks to two comrades from graduate school days, Grier Nicholl, now with Augsburg College, and Robert Merideth, now with the University of California at Davis, for their advice and moral support while I was working on this book.

American institutions that have aided my research include the Library of Congress, the National Archives, the State Library of Oregon, the Boston Public Library, the Rhode Island Historical Society, the *New York Times* archives, and the libraries of New York University (Washington Square Branch), Harvard, and the University of Minnesota.

While working on this book I had the good fortune to be living in Argentina and Spain, countries, to say the least, very much on Sarmiento's mind. For this circumstance, and for a leave of absence during the fall of 1967, I am grateful to the United States Foreign Service, with which I was then associated.

I am also grateful to the Tozer Foundation of Minneapolis and the Instituto de Cultura Hispanica of Madrid for grants which aided my research and writing.

At Princeton University Press I would like to thank Roy Grisham, who patiently guided the project through the early stages; Linda Peterson, who deserves much credit for whatever quality the writing in this book has; and Jan Lilly for her excellent design.

A last and special acknowledgment is due my wife, Mae Shafter Rockland, who not only provided home environments on three continents conducive to my work under, at times, the most difficult circumstances, but who also was a most perceptive critic of the several drafts and made many valuable suggestions. More important, she has always matched my own enthusiasm for Sarmiento.

M.A.R.

Princeton, New Jersey
October 1969

Introduction

The most startling fact about Domingo Faustino Sarmiento is that virtually no one in the United States has ever heard of him.[1] Sarmiento, who some feel is the outstanding figure in the long history of the many nations of Latin America, and who moreover is the Latin American who most concerned himself with the United States, is unknown to all but a few experts in this country. Not a single work by or about him can be found in most American* bookstores. Only one of his works has been translated into English—a hundred years ago. When foreign commentators on the United States are discussed in university courses, Sarmiento is not among them.

This should not surprise us, since the great men of Latin America, except for a few generals of the revolutionary period, remain anonymous in North America. This is true because Americans have always sought their models and what they have considered their natural cultural alliances in Europe, without imagining that they might have a close cultural affinity with other nations of this hemisphere and their leaders. Americans have regarded Latin America as really just one, very foreign land, extending from the Rio Grande to the Straits of Magellan, teeming with disease and racked by revolution, a cultural backwater unworthy of serious consid-

[1] As one American commentator has said, "Even a superficial knowledge of Sarmiento has long been overdue in North America" (Allison Williams Bunkley, *Sarmiento Anthology* [Princeton, 1948], p. 5).

* Throughout this essay the terms "American" and "the United States" will be employed whenever practical instead of "North American" and "North America." The rationale for this usage will be found in the Notes on the Translation, pp. 110-11.

3

eration. The great cultural, political, social, economic, racial, and geographical differences among the Latin American nations, conflicting as they do with this mono-lithic conception, have been all but ignored.

But when these nations are examined carefully, many similarities between them and the United States are dis-covered. The author of *American Commonwealth*, Lord Bryce, in his less well-known work *South America, Ob-servations and Impressions*,[2] found many parallels be-tween the United States and the Latin American nations and thought that Argentina in particular bore a striking resemblance to the United States, more so than any Eu-ropean nation. Among the parallels between Argentina and the United States pointed out by Bryce are the ex-istence in both nations of great expanses of exploitable land and an almost obsessive literary and mythological interest in the land; an almost identical frontiersman tradition illustrated by the figures of the cowboy and the gaucho; a similar dichotomy of country and city; an almost identical ethnic mixture; a similarly fluid class structure; almost identical constitutional and political structures; and a similarly strong tradition of the separa-tion of church and state. Bryce concluded by calling Ar-gentina "the United States of the Southern Hemi-sphere."[3]

These similarities between Argentina and the United States suggest that not only Hispanists but students of the United States as well have a legitimate interest in Latin America, particularly in Argentina. The similari-ties imply that perhaps the United States is more *Ameri-can* in the hemispheric sense, that is, perhaps it has a closer affinity with other New World nations, than has heretofore been supposed. Perhaps, also, its affinity with

2 (New York, 1912). 3 *Ibid.*

Europe has been overemphasized. After all, no *European* nation has been described as "The United States of Europe." Rich new ideas about our civilization might result from considering it in relation to other American nations; we might find it illuminated from perspectives which have not as yet even been imagined.

This is why the figure of Domingo Faustino Sarmiento is so important to the study of the culture of the United States, for, in addition to being a most representative Argentine (Mrs. Horace Mann once told Sarmiento that he was "not a man, but a nation"),[4] he is also the most important and serious student of the United States that that country and, indeed, Latin America has produced. And more than any other Argentine, Sarmiento dedicated himself to making Bryce's view, that Argentina was the United States of the Southern Hemisphere, a reality.

Though the United States figures prominently in the whole of the *Obras completas*, *Travels in the United States in 1847* is Sarmiento's most complete statement on the United States. It is my hope that with its publication in English *Travels* will assume its rightful place among the great commentaries on the United States written during the last century by foreign visitors to our shores. I believe *Travels* illustrates my contention that there is much rich material to be found by the student of the civilization of the United States in such seemingly out of the way places as along the high peaks of the Andes Mountains and near the waters of the River Plate.

---

[4] Sarmiento, *Obras completas*, 2nd edn. (Buenos Aires, 1948-1956), XLVII, 287. Subsequent references to Sarmiento's *Obras* will be to this edition unless otherwise indicated.

1. Sarmiento and the United States

Domingo Faustino Sarmiento has been described by various authors as "the greatest Spanish American figure of his epoch," "the most striking figure in the eventful Latin American historical drama" of the nineteenth century, and as "perhaps the greatest man of letters in the history of Argentina."[5] Another writer says that, "In the literature of Spanish America . . . [Sarmiento's] figure stands out above all the rest."[6] Another goes further and describes him as "the most powerful brain America has produced."[7] And still another writer goes so far as to claim that "America has not produced another man like him nor does Europe have in its history a personage that resembles him."[8] The father of public education in that part of the world, Sarmiento is often referred to as the Horace Mann of Argentina and of South America, while some insist that because of his dramatic contributions during the period of national unification he is also the Abraham Lincoln of his country.[9]

The great men of the period when the Latin American nations were being formed were usually philosophers or generals, only occasionally both. Sarmiento was that rare combination of thinker and doer, a uni-

[5] Jose de Onís in the Introduction to *Travels; A Selection*, trans. Inés Muñoz (Washington, 1963), p. ix; Allison Williams Bunkley in *The Life of Sarmiento* (Princeton, 1952), p. ix; John A. Crow in *The Epic of Latin America* (New York, 1946), p. 601.

[6] Federico de Onís, *España en América* (Madrid, 1955), p. 125.

[7] Carlos Pellegrini as quoted in W. Rex Crawford, *A Century of Latin American Thought* (Cambridge, Mass., 1961), p. 42.

[8] Ricardo Rojas, *El pensamiento vivo de Sarmiento* (Buenos Aires, 1941), p. 18.

[9] See Jose P. Barreiro, "Paralelo de Sarmiento y Lincoln," *Comentario* (Buenos Aires), VI (October-November-December 1958), 18.

6

versal man, or, as one writer has described him, "a whole world of thought and action."[10] Few men have done so much in their lives and been masters of so many fields on any continent. Sarmiento was Latin America's most outstanding educator, a superb writer and journalist, an influential sociologist and philosopher; and during his long career he was at one time or another a revolutionary leader, a general, an ambassador, governor of a province, senator in the national legislature, a cabinet minister, and president of his country. "In him," as one writer has said, "journalism does not kill the writer, the writer does not kill the teacher, the teacher the statesman, nor the statesman the sociologist and political philosopher. He was all of these at once."[11]

Sarmiento was born in 1811 into a poor family living in the small city of San Juan, which is in the western part of Argentina, against the towering Andes. He liked to say that he was one year younger than the Republic, since 1811 was the year after Argentina declared its independence and initiated actions which ultimately drove the Spaniards from that part of the New World. With independence won, the Republic entered a long period of anarchy during which groups of gaucho ex-soldiers, led by *caudillo* chieftains, roamed the land, ruling by the sword, taking up one cause after another with seeming abandon. It was inevitable that the young Sarmiento should be drawn into these struggles, and because of them a good number of his early years were spent on the move as he ran from one band or another, on one occasion narrowly escaping death at the hands of a lynch mob. These experiences made him decide as

[10] Jose de Onís in the Introduction to *Travels; A Selection*, p. ix.
[11] Alberto Palcos, *Sarmiento* (Buenos Aires, 1962), pp. 277, 278.

a youth to dedicate his life to eradicating the anarchic forces which were pulling his nation apart and which unfortunately continue to do so.

Sarmiento early came to the conclusion that it was the lack of educated and enlightened men which kept Argentina and the rest of South America in what he considered a semisavage state. When Juan Manuel Rosas rose from among the other *caudillos* to become dictator of Argentina in 1829, Sarmiento elected to fight him not only with the sword but with schools, since, he reasoned, "an educated people would never elect a Rosas."[12]

Sarmiento's own education was meager, consisting of several years of elementary education and of reading all the books he could obtain, usually by French authors of the revolutionary period, from the few men in San Juan who had libraries. One book he came across was Benjamin Franklin's *Autobiography*, and after reading it he formed a lifelong attachment to Franklin and determined that he too would be a self-made man. One writer has said that "throughout Sarmiento's future life, Franklin was to be his most important single model,"[13] and there are ninety-five references to Franklin in Sarmiento's *Obras completas* and a Benjamin Franklin library in San Juan, founded by Sarmiento, to attest to this. "I felt as if I were Franklin," Sarmiento was to write in *Recuerdos de provincia* (1850), the charming account of his childhood and youth; "and why not? Like Franklin I was very poor and studious, and I felt that, with luck, and following his example, I might someday succeed in being like him, in obtaining an honorary doc-

[12] Quoted in Allison Williams Bunkley, *The Life of Sarmiento*, p. 446.
[13] Bunkley, *Sarmiento Anthology*, p. 10.

torate and making a place for myself in American letters and politics."[14]

In addition to trying to educate himself as best he could, Sarmiento was as a youth already interested in the education of others. In rural Andean towns on both sides of the frontier with Chile, wherever the fortunes of civil strife led him, he would earn his keep by teaching the village children to read and write. In San Juan, in 1838, he went one step further and, with some friends, enterprisingly founded a small school for girls, the first of many schools he was to be associated with.

A short time later, his outspokenly liberal views made it necessary for him to continue his activities in a more friendly climate, across the Andes from San Juan in Santiago, Chile. He had also founded a small newspaper, *El zonda*, in 1839, and when he proceeded to attack Rosas in its pages he was immediately arrested and released only on condition that he leave the country.

In Santiago, Sarmiento, already a budding educator, was befriended by Manuel Montt, Minister of Education and later President of Chile, who encouraged his recommendations for educational reform. Sarmiento presented a scheme for a revised and simplified spelling of Spanish at the University of Chile, where he was appointed to the Faculty of Philosophy and Humanities. He also published a book on methods of teaching reading, *Método de lectura gradual*, which eventually was used throughout the Chilean elementary school system.[15] But his most significant accomplishment in the educational field during these early years was his founding in 1842 of the Escuela Normal de Preceptoras in Santiago, the first normal school in Latin America, anticipated in

[14] *Obras*, III, 168.   [15] *Obras*, XXVIII, 87-111.

the Western Hemisphere only by the one Horace Mann founded at Lexington, Massachusetts in 1839.

In addition to distinguishing himself as an educator, Sarmiento began in earnest his career as journalist and writer while in Chilean exile. He founded *El progreso*, the first daily newspaper in Santiago, and through its columns entered Chilean political life. This was not the most prudent activity for an alien and a political exile to be engaged in. In the elections of 1841 he came out in favor of the presidential candidate of Montt's party. When this candidate subsequently won, Sarmiento provided a perfect scapegoat for the losing party, which cried for the foreigner's blood. With each passing day his situation in Chile became more difficult.

The precariousness of his position was increased by the attacks he was continually making in the press on his old foe, Rosas. The Argentine diplomatic representatives in Santiago regularly complained to the Chilean government, demanding that his pen be silenced. The Argentines were particularly incensed by the publication in 1845 of Sarmiento's most complete indictment of Rosas, his masterpiece and one of the greatest works in the Spanish language, *Facundo*.[16] In glorious prose, it is the half-fictional, half-historical account of the life of the gaucho tyrant, Juan Facundo Quiroga, Rosas' associate in western Argentina. As a youth, Sarmiento had been ordered whipped and imprisoned by a local representative of Facundo in San Juan, and he later wrote: "In the eighteenth year of my life, I entered a jail and came out with political ideas."[17]

In *Facundo* we find more than political ideas: it contains the most complete statement of Sarmiento's po-

[16] *Obras*, VII.
[17] *Recuerdos de provincia*, *Obras* (1st edn.), III, 154.

10

litical philosophy. The subtitle of the book, *Civilización y barbarie,* suggests its thesis: that Argentina was the site of an age-old struggle between civilization and barbarism; that civilization was represented by rationalism and intellectualism, by a settled life, and by cities, while barbarism was represented by the wilfulness and personalism of the gauchos, by the nomadic life, and by the plains. There were two powers in Argentina: "One of these powers was civilized, constitutional, European; the other barbarous, arbitrary, South American." Rosas and Quiroga he saw as "the climax" of the barbarism of the plains, and he felt that Buenos Aires, "the only city in the vast Argentine territory in communication with European nations . . . would ere now have become the Babylon of America, if the spirit of the pampa had not breathed upon her. . . ." The cities were "small oases of civilization surrounded by an untilled plain" and "the only means of developing the capacity of man," while plains, he felt, "prepare the way for despotism."[18]

The novels of James Fenimore Cooper, especially *The Prairie,* are undoubtedly one of the influences at work in *Facundo.* Sarmiento states at one point in the book that Cooper "is the only North American novelist who has gained a European reputation, . . . and he succeeded in doing so by removing the scene of the events he described from the settled portions of the country to the borderland between civilized life and that of the savage. . . ." This is where the action of *Facundo* takes place and where Sarmiento himself battled for the survival and unification of Argentina. Sarmiento makes several other references to Cooper in *Facundo,* drawing paral-

[18] *Life in the Argentine Republic in the Days of the Tyrants* [English title of *Facundo*], trans. Mrs. Horace Mann (New York, 1961), pp. 108, 27-29.

11

lels between American and Argentine plainsmen and frontiersmen. Also, he is enough of a romantic to have, as did Cooper, an ambivalent attitude toward the barbarism he hoped to overcome. At one point he writes of Rosas: "Yes, he is great, tremendous; for the glory and the shame of his country."[19] These parallels between Sarmiento and Cooper have led at least two Argentine critics to suggest that, more than merely influencing Sarmiento, Cooper's works were instrumental in the development of his basic thesis of civilization versus barbarism.[20] What is certain is that, given his reading of Franklin's and Cooper's works, Sarmiento must have been much more interested in the United States before his first visit there in 1847 than most Argentine historians have supposed.[21]

Spurred by Sarmiento's publication of *Facundo* and his ever-increasing journalistic activities against the Rosas regime, the Argentine government finally requested his extradition to face charges of treason in Buenos Aires. The Chileans, with Manuel Montt arguing for Sarmiento, refused, but it was clear that his continued residence in Chile was putting a strain on Chile's relations with Argentina. This, together with the antagonisms his

[19] *Ibid.*, pp. 33-34, 40.

[20] Antonio de la Torre, in the Introduction to *Estados Unidos*, p. 17; De la Torre mentions that Raul Orgaz holds to this same theory. (All references to *Viajes* are to the three-volume Hachette edition, published in Buenos Aires: *De Valparaiso a Paris* [1955], *España e Italia* [1957], *Estados Unidos* [1959].

[21] For an example of an Argentine historian who feels that Sarmiento was essentially ignorant of the United States prior to his 1847 visit, see Joseph B. Barrager, "Sarmiento y los Estados Unidos," *Historia* (Buenos Aires), VI (April-June 1961) 25. Merle E. Simmons has written an excellent article on Sarmiento's attitudes toward the United States prior to his 1847 visit. See "Los Estados Unidos en el pensamiento de Domingo Faustino Sarmiento antes de su primera visita a Norteamerica," *Revista de historia de America* (Mexico City), Nos. 35-36 (January-December 1953), 59-95.

participation in political life in Chile had occasioned, led Montt, who had begun to fear for Sarmiento's life, to conclude that it would be best for all concerned if Sarmiento left the country for a while. Montt proposed a trip under the auspices of the Ministry of Education to study educational systems on other continents. This was not a charitable gesture, for Montt knew that the trip would be as valuable to Chile as to Sarmiento: Sarmiento would test his educational theories against what he saw and return with ideas for improving the schools of Chile.

Sarmiento was enthusiastic about Montt's proposal. In October of 1845 he sailed from Valparaiso, not to return for two and a half years. During this trip he was to discover new worlds to bring back to South America and, further, he was to form his lifelong attachment to the United States.

His travels in Europe were a rude shock. He went there looking for an example or model for the progressive nation he hoped to see created on the banks of the River Plate, but he was to discover that despite Europe's art treasures, despite the existence there of the intellectuals who had educated him with their books, life on that continent offered little that was not already typical of conditions in South America. Later he was to write: "I have just come from going about Europe, from admiring her monuments, prostrating myself in front of her science, and I am still astonished by the wonders of her arts. But I have seen her millions of peasants, proletarians, and mean workmen, and I have seen how degraded and unworthy of being counted as men they are. The crust of filth which covers their bodies and the rags and tatters in which they are dressed do not sufficiently reveal the darkness of their spirits; and with regard to

13

politics and social organization that darkness is enough to obscure the minds of the wise men, of the bankers, and of the nobles" (p. 176).[22]

Of all the European countries, France was a particular disappointment, since, like all South American intellectuals of the day, Sarmiento had looked to France and the ideals spawned and institutions created by the French Revolution. Approaching the coast of France, he had felt that he was coming home, that France was the "land of [his] dreams" and Paris "the fount of our intellectual life." He had felt "respect comparable to the vague awe of a child about to take his first communion," or "rather like a member of the family who has been born abroad and now approaches his ancestral home with a beating heart."[23]

But upon mooring in Le Havre, his boat was immediately attacked by "an ignoble mob of elegantly dressed servants who assaulted us, shouted at us, scaled the boat by means of the hawsers, surrounded us like flies, made us nauseous with their stinking breath, and tried to get a card with the name of the hotel which sent them into our hands or pockets. It was impossible to speak to them, shake them off, startle them with a movement of the hands, flee, or hide. Ah, Europe! Sad mixture of greatness and abjection, of wisdom and brutalization, sublime and filthy receptacle of all that both elevates and degrades man, kings and lackeys, monuments and pesthouses, opulence and savagery." "I haven't been able to rid myself for two days of the bad effect of this first

[22] The edition of *Travels* principally used for my translation is *Estados Unidos*, the third volume of Sarmiento's *Viajes* as published in 1959 by Hachette of Buenos Aires. All page numbers in the text refer to the translation that follows.

[23] Quoted in Edmundo Correas, *Sarmiento and the United States* (Gainesville, Fla., 1961), p. 5.

impression," he wrote to a friend.[24] Indeed, he was not able to rid himself of this impression during all the time he stayed in France. France was simply a hopelessly backward place with regard to the things he considered important: how the common man lived, his level of education, and the extent to which he participated in the political life of his country. France and the rest of Europe were, he felt, like South America, still in a state of barbarism.

Later, when he had had an opportunity to see something of the United States, he wrote, comparing it with France, that

> The only country in the world where the ability to read is universal, where writing is practiced by all in their daily lives, where 2,000 periodicals satisfy public curiosity, and where education, like welfare, is everywhere available to all those who want it is the United States. Is there any country in the world which can compare with it in these respects? In France there are 270,000 voters; that is, among 36 million individuals in the oldest civilized nation, only 270,000, according to the law, are not considered beasts. Reason is not recognized as the important factor in governing.

> In the United States, every man has a natural right to a role in political affairs, and he exercises it. On the other hand, France has a king, 400,000 soldiers, fortifications in Paris which have cost 2 billion francs, and a people dying of hunger. (p. 152)

Sarmiento even became disillusioned with the French Revolution, deciding that, rather than representing progress, it had only replaced one despotism with another.

[24] *De Valparaíso a París*, pp. 183, 184.

"The *Times* once said," he wrote, "that if France had abolished the passport liberty would have advanced more than it has in half a century of revolutions and advanced social theories . . ." (p. 161). France might have literature, but the United States had "liberty, wealth, the most complete civilization, . . . rights, and equality."[25]

But Sarmiento had not come to Europe solely to explore its relative merits as a model for Argentina; he was also on assignment by the Chilean government to investigate the educational systems of the countries he visited and to make recommendations for improvements in Chile. With this in mind, he traveled extensively, making notes on the educational institutions he inspected on the Continent and later in the United States, and upon returning to Chile he published a book in the form of a report to the Ministry of Education entitled *Educación popular* (1849).[26] The report was written much in the manner of Horace Mann's *Seventh Report of the Secretary of the Massachusetts Board of Education*, based on his European trip a few years before (1843).[27]

While abroad, Sarmiento wrote long letters to friends in Chile, Argentina, and Uruguay on what he saw and learned on his travels, and on his return to Chile these were collected as *Viajes en Europa, Africa i America,* the third and longest section of which is *Estados Unidos* or *Travels in the United States in 1847.*

Circumstances almost kept Sarmiento from writing *Travels*, for toward the end of his stay in Europe he took stock of his funds and discovered that he had only six

---

[25] *Obras*, IV, 279.   [26] *Obras*, XI.
[27] Mary Tyler Peabody Mann, *Life and Works of Horace Mann* (Boston, 1867), III, 230-418.

hundred dollars left, while the return trip to Chile alone, by even the most direct route, cost seven hundred. He decided, however, to take his chances and push on to North America, because, as he asked himself, "Could I as a schoolteacher on a world trip of exploration to examine the state of primary education return to [South] America without having inspected the schools of Massachusetts, the most advanced in the world? In my search for data on immigration, . . . how could I manage without visiting the United States, the country to which two hundred thousand emigrants steer each year? As a republican, and having witnessed what form the republic has taken in France, could I return without having seen the only great and powerful republic that exists on the earth today? Well," he told himself, "where reality fades away, the imagination takes over" (p. 211), and he resolved to get to the United States one way or another and to finance the rest of the trip by working his way if necessary.[28]

Sailing from Liverpool on August 17, he arrived in the United States on September 15, 1847. He was to remain in this country for less than two months, but they were to be two of the most important months in his life.[29] He had come from Europe disillusioned, but now he saw that his hopes for the Argentine Republic were

[28] Luckily, when Sarmiento reached the United States he encountered Santiago Arcos, a wealthy Chilean who insisted upon becoming his traveling companion and on helping to support him until he returned to Chile.

[29] There is a tendency among Argentine Sarmiento scholars to exaggerate the extent of Sarmiento's first visit to the United States, perhaps because it is difficult to imagine that he could have written *Travels* after a stay of less than two months. With the publication of Sarmiento's expense notebook, however, it is possible to ascertain the exact period of his stay as September 15 through November 4, 1847. See *Diario de gastos*, ed. Antonio P. Castro, Publications of the Sarmiento Museum, IV, No. 2 (Buenos Aires, 1950); and pp. 309-316.

17

not unrealistic. "The proof is in the United States," and its success was not incapable of being transplanted to other lands. The United States, he felt, was the vanguard of a general movement in the direction of free and progressive societies which was about to sweep the world. "How it excites me," he wrote, "to think that the moment is coming when the sufferings of centuries and of millions of men, as well as the violations of sacred principles by superstitions elevated to the level of theory and science, will confront a reality which will destroy them. The hegemony of the Republic, when it is strong and rich by hundreds of millions, is not far off. The progress of the American population indicates that this is so" (pp. 180-181). Now he could hope for the establishment of free institutions in Argentina or wherever tyrants reigned in South America. The United States had shown the way by its example, and South America would follow it to freedom. "Educated as you and I are," he wrote to a friend, "under the iron rod of the most awful tyrant, and fighting him unceasingly in the name of right, of justice—in the name, in short, of the Republic—we have, as have so many others who wished to realize plans arrived at through conscience and human intelligence, taken heart on seeing in the midst of the leaden night which weighs upon South America that halo of light shining from the North. At last we have told ourselves, in order to endure the evils of the present: 'The Republic exists, strong, invincible; her lamp is lit; and someday justice, equality, and law will come to us when the South reflects the light of the North'" (p. 116).

But just as he had not gone to Europe as an agent of the future Argentine Republic, neither was this his role, at least ostensibly, in the United States. He had come

18

to complete his report to the Chilean government by examining North American education. "The principal object of my trip," he wrote, "was to see Mr. Horace Mann, Secretary of the Board of Education, the great reformer of primary education, who like myself had traveled through Europe in search of methods and systems, a man who combined an inexhaustible quantity of good will and philanthropy with a rare prudence and a profound wisdom in his acts and in his writings" (pp. 242-243).

It appears that Sarmiento knew nothing of Mann until shortly before arriving in the United States, for, as he writes in *Educación popular,*

It was in England that, for the first time, I came across Horace Mann's work, published in the United States and republished here, entitled *Report of an Educational Tour in Germany, France, Holland, and Parts of Great Britain and Ireland.* Mr. Mann is the . . . citizen who most deserves credit for having encouraged primary education to achieve the position it now has. . . . Traveling from the northern part of America, and guided by the same motives, Mr. Mann preceded me by two years in the enterprise which I have undertaken starting out from the southern part of the hemisphere. We traveled through the same countries and examined the same schools, and, except for slight differences occasioned by the peculiarities of our respective languages, his observations corroborate and complement mine. From the moment this important work fell into my hands, I knew where I wanted to go in the United States.[30]

30 *Obras,* XI, 67.

19

Sarmiento had the good fortune of being able to secure a "manna from heaven" letter of introduction during his Atlantic crossing, from a person he describes as "a United States Senator who knew Horace Mann" (p. 213), and as soon as he could, he traveled to see Mann.[31]

> He lived outside of Boston, and I had to take the railroad to get to East [West] Newton, the small village where he resided. We spent many long hours talking on two consecutive days. He told me of his tribulations and of the difficulties which had beset his great work, such as popular prejudices on education, local and sectarian jealousies, and the vulgar pettiness which may bring the best of institutions to ruin. The legislature of the state had itself been at the point of canceling out his work, of dismissing him, and of dissolving the Commission on Education, yielding to the lowest motives—envy and conformity. His work was immense and the compensation tiny, but his pay was in the fruits already harvested and in the future which he was opening for his country. He was creating near his house a normal school, which I visited with his wife [Mary Peabody Mann]. . . . The number of teachers in [Massachusetts] . . . is greater than the whole of the permanent army of Chile and a third the size of the United States Army.   (p. 243)

When Sarmiento arrived in West Newton, the Manns had just recently settled in a new house they had built

[31] According to Justo Garate Ariola ("Novedades acerca de Sarmiento," *Nueva Era* [Tandil, Argentina], August 23, 1949), there were no United States Senators on Sarmiento's ship, the *Montezuma*. However, Garate notes that George Bliss, a Massachusetts politician, was aboard and he feels that it was probably Bliss who gave Sarmiento the letter to Mann.

near the normal school.[32] During the two days they were together Sarmiento and Mann conversed at length on educational subjects, either in Mann's study or while strolling about the town. Mann knew no Spanish and Sarmiento essentially no English, so Mary Mann did the translating, speaking French with Sarmiento. Many years later she described the visit in a letter to Henry Barnard:

My dear Mr. Barnard:

I have of late had a very interesting correspondence with . . . D. F. Sarmiento. He visited in West Newton many years ago where he gave us a great deal of information about Chili [sic] from which kingdom he had been sent to Europe just two years after my husband went, to visit schools and colleges. He followed very closely on our footsteps and went still further. We were very much pleased with him. He could not speak English then and I talked with him in French one whole day.[33]

Horace Mann gave Sarmiento a complete set of the *Common School Report and Journal* and the *Abstract of School Returns,* as well as a collection of his speeches and other reports.[34] He also gave him "many letters of introduction to learned men, pedagogues, and prominent people. His name alone," Sarmiento found, "was, wherever I went, a passport for me" (p. 248).

[32] Some years later Nathaniel Hawthorne and his wife (Sophia Peabody Hawthorne, Mary Mann's sister) would temporarily occupy this house, whose more than adequate furnace gave Hawthorne "ideas of writing a story about a house built over hell with evil spirits rising out of the hot air radiators" (Louise Hall Tharp, *The Peabody Sisters of Salem* [Boston, 1950], p. 222). Hawthorne wrote most of *The Blithedale Romance* while living in the Mann house in West Newton.

[33] Letter of July 21, 1865, in Alice Houston Luiggi, "Some Letters of Sarmiento and Mary Mann 1865-1876, Part I," *The Hispanic American Historical Review* (May 1952), pp. 188, 189.

[34] *Las escuelas, Obras,* xxx, 58.

When Sarmiento left West Newton neither he nor the Manns could have been aware of the importance his two days there would have for the future of education in South America. Mann did not give Sarmiento new ideas so much as he confirmed in him ideas already present and slowly gathering strength: that a democratic political and social context was the best atmosphere in which education might flourish; and that an educated populace was the greatest resource upon which a nation might draw.[35] The greatest number of pages in *Educación popular*, and the most enthusiastic ones, are devoted to education in the United States, most particularly in Massachusetts, and Mann's name figures throughout them. Sarmiento was obviously enchanted with Mann, and he wished to emulate him. "Can you think of anything more beautiful," he wrote, "than Mr. Mann's obligation as Secretary of the Board of Education to travel a part of the year, call an educational meeting of the population of every village and city where he arrives, mount the platform and preach a sermon on primary education (demonstrating the practical advantages which accompany its wide diffusion), stimulate the parents, conquer selfishness, smooth out difficulties, counsel the teachers, make suggestions, and propose improvements in the schools which his science, his good will, and his experience suggest to him?" (pp. 244-245). An Argentine writer has said that probably no one "has ever been so faithful to the teachings of Horace Mann" as Sarmiento,[36] and in Argentina their relationship has become part of the national mythology. The statement by an American writer that "It will always be

[35] See Michael Aaron Rockland, "Argentina's Great Educator," *The Bulletin Board* (Buenos Aires), November 1963, p. 7.
[36] Emilio Carilla, *El Embajador Sarmiento* (Santa Fe, Argentina, 1961), pp. 73, 74.

a source of pride and satisfaction to the people of the United States that the torch of learning, so long and triumphantly held aloft by Sarmiento, the greatest educator of . . . the Spanish American republics, should have been kindled by the patriarch of North American schoolmen, Horace Mann,"[37] will be true when Sarmiento's name becomes a household word in the United States just as "Horacio" Mann's is in Argentina.

Encouraged by Horace Mann and guided by his ideals, Sarmiento continued his investigations in the United States. For two months he traveled about the eastern part of the country, visiting all the major cities and journeying by stagecoach to Pittsburgh and by steamboat from Pittsburgh to New Orleans on the Ohio and Mississippi Rivers. He set sail for South America on November 4. "The North American world was ending," he wrote, "and we began to sense through anticipation the Spanish colonies toward which we were heading."

Arriving back in Chile in February 1848, Sarmiento returned to his customary pursuits: educational projects, writing, teaching, and political agitation against the Rosas regime. In 1850 he published *Agiropolis*, in which he proposes an Argentine Constitution based on the federalist principles of the United States Constitution.[38] A year later he published *Recuerdos de provincia*, an account of his childhood which was also a reply to the propaganda of the Rosas regime against him and his family.

With several other important books published and his fame as writer, educator, and political figure grow-

[37] Percy Martin, "Sarmiento and New England," *Hispanic American Essays*, ed. A. Curtis Wilgus (Chapel Hill, N.C., 1942), p. 340.
[38] *Obras*, XIII.

ing, Sarmiento continued his activities in Chile until 1851, when word reached Santiago that an army had been organized in Uruguay to overthrow Rosas. Together with other exiles, he immediately sailed for Montevideo, where he was given the rank of lieutenant colonel and charged with writing the army's newspaper. In 1852 the decisive battle of Caseros was fought, and Rosas, after almost a quarter of a century of domination, fled to Europe.

But Sarmiento's initial happiness over Rosas' overthrow was frustrated when he found himself in disagreement with the new government, which had been organized as a Confederation but which had chosen as its president General Urquiza, an ex-lieutenant of Rosas. Unwilling to lend his name and prestige to the Urquiza-led Confederation, and fearing that his continued presence would soon lead to further civil war, Sarmiento again reluctantly left Argentina with others of like sentiment and took the well-traveled route to Chile and a self-imposed exile.

During the next few years he maintained a Chilean residence but was in and out of Argentina on brief educational and political missions. In 1855, eager to participate more fully in national life, he returned to Argentina to stay. He was named Director of Schools by the Buenos Aires Provincial Government and also founded an educational journal, the *Anales de educación común*. He returned to journalism, taking over the editorship of the newspaper *El nacional*, and soon he was running for office for the first time, winning successive elections to the Buenos Aires City Council and to the National Congress as Senator from San Juan. It was during this period that he also participated in the struggle to keep

Roman Catholicism from becoming the official religion of Argentina.

In 1860 Sarmiento was named Minister of Government and Foreign Relations of the Buenos Aires Provincial Government by his old friend and political associate Bartolome Mitre, then Governor. Later in the same year—his affinity for the United States being well known and a temporary peace between Sarmiento and Urquiza having been arranged—he was asked to serve as the Confederation's Minister to the United States. But before this appointment could take effect, civil war again broke out. Sarmiento went to western Argentina at the head of troops, while Mitre led the Buenos Aires army. By 1861 the Confederation had been smashed, and Sarmiento and Mitre proceeded to form the Federation which has remained Argentina's form of government until today.

Mitre was the clear favorite to win the presidency, and he proposed that Sarmiento fill the vice-presidential spot on his ticket. After considering the offer for some time, Sarmiento declined; he is supposed to have told Mitre that he would support him in the approaching election but was "reserving the second presidency for myself." Instead of running for Vice President, Sarmiento decided to seek election as Governor of San Juan Province. As a native son who had just distinguished himself by pacifying the western region of the country, Sarmiento was easily elected.

As Governor of San Juan he had his first opportunity to put into practice the ideas which had been maturing within him through all the years of revolution and exile. True to form, he first of all built schools and founded public libraries. He laid out roads and had the first official maps of the province drawn up. But after their initial enthusiasm, the people of San Juan began to grumble at the taxes which were being collected to support Sarmiento's projects. To complicate matters, a revolt broke out in the neighboring province of La Rioja, led by the *caudillo* El Chacho. Sarmiento was asked by the national government to put down the uprising, and he accordingly raised an army and declared a state of siege in San Juan and La Rioja Provinces. This action proved decidedly unpopular in Buenos Aires and in the western provinces. It was felt that in declaring a state of siege Sarmiento had overstepped the powers delegated to him by the national government. Matters went from bad to worse when El Chacho was murdered while a prisoner of troops under Sarmiento's command, and Sarmiento, though apparently not involved, was held responsible.

President Mitre, knowing of Sarmiento's frustrations as Governor and his unhappiness over the calumny being heaped on him for the El Chacho affair, decided to nominate him Minister to the United States again. Sarmiento was pleased for more reasons than one to accept the appointment. As soon as he could gather his legation staff, he sailed for the United States.

On May 15, 1865 he landed in New York City, where he was to serve the Argentine government for over three years as Ambassador to the United States. Unfortunately this extended stay was not to produce a major work on the United States, as did his much shorter stay two decades earlier. Sarmiento was, nevertheless, a most unorthodox diplomat, and he organized his legation more like a floating seminar than a political and administrative arm of the Argentine government. He settled in New York rather than in Washington to avoid diplomatic corps life (he once described embassies as "havens for the lazy")[39] and because he wished to be at the center of literary, artistic, commercial, and industrial life—in contact with American society, in short, rather than with the United States government. "If a diplomat's mission is to cultivate good relations," he later wrote, "I have more than fulfilled mine. . . . I have invested the money which another would have spent on dinners and a carriage in traveling about the United States, studying its institutions, visiting its public establishments, and getting to know its people, while the diplomatic corps plays cards in Washington."[40]

He felt that his legation should be "a center of study," and he wrote a friend: "I rise at five o'clock in the morning. . . . I am writing, translating, compiling, and publishing two books at once. I send off letters that are becoming more frequent and more full of interesting things each day. I am also publishing some articles in the daily press. . . . Having some mental energy left over (my head is the most powerful part of my body), I sometimes send letters [to Argentine newspapers] . . . which you will soon begin to see."[41]

Sarmiento believed that he had a double mission in the United States: to inform Americans about Argentina —his primary mission, to be sure—but beyond this, to inform himself and his countrymen about the United States. As one Argentine historian has written, not only was Sarmiento "the messenger of Argentine letters and ideals in the country of Washington, but, contrary to normal practice, he . . . also tried to spread knowledge

39 In an undated letter to Bartolome Mitre, *Sarmiento-Mitre correspondencia, 1846-1868* (Buenos Aires, 1911), p. 364.
40 *Obras*, XLIX, 282, 283.
41 Letter of August 6, 1865 to Aurelia Velez, *Obras*, XXIX, 45.

of the latter country in the former."[42] At one point, Sarmiento wrote to a friend: "I shall make this country known in Argentina, and their relations will always be cordial."[43] Nicolas Avelleneda, who succeeded Sarmiento as President of Argentina, once wrote that "Sarmiento is the first who has explained American institutions to us; he is more familiar with them than the judges of the Supreme Court in Washington."[44]

Involvement in intellectual rather than political activity during the early months of Sarmiento's diplomatic mission was almost a necessity, due to the fact that the trunk containing his credentials and a letter from Mitre to Lincoln had been lost during his trip to the United States. New papers addressed to President Johnson were necessary in any case, since Abraham Lincoln had been assassinated the month before Sarmiento arrived. While awaiting new credentials he traveled to Philadelphia, Baltimore, and Richmond to view the effects of the war on those cities, and in Washington he was invited to share the official stand reviewing the parade of the 200,000-man Army of the Potomac along with President Johnson, Secretary of State Seward, and Generals Grant, Sherman, and Meade. The next day he attended the trial of those implicated in the Lincoln assassination.

He was finally received officially by Andrew Johnson in the White House on November 9. Sarmiento thanked Johnson for receiving him, expressed sorrow at the death of Lincoln, and mentioned that the Argentine

[42] Amaranto Abeledo, "En torno a los viajes de Sarmiento a los Estados Unidos," *Revista de educación* (Buenos Aires), March 1957, pp. 3, 11.

[43] *Obras*, XLIX, 283.

[44] Quoted in Oscar Antonio Montaña, "Sarmiento, Embajador en Estados Unidos," *Sarmiento, Cincuentenario de su muerte* (Buenos Aires, 1938), V, 153.

Constitution and form of government owed much to its American model. President Johnson replied: "Believe me, sir, that it is a source of enduring gratification to the people of the United States, that they have framed for themselves a constitution for civil government, which so many of the new, enterprising, and enlightened states, which are growing up on this continent, have thought worthy to be adopted by them as a model. The fact, however, is one which had brought with it to us a great responsibility—the responsibility of conducting the administration of our cherished system in such a manner as to maintain, preserve and increase the confidence of mankind. . . ."[45]

This was one of Sarmiento's very few contacts with official Washington. He considered it more important to be known as an educator than as a diplomat in the United States, so that he was more often present at educational than political meetings. August 1865 found him at the American Institute of Education Congress at Yale University, where his recently published pamphlet *The Argentine Republic, Its Resources, Character and Condition*,[46] was distributed and part of a paper he had pre-

[45] United States National Archives, State Department Division, *Argentine Republic*, Outgoing Correspondence, Vol. VI, September 28, 1838 to October 31, 1896; letter undated, but probably written on November 9, 1865. Sarmiento was not to see Johnson again except at the impeachment proceedings in the spring of 1868. On May 22, 1868 he wrote a long letter marked *Confidencial* to the Minister of Foreign Relations in Buenos Aires, which included the following remarks: "In vain would I try to give you a complete picture of this famous trial which, in my opinion, is the most important event of our century. . . . Republican institutions have emerged sound from this terrible ordeal" (*Obras*, XXXIII, 29).

[46] Subtitled "Letter From the Argentine Minister" (New York, 1865). The pamphlet was eight pages long, written in excellent English (doubtless translated by Edward Davidson, the American employed as Argentine Consul in New York). The pamphlet begins: "A number of letters have been lately received by the Consul of the Argentine Re-

pared for the occasion read. He also briefly addressed the Congress in Spanish, his translated words including the following remark: "To prove to you that my country has gone some way along the road that has brought so many good things to the United States, I offer myself as proof of the high estimation in which education is held. I am, and proud of it, a South American schoolteacher. I have been a superintendent of schools and have directed public education; I have been a Minister . . . and have signed decrees for the erection of a hundred school buildings. I am an Ambassador now, but as you can see by my interest in being here among you, I still remain, by preference and vocation, a schoolteacher."[47] The next year he attended the meeting of the National Teachers Association in Indianapolis. Sarmiento was made an honorary member of the Association and was asked to speak on "Education in Argentina." He insisted on being introduced not as the Argentine ambassador but as a friend of Horace Mann, and stressed again his true vocation: "If my fellow citizens honor me by asking me to guide the destinies of my country, I will be in the presidency of the Republic, as always, above all a schoolteacher."[48]

---

public, in New York, from parties desirous to emigrate to that country, and anxious to have some details respecting it. That a general answer may be given to these inquiries, the minister of the Argentine Republic has, at the request of the Consul, addressed him the following letter." There follows a long letter from Sarmiento to Davidson, with a general description of Argentina and also a defense of Argentina's position in the war with Paraguay.

[47] Sarmiento's remarks were translated by Professor Greenleaf of Brooklyn College. Sarmiento wrote a report on this Congress which is found in *Escuelas, Obras*, xxx, 145-164. His own paper is found on pp. 165-176.

[48] Sarmiento's speech is found in *Obras* (1st edn.), xxi, 237-242. On this occasion, Sarmiento read his own speech in English. See also *Proceedings and Lectures of the National Teachers Association at Their*

Attending as many conventions and other educational meetings as possible, Sarmiento became in effect an unofficial representative of the schools of South America. He devoted so much of his time to sending information on education to Argentina and to the other Latin American countries that there was a good deal of truth in his statement that he served in the United States as "Superintendent of Schools of South America."[49] He became a clearinghouse for educational projects in the Americas and his legation a center of North and South American cultural interpenetration.

Ambas Americas, a magazine he published in New York during these years, was his chief vehicle for keeping in contact with educators throughout the hemisphere. The magazine went through four numbers[50] and then died when Sarmiento returned to Argentina, but while it lasted it received considerable support throughout the Americas, including a subscription for two hundred copies from President Juárez of Mexico. The magazine contained letters from American educators and concerned itself particularly with the current controversy over a national office of education in the United States. *Ambas Americas* was probably, as one writer suggests, "the first example of inter-American publication."[51]

In addition to founding *Ambas Americas*, contributing letters and articles to the periodicals of both hemi-

---

Annual Meetings, Held in Indianapolis, Indiana, August 1866 (Albany, 1867), pp. 77-79.

[49] Quoted in Alberto Palcos, *The Pan American Ideals of Sarmiento* (Buenos Aires, 1938), p. 15.

[50] Sarmiento wrote in his "Diario de un viaje de Nueva York a Buenos Aires" that "the fourth and last number was run off and bound barely twenty hours before leaving" the United States (*Obras*, XLIX, 291).

[51] Ernesto Nelson, in the prologue to the facsimile edition of the first number of *Ambas Americas* (Buenos Aires, 1943), p. 1.

spheres, and writing pamphlets on Argentina for distribution in English in the United States, Sarmiento was simultaneously at work on two books almost from the moment his ship docked in the United States. The first, *Vida de Lincoln*, was essentially a compendium of condensations of some of the more interesting American works on Lincoln which were then pouring from the presses, translated by Sarmiento himself into Spanish.[52] Sarmiento intended his life of Lincoln for the elementary schools of Argentina, and most of the copies of the book were shipped to Buenos Aires. The first edition came out in November 1865, published by Appleton in New York. A second edition appeared in 1866. Sarmiento had hoped to include some verses on Lincoln by the Argentine educator and writer Juana Manso, in the first edition, but they arrived too late.[53] Miss Manso's poem does appear in the second edition. As we shall see, Sarmiento at one time hoped to publish a third edition of the book with Miss Manso's poem translated into English by Henry Wadsworth Longfellow.[54]

In addition to *Vida de Lincoln*, Sarmiento was working on a book on education in the United States, *Las escuelas: Base de la prosperidad y de la Republica en los Estados Unidos*. The title suggests how very committed he was to the theory that a successful political and economic system—a successful society, in short—is depend-

---

[52] *Obras*, XXVII.

[53] Sarmiento wrote to Miss Manso on November 20, 1865, saying: "If your verses had arrived on time I would have put them in at the end of the book. If there is a second edition, I will add them" (*Obras*, XXIX, 277).

[54] In a letter of June 28, 1866 to President Mitre he wrote: "The Lincoln book is heading for its third edition" (*Sarmiento-Mitre correspondencia*, p. 367). However, I have found no evidence that the third edition was ever published, and no Argentine historian refers to it with certainty.

ent on the educational level of the people, an idea which had been confirmed in him by Horace Mann twenty years before. Indeed, the inspiration for the book's title may have been a Horace Mann lecture entitled "The Necessity of Education in a Republican Government," which had appeared in Mary Mann's *Life of Horace Mann*.[55] Sarmiento was given a copy of the *Life* by Edward Davidson, an American serving as Argentine Consul in New York, who, Sarmiento later wrote to Mary Mann, "knew of my enthusiasm for Mr. Mann."[56] With the aid of her book and numerous documents which Mary Mann was soon to send him, Sarmiento wrote a short biography of Mann which is the most important part of *Escuelas*. Mary Mann, as we shall see, was involved with almost everything Sarmiento published—and did—while in the United States.

Sarmiento first wrote to Mary Mann, who was then living in Concord, shortly after he arrived in the United States. On July 8 he had seen a notice in the New York papers describing the erecting of a statue of Horace Mann on the lawn in front of Bullfinch's State House in Boston, and he wrote to her that day saying:

> I have seen in the newspapers that a statue to the memory of Horace Mann has been raised up on the lawn of the State House. . . . If I had known in time, I would have run or, more accurately, flown in order to add my applause to that of the multitude honoring that great man. . . .[57]

[55] Carilla supports this theory in *El Embajador Sarmiento*, p. 72.
[56] Letter of July 8, 1865, *Obras*, xxx, 57-60.
[57] Sometime later, when Sarmiento was in Boston, he had an opportunity to see the new Mann statue for himself. He left Tremont House, where he was staying, and, after strolling around Boston Commons and visiting with Franklin's statue in front of the Boston City Hall, he walked over to the State House. These were his thoughts:

Perhaps you will not remember me; but if an appreciation of Mr. Mann were helpful in gaining your friendship, let me assure you that no one has had a greater estimation of his character and service to humanity. In 1847, I had the honor of meeting with him in his home in West Newton; and, if memory does not fail me, you yourself served as interpreter during our long conversations on educational matters and were kind enough to familiarize me with the customs and characteristics of the town in which you were living. . . .

Sarmiento describes the help Mann gave him and then continues:

Armed with these documents and a collection of his lectures, reports, and speeches, and nourished with his oral instructions, I returned to South America and during these years have done nothing else but follow in his footsteps, his great work in organizing education in Massachusetts serving as my model. . . .

From this you may infer that the name of Mr. Mann was for me, during all of my work and struggles for education, what the works of Saint Augustine were for the missionaries of the Church.[58]

During the period between Sarmiento's visit to West Newton and Mann's death in 1859 there is evidence of some communication between them. In *Escuelas* Sar-

---

"One does not find himself every day at the foot of the statue of a man you have known when alive, one who could be called your friend and collaborator in the same field, who was nourished by the same ideas— although we used different methods and had different results because of the terrain in which each worked. . . . I was tempted to say hello to him, to smile to him, and to ask him if he remembered that traveler he received in West Newton in 1848 [*sic*]" (*Obras*, xxx, 198).

[58] Letter of July 8, 1865, *Obras*, xx, 57-60.

1. A portrait of Sarmiento in 1845, shortly before his visit to the United States.

2. A daguerreotype of Mary Peabody Mann taken around the time of her marriage to Horace Mann in 1843.

3. Horace Mann in an engraving from a drawing
executed by Sophia Peabody Hawthorne in 1865,
several years after his death.

4. The Argentine Legation in the United States in 1865. Ambassador Sarmiento is seated at the left.

miento mentions that after he left the United States in
1847 Mann wrote to him "in Chile on educational subjects,"[59] and included in Mary Mann's answer to Sarmiento's first letter to her in 1865 were the following remarks:

> I remember well the very pleasant visit you made to
> W. Newton and how much I regretted that my French
> parlance was so rusty, but in spite of that, you gave
> us much pleasant information and left an impression
> both of your own earnestness and devotion to the
> highest interests of your country, which often caused
> you to be spoken of between us—for no persons in-
> terested my dear husband so much as those who were
> wise and philanthropic enough to see and feel that
> only through the cultivation of man's whole nature
> could society ever reach that destiny which the Crea-
> tor marked out for it. When your book came, we were
> interested in that, and I hope you received our ac-
> knowledgements for it.
> . . . I have also three sons who have often heard me
> speak of you and who feel an interest in everyone who
> had a regard for their father.[60]

[59] *Obras*, xxx, 198. In a review of *Escuelas* entitled "Educational Lessons for South America," published in *The American Journal of Education* (September 1866), p. 535, attention is given to Sarmiento's statement on his contact with Mann after 1847.

[60] This first letter from Mary Mann to Sarmiento is reproduced in
Spanish in *Escuelas, Obras*, xxx, 60-63. A copy of the English original
was discovered by Horace Mann III in 1953 and printed privately by
Alice Houston Luiggi (it was discovered too late for her collection of
Sarmiento letters published in the *Hispanic American Historical Re-
view*). There are substantial differences between the English version
found by Horace Mann III (quoted here) and Sarmiento's translation.
The book mentioned by Mary Mann is undoubtedly *Educación popu-
lar*, with its many references to education in Massachusetts and to
Horace Mann.

A shared dedication to Horace Mann's memory was to provide the basis for the friendship between Sarmiento and Mary Mann which now developed. Mary Mann saw Sarmiento as carrying forward her husband's work. Early in their relationship, she wrote to him: "I have never been more gratified than by learning from you that my dear husband's labors have borne fruit in such a garden of Eden. I suspect it owes all of its prosperity to you, but I must find that out from someone else than yourself."[61] Sarmiento similarly once wrote to Mary Mann: "It will be a historical fact of great influence in South America that the woman who helped Horace Mann in his great work in the north lent her sympathetic cooperation to his followers in the southern part of America."[62] On another occasion he wrote: "You will have had the supreme happiness of sustaining and inspiring two workers at the geographical extremes of

[61] Unpublished letter of July 22, 1865, Mary Mann Folder, Archives of the Sarmiento Museum, Buenos Aires. Almost all of Mary Mann's letters to Sarmiento are unpublished (five are published in the *Obras*) and are to be found, together with several letters from other Americans to Sarmiento, in this folder in Buenos Aires, hereafter cited as MMF. Some years after Sarmiento's death, in 1913, all letters in the possession of his heirs were turned over to the Museo Histórico Nacional. When the Sarmiento Museum was created in 1938, the letters were moved there and now make up the greater part of the archives.

[62] Letter of May 31, 1866, *Boletín de la Academia Argentina de Letras*, IV, No. 14 (1936), 301.

The great majority of Sarmiento's letters to Mary Mann are published in the *Boletín*, in seven installments: Vol. III, Nos. 9, 10, 11-12 (1935); and Vol. IV, Nos. 13, 14, 15, 16 (1936). This collection will be cited hereafter as *BAAL*. The originals of these letters are now in the Archivo General de la Nación in Buenos Aires. They were discovered by a Costa Rican diplomat at an auction of old items, mostly junk, in Washington in 1933. Fortunately, this gentleman, Manuel Gonzalez Zeledón, was familiar with Sarmiento and recognized the great value of the letters. He purchased the letters and sent them to the Argentine Sarmientista Alberto Palcos, who supervised their classification in the National Library. They were removed from the Library several years ago and placed in the National Archives.

America, and my name is now being sanctified by being associated with yours."[63]

When Sarmiento became interested in having busts sculpted of Mann and Lincoln, "the two men I love the most,"[64] Mary Mann was happy to help him with this project. She contacted William Rimmer, the distinguished American sculptor, who was a distant relation: "I write now to say that my sister [Elizabeth Peabody] has seen Dr. Rimmer, to whom she wrote on the very day she gave you an introduction to him and he would be most happy to cut the heads for you. He thinks with you that they are eminently representative American heads and he had longed to do them both. He was delighted too with the thought of sending a work into the Argentine Republic of which he seemed to know something. Possibly you have changed your mind upon the subject, but if not I shall be glad, for he is the most able artist in the country, tho not as extensively known by works as some who are his inferiors. . . ."[65] Sometime later, Sarmiento wrote to Mary Mann on the same subject: "Mr. Rimmer, the artist, writes me that he has finished the busts of Mann and Lincoln and that the former will be in your house. So, at this time, a year from now, we will have erected statuary to the object of our cult at the opposite end of America."[66] The Rimmer busts are today in the Sarmiento Museum in Buenos Aires.

Sarmiento and Mary Mann met only four times while he was in the United States as Ambassador, twice in Con-

63 Letter of May 20, 1866, *BAAL*, IV, No. 14 (1936), 297.
64 Letter of May 12, 1866, *BAAL*, III, No. 9 (1935), 83. This letter is marked *Confidencial*. In it, Sarmiento communicates the fact that the two busts cost him six hundred dollars.
65 Letter of November 7, 1865, MMF.
66 Letter of July 7, 1866, *BAAL*, III, No. 9 (1935), 88.

cord and twice in Cambridge, where she moved in 1866. The record of these visits is most incomplete. However, their long and full correspondence—of which, in Argentina and the United States, I have been able to discover a total of 176 Sarmiento letters and 195 Mary Mann letters—demonstrates the extent of their friendship. The correspondence continued until Mary Mann's death in 1887 and provides magnificent portraits of Argentina and New England in the second half of the nineteenth century.[67]

Sarmiento almost always wrote his letters in Spanish; Mary Mann wrote hers in English. His first letters were translated into English by the Legation Secretary, Bartolito Mitre, President Mitre's son, who knew the language well.[68] But in her letter of September 25, 1865 Mary Mann announced: "I am happy to say that I can read Spanish. Once I could speak it a little (after a resi-

[67] The breakdown of the locations of the letters is as follows:

SARMIENTO		MARY MANN	
147 letters	*BAAL*	190 letters	MMF
23 letters	Mary Mann Papers, Library of Congress	5 letters	Published in *Obras*
3 letters	Published in *Obras*		
3 letters	Sarmiento Museum, Buenos Aires		

In the MMF are twenty-three letters to Sarmiento from other Americans, such as Elizabeth Peabody, Henry Wadsworth Longfellow, Ulysses S. Grant, and the sons of Horace and Mary Mann.

[68] Sarmiento had some familiarity with English prior to coming to the United States as Ambassador in 1865. His reading comprehension was good, and he had once had some English lessons from a Mr. Richard in Chile. Aboard ship on his way to the United States in 1847, however, he remarks that "my poor English led me to spend much time on board with a Jewish family that spoke French" (*Travels*, p. 213) and we know that he spoke French with Mary Mann during his visit to West Newton in 1847. Between 1847 and 1865 there is no evidence of his having studied English further, but toward the end of his three years as Ambassador his ability improved to the point where he began occasionally to write to Mary Mann in English, without Bartolito Mitre's assistance.

38

dence of more than a year in Cuba) tho I did not dare to try it when I saw you in W. Newton."[69] When Sarmiento received this news he was ecstatic. "I am thrilled," he wrote in Spanish on September 28, "to learn . . . that you know Spanish, that you at least know it better than I know English—since I do not speak a word. God has sent you to me as a guiding angel, and you must accept this providential mission with Christian resignation."[70]

The discovery that the English she had been reading was not Sarmiento's but Bartolito Mitre's was a keen disappointment to Mary Mann. "I read your letter with love," she replied. "But I am as much grieved that you cannot speak English as you are glad that I can read Spanish."[71] She was disappointed not only because their communication would be more difficult than she had expected but because she feared that Sarmiento's diplomatic mission would be less successful if he could not speak with Americans in their native tongue. In a letter to Juana Manso, with whom she had been put in contact by Sarmiento, Mary Mann wrote: "If Mr. Sarmiento were to speak English a little more, he would be known here better than through any other means, since he already has friends [and] admirers."[72]

[69] Mary Mann went to Cuba in December 1833, accompanying her sister, Sophia Peabody (later Mrs. Hawthorne), who was ill. They lived for a little over a year with the family of a wealthy planter, Sophia as a guest and Mary as governess. They returned to Massachusetts in May 1835. Over the years Mary Mann worked away at a novel based on her Cuban experience. *Juanita: A Romance of Real Life in Cuba Fifty Years Ago* was finally published just after her death in 1887. For more information on the stay in Cuba, see Tharp, *The Peabody Sisters of Salem*, Chap. 7.

[70] *BAAL*, IV, No. 15 (1936), 451.

[71] Letter of October 1, 1865, MMF.

[72] Letter of August 27, 1866, quoted in "Sarmiento y las Lenguas Vivas," *Universidad* (Santa Fe, Argentina), April-June 1962, p. 156. Mary Mann's letter was originally written in English. What is presented here is a translation from the Spanish rendering of the letter published

But regardless of the progress he would make in improving his English, Sarmiento was to call on Mary Mann to fulfill the "providential" mission for which her sojourn in Cuba years before had qualified her. Shortly after he first contacted her in 1865, he engaged her as translator and editor of his articles, speeches, and books. Her outstanding achievement in this area was the translation of *Facundo*, the only English translation which has been made of this book. Two paperback editions of her translation were in print recently, and generations of American university students have read *Facundo* in English without realizing the significance of the name "Mrs. Horace Mann" on the title page.[73]

When Sarmiento went to the United States as Ambassador, he took numerous copies of *Facundo* (mostly of the French edition) along in his trunks and made a custom of giving them to new friends and acquaintances and placing them in libraries wherever he traveled. In 1865 he wrote to a friend in Argentina about the effect of *Facundo* on his American friends: "This book serves me as a means of introduction. Being Minister isn't everything, and being an educator is not so distinguishing a title in a nation of professors and teachers. But I still have my *Facundo*, my parrot and my cannon. No one resists it."[74]

Sarmiento sent a copy of *Facundo* to Mary Mann with his letter of July 28, 1865, introducing it thus in English: "I send you a little book entitled: *Civilization &*

---

in *Universidad.* Mary Mann's correspondence with Juana Manso was to bear fruit in Miss Manso's translation of Volume II of Mary Mann's *Life of Horace Mann,* the *Lectures and Annual Reports on Education* (Cambridge, 1867). Miss Manso's translation was entitled *Lecturas sobre la educación* (Buenos Aires, 1868) and was dedicated to Mary Mann.

[73] The two editions are published by Collier (New York, 1961) and Hafner (New York, 1960).

[74] Letter of October 15, 1865 to Aurelia Velez, *Obras,* XXIX, 67.

Barbarie, that I wrote some twenty years ago, in order to explain the causes of the civil wars we have been subjected to during nearly half [a] century. Between the cities and towns, where the little culture we got, took shelter, and the half wild inhabitants of the prairies (pampas), scattered on the plains like your squatters & pioneers, there was a continual strife; the latter, like Arabian hordes, used to charge against the cities, taking, sometimes, possession of them and imposing at their will petty tyrants and rulers for life. Spaniards did not follow the wise policy of your New-England ancestors in establishing schools to continue, through them, the civilized practices and traditions of Europe. This circumstance explains about one half of those civil wars now raging among their descendants."[75]

Soon afterwards, he wrote again about *Facundo*: "Are you blessed with an abundance of spare time and good will to undertake the translation of Civilization and Barbarism? . . . Were you disposed to do it, I would feel particularly proud to see on the title page of a book written by Mr. Sarmiento the name of Mrs. Mary Mann."[76] Mary Mann responded that "Ben [her son, Benjamin Pickman Mann] and I think we shall undertake the translation—I think we can do it in six months, tho he is very busy preparing for college—and as to myself there is no end to my occupations."[77] Sometime later she again wrote on the subject: "I have actually begun

[75] *BAAL*, IV, No. 16 (1936), 591.
[76] Letter of September 23, 1865 (in English); *BAAL*, IV, No. 16 (1936), 595.
[77] Letter of September 25, 1865, MMF. This is the same letter in which Mary Mann announced that she knew Spanish. It seems curious that Sarmiento would ask her to translate *Facundo* without knowing of her experience with Spanish, but this is the case. In his letter of September 23 he asked, "Have you a friend by you who can read Spanish?" He apparently thought she might translate *Facundo* word by word, with dictionary in hand.

to translate the 'Civilization' etc. I do not know when it will be completed, but with the occasional aid of my sons, it may not be very long." She would do it, she wrote, "all in friendship & good will & if I can get a publisher to undertake it I will *share the profits* with you . . . & perhaps we shall make a great deal of money! It will be no matter if we do not make any."[78] The book was finally published in 1868 under the English title of *Life in the Argentine Republic in the Days of the Tyrants.*[79]

Mary Mann took on other translation chores for Sarmiento while he was in the United States. She put into English his most important speech as Ambassador, his address of December 27, 1865 to the Rhode Island Historical Society entitled "North and South America." An early example of the Pan Americanism which later would express itself in the Good Neighbor Policy of Franklin Roosevelt and the Alliance for Progress of John Kennedy, the address called for strengthened ties in the hemisphere through inter-American educational projects and suggested that the United States interest itself in the political, economic, and cultural development of South America. But this speech also had a good deal of bite to it—which is why, in the *Obras completas,* and whenever it is referred to by Argentine scholars, the title used for the speech is "La doctrina Monroe."

[78] This letter (MMF) is dated January 3, 1865, but it was almost certainly written on January 3, 1866. Sarmiento was not in the United States in January 1865. Sarmiento and Mary Mann often dated their letters with the previous year during the first one or two months of the new year, a not uncommon slip.

[79] The title page reads: "*Life in the Argentine Republic in the Days of the Tyrants Or 'Civilization and Barbarism,'* From the Spanish of Domingo F. Sarmiento, L.L.D., Minister Plenipotentiary From the Argentine Republic To the United States, With a Biographical Sketch of the Author By Mrs. Horace Mann, First American from the third Spanish Edition" (New York, 1868).

Going far beyond the attitude toward American expansionism expressed in *Travels* (discussed in part II of this essay), Sarmiento declared that "The Monroe Doctrine has lost its sanctity and ceased to be a protective barrier of separation to become in itself a threat." He continued, "Who was to believe that there would come a day when the Republic would cast shadows all around itself: slavery to the South, conquest to the West, a menace to the North, and a challenge to Europe." The Society voted to publish Sarmiento's speech as a pamphlet.[80]

In addition to translating Sarmiento's books and speeches, Mary Mann wrote or inspired many of the articles and reviews which appeared on Sarmiento and his works in American periodicals during these years, including a number on Sarmiento as an educator and aspiring presidential candidate.[81] Most of these articles

[80] *North and South America, A Discourse Delivered Before the Rhode Island Historical Society, December 27, 1865, By his Excellency, Domingo Faustino Sarmiento, Argentine Minister to the United States* (Providence, R.I., 1866). In *Obras*, XXIX, 86, the editor refers to a review of Sarmiento's speech in *The Herald* (presumably the *New York Herald*). The date is not given, and I have not been able to locate the particular issue, but the editor provides the following quotation from the *Herald* article, which I have retranslated into English: "It [Sarmiento's speech] may be included among the most outstanding examples of American genius."

[81] The following articles appear to have been authored by Mary Mann: "Letter of His Excellency Col. Sarmiento to Hon. Charles Sumner," *The Massachusetts Teacher*, XXI (August 1868), 289-294; "Letters of Hon. Charles Sumner and Colonel Sarmiento," *The Massachusetts Teacher*, XXI (September 1868), 335-337; review of *Escuelas*, *The Massachusetts Teacher*, XIX (August 1866), 289-290; review of *Vida de Lincoln*, *The Christian Examiner*, LXXX (January 1866), 133-138; review of *Vida de Lincoln*, *The Commonwealth*, IV, No. 19 (January 6, 1866), 1; "Educational Biography: Señor D. F. Sarmiento," *The American Journal of Education*, XIV (December 1866), 592-598. These articles are either initialed or signed by Mary Mann or are indisputably linked with her by evidence in the Sarmiento-Mary Mann correspondence. Several other articles were probably also written by Mary Mann, though there is no clear evidence: "Educational Lessons

are unsigned or simply initialed, testimony to the disinterested spirit which motivated her. Sarmiento once wrote to a friend, "When I publish anything, the newspapers and magazines always speak of it. Then I look at the article closely and discover a sentence taken from a letter of mine to her. Then I know that she wrote the article."[82]

Mary Mann was particularly helpful to Sarmiento in his political career. For Sarmiento, it was useful to have someone he could talk to candidly about his aspirations, someone who could be trusted entirely with the details of his political career, and his letters to Mary Mann are full of the strategies of an absentee candidate for the presidency of his country. A letter to Henry Barnard suggests the extent of Mary Mann's involvement in Sarmiento's political fortunes: "This talk of the Presidency for Mr. Sarmiento must only be between him and me and you. I should not dare to confide it to anyone else."[83] Projects such as the translation of *Facundo* were carried out by Mary Mann with full appreciation of the favorable effect they might have on Sarmiento's candidacy by contributing to his prestige with his countrymen.

Perhaps more important than anything else she did for him, Mary Mann helped Sarmiento by presenting him to the people he needed to know to carry out his mission in the United States. In her second letter to him,

---

for South America," *The American Journal of Education*, XVI (September 1866), 533-538; review of "North and South America," Sarmiento's speech to the Rhode Island Historical Society, in *The Massachusetts Teacher*, XIX (March 1866), 111; reviews of *Life in the Argentine Republic in the Days of the Tyrants* [*Facundo*], in *The Christian Examiner*, LXXXV (September 1868), 185-196 and *The New Englander*, XXVII (October 1868), 666-679.

[82] *Obras*, XLIX, 286.

[83] Letter of September 18, 1866, Luiggi, "Letters, I," p. 199.

she wrote: "If I remember aright, you are a man of progress in the highest sense of that word and, therefore, I cannot add to your stores except by pointing you to the minds most worthy to be known."[84] And Sarmiento, referring to Mary Mann's efforts on his behalf, once wrote to a friend that "Wherever I went, I found friends her forethought had made for me."[85]

Among the first people she introduced him to were, of course, her sons, Horace Mann, Jr., George Combe Mann, and Benjamin Pickman Mann. Sarmiento took an interest in each of them. In a letter to Mary Mann in 1867, he wondered if someday a university might be founded in Argentina with young Horace as president. "I can't make promises," he wrote, "but let us for the moment pretend. . . . If I get to have real influence in my country we are going to need a president for one of the universities who can organize it effectively. Would it not have a great moral effect if the son of Horace Mann, graduated from the University at Cambridge, were entrusted with these reforms?"[86] Unfortunately this was never to be, since Horace Mann, Jr., who had accompanied Henry David Thoreau on his Minnesota trip in the spring of 1860, a last attempt to regain his health, was himself dead of tuberculosis by 1868. George Mann was commissioned by Sarmiento to make a study of selected American colleges, which the Ambassador then remitted to the Ministry of Education in Buenos Aires. Benjamin Mann, being the youngest of the boys, was usually about the house when Sarmiento called on Mary Mann in Concord or Cambridge and, as we have already mentioned, he apparently helped his mother

84 Letter of July 22, 1865, MMF.
85 *Obras*, XLIX, 286.
86 Letter of October 3, 1867, *BAAL*, IV, No. 13 (1936), 118.

with her translation of *Facundo*. After graduating from
Harvard in 1870, he was sent by the United States Department of Agriculture to Brazil to classify insects
harmful to crops. While in that part of the world he
became, with Sarmiento's assistance, a correspondent
for the Argentine newspaper *El nacional,* under the
pseudonym "Hamaha."

Of greater interest than Sarmiento's relationships with
the Mann sons is his friendship with Mary's sister, Elizabeth Peabody, the founder of the kindergarten movement in America. Elizabeth, who lived with Mary during these years, was usually at home when Sarmiento
visited. Also, there is evidence that she called on him
in New York City before sailing to Europe to study primary education methods in 1867,[87] and Sarmiento apparently saw Elizabeth twice in Europe when he went
to the Paris Exhibition that summer.

There exist several letters that passed between Sarmiento and Elizabeth Peabody. With one she took the
liberty to send "The Aesthetic Paper [sic] which was an
attempt at a periodical publication that I made, that
never reached beyond the first number. It contains several articles—also one paper of my own which I wish
you would read at some leisure hour for it contains very
earnest thoughts of mine upon integral education. It is
called 'The Dorian Measure.' "[88] The one published
number of *Aesthetic Papers* included Henry David
Thoreau's lecture on "Civil Disobedience." There is

[87] See Cesar H. Guerrero, *Mujeres de Sarmiento* (Buenos Aires, 1960),
p. 261.

[88] Undated, MMF. This letter also contains the following interesting
remark: "I want you to speak English because I think you may be of
infinite service in advising our people about Reconstruction—having
lived yourself such an Alfred the Great Life for your own rising nation."

also an extremely interesting letter of six long pages from Elizabeth on the occasion of the death of Sarmiento's natural son, Dominguito, in the war against Paraguay in which Argentina, Brazil, and Uruguay were then engaged. It is written in her inimitable rambling style and handwriting; she writes in all the margins and even diagonally across the page atop other writing. Students of Elizabeth Peabody and American Protestantism will be interested in studying this letter, filled as it is with her very personal Christian theories. Unfortunately, there is room for only a sample:

> The letter from you which my sister read to me this morning, has gone to my heart of hearts. . . . I pray that the cup of this great sorrow may pass from your lips,—and *transfiguration* preclude the necessity of the *resurrection from the dead*. But, in the hope of the latter, if you cannot have the former, may you find tranquility & rest—as I do *for* you. For I do not believe any veil of death will fall over your eyes so thick, that you will not, *in your conscious existence* & identity, behold—though perhaps from *the other side*—the radiant harvest of the upright in heart— *the light sown—springing up in South America*— within & without the bounds of your own Argentine Republic.
>
> With the most respectful sympathy—
> Yours—
> Elizabeth P. Peabody[89]

One wonders what poor Sarmiento was able to make of this letter and whether it comforted him.

[89] The letter (MMF) is dated "February 6th," and is almost certainly from the year 1867.

Elizabeth Peabody was so affected by the death of Sarmiento's son that she wrote an article for *The Radical* about it. After paying tribute to Dominguito, Elizabeth used her article to defend Argentina's position in the war. "The American public," she writes, "has been so little in the habit of turning its attention to the details, or even to the important events of South American current history, that the merits of the war of the allies against the Paraguayan tyrant, are little understood. I say Paraguayan tyrant, because it is eminently against the tyrant that the war is waged, and not against the people who by his defeat would be released from a barbarous and demoralizing bondage."[90] That Sarmiento had friends in the United States willing to write what amounts to pro-Argentine propaganda speaks well of his skill and influence as a diplomat.

Little connects Sarmiento with Mary Mann's other sister, Sophia Peabody Hawthorne, and in fact Mary Mann appears to have tried to keep Sarmiento from knowing Sophia. Hawthorne had died in 1864, and Sophia was living at Wayside in Concord during the period when Sarmiento was in the United States. While Mary and Elizabeth can be clearly identified as liberals within the prevailing political and cultural ethos of the time, Sophia was identified with her husband's more conservative or apolitical attitudes. I refer to Hawthorne's views on Brook Farm, his defense of and assistance to Franklin Pierce, and his more "moderate" attitude toward slavery. The fact that Sarmiento was never presented to Sophia supports the idea of a continuing schism between the sisters advanced in Louise

---

[90] "Death of Capt. Sarmiento and Lieutenant Paz," *The Radical*, III (September 1866-June 1868), 28. Sarmiento had a son and daughter, both born out of wedlock, though both recognized and cared for by their father. Sarmiento was briefly married to the mother of his son.

Hall Tharp's *The Peabody Sisters of Salem*. In a letter
to Sarmiento, Mary Mann mentions a drawing of Horace
Mann "in preparation by a friend," without telling him
that this "friend" was her sister.[91]

In addition to acquainting him with her distinguished
family, Mary Mann introduced Sarmiento to the great
literary and philosophical minds of Concord and Cambridge. Among these men, Sarmiento could not have
made a more valuable acquaintance than Ralph Waldo
Emerson, with whom he spent two evenings in Concord
and whom he saw a third time in Cambridge at a farewell party given for the Argentine Minister in 1868 by
Mary Mann. Sarmiento first became familiar with Emerson and his works through Mary Mann's letters:

> Have you read the works of Ralph Waldo Emerson?
> He has written "Essays," "Representative Men," "Eng-
> lish Traits," "The Conduct of Life" and some ex-
> quisite poems—and is *the* poet, in my estimation. I
> wish I could say he is a representative American, but
> that would be saying too much for our people, few of
> whom are so advanced in thought as he. He resides in
> Concord, which makes it a shrine, and when you come
> you must see him. If you have time I hope you will
> read his books first. He was originally a Unitarian
> minister, but left preaching for any special denomina-
> tion on account of his peculiar views, some of which
> made him unacceptable. In his perfect freedom of
> thought & the expression of it he does represent the
> theory of American mind, the law of which is progress
> & free thought. Dogmatic religion is contrary to its
> genius. He wrote a beautiful analysis of our good

---

[91] Letter of July 22, 1865, MMF. Sophia's drawing appears as the
frontispiece to Volume I of Mary Mann's *Life of Horace Mann*.

President who was so cruelly murdered. He was truly a representative American, who grew daily with the growth of his time.[92]

Emerson is a chief subject in several subsequent letters in which Mary Mann is trying to induce Sarmiento to come for a visit to Concord. "I hope you will come in October," she writes in a letter dated simply September 1865:

> Everyone will be in his own place then and Mr. Emerson's daughter will be married (on the 30th) having him more at leisure. The beautiful New England weather will have come, and every one will feel strong to carry out his wishes. I shall not allow you to stay at the Hotel except for your apartments, for they do not have a nice table & I always do! So you will be obliged to get up in the morning and eat New England breakfasts in order that my sons, who are not at home always at noon, may have the pleasure of knowing you—and we will ask the pleasantest people to come to dine, as we want them. I live very simply, but you shall surely have good and wholesome food, good country milk & butter, & we will forget that you have ever been Governor or Diplomatic Minister or hero. No, we cannot forget that. . . .[93]

On September 25, she again mentions Emerson:

> Let me know, if you please, when you are ready to come, that I may not only have my turkey ready to welcome you (the turkey is the symbol of welcome at N. England dinner tables,) but my philosopher, who is better than the turkey, and who is the host of Concord. Sometimes he steals my guests, which is the

---

[92] Letter of July 22, 1865, MMF.   [93] MMF.

only sin I can convict him of, for he is as charming and good as he is great—and the worst of it is that he is such a delightful thief that he is not to be resisted.[94]

Sarmiento apparently spent three days in Concord. During this time he had a turkey dinner at Mary Mann's house, with Elizabeth Peabody in attendance and Ralph Waldo Emerson there as a guest, and two days later he again spent several hours with Emerson at his home and was invited to dine with him.[95] Emerson thanked Sarmiento for the gift of a copy of *Facundo*, and he encouraged Mary Mann to continue with her translation of the book. Sarmiento had sent a copy for Emerson along with his letter of July 28 in English, saying, "I add one more copy to the address of Mr. Emerson, whom I will be glad to pay my respect, when I have the pleasure of visiting Concord. . . ."[96] In her next letter Mary Mann mentioned that "My sister took . . . [the] book to Mr. Emerson last evening."[97] Emerson apparently read it with interest, because Mary Mann later wrote in the Preface to her translation of *Facundo* that "When R. W. Emerson read the book he told Colonel Sarmiento that if he would write thus for our public, he would be read."[98] Emerson read French quite well, but he spoke it poorly. As Mary Mann wrote to Sarmiento, "So few New England people speak either Spanish or French. . . . Mr. Emerson, poet and philosopher as he is, does murder the French language when he tries to pronounce it."[99] After Sarmiento left Concord, Mary Mann wrote to him: "I'll not think we shall allow you to speak

---

[94] MMF.　　　　[95] See *Obras*, XXIX, 67 and XXX, 202.
[96] *BAAL*, IV, No. 16 (1936), 592.
[97] Letter of August 7, 1865, MMF.
[98] P. 11.　　　　[99] Letter of October 1, 1865, MMF.

French when you visit Concord again. You must talk *American,* as Mr. Emerson said, & it is no matter how many blunders you make."[100]

Sarmiento described his meetings with Emerson as filled with good talk: "We spoke about everything: education, schools, the weather," anything appropriate to men "who represent different and yet similar countries, literatures, civilizations, and customs and who are put in intimate contact for the first time. 'Does it snow in your country?,' he asked. 'A little,' I replied. 'There is much to be learned from the snow,' he said."[101] Sarmiento was enchanted by this phrase, and he would repeat it several times in future writings.

Emerson made a great impression on Sarmiento, and there are seventeen references to him in the *Obras completas.* When Emerson died, Sarmiento wrote a long obituary for the Argentine press titled "Los dioses se van," which began: "News of the death of Emerson has arrived, he who was the poet-philosopher of the United States and whom we had the pleasure of counting among our friends. . . . A word from the River Plate which goes with conscience and love to unite with friends in the United States will not be ignored by those who survive in Concord."[102]

Sarmiento also met and corresponded with Henry Wadsworth Longfellow, and they too became friends. He was introduced to Longfellow in Cambridge a few days before his first visit to Concord. The occasion was

[100] Letter of November 12, 1865, MMF.

[101] *Obras,* xxx, 202.

[102] *Obras,* xlv, 348-350. One wonders what Emerson thought of Sarmiento. But unfortunately Sarmiento is not mentioned in any of the published letters or journals of Emerson, and Carilla (*El Embajador Sarmiento,* p. 106) states that the unpublished journals in the Houghton Library at Harvard do not contain a reference to Sarmiento. This is very curious and disappointing.

a dinner in Sarmiento's honor offered by the Harvard astronomer Benjamin Apthorp Gould, whom he had met through the good offices of Mary Mann. Longfellow was invited to the dinner, and he made the following notation in his journal for Thursday, October 12, 1865: "We go in the evening to a supper at Dr. Gould's, where we meet Sr. Sarmiento, Minister of the Argentine Republic, and I have the chance to try my Spanish; the first time for six years or more."[103]

Longfellow, who was Professor of Romance Languages at Harvard and had visited Spain as a young man, spoke and wrote Spanish well. When Sarmiento met him he wrote to a friend, "I passed many agreeable hours with Longfellow, reputed to be the best contemporary poet in the English language. He speaks Spanish better than you and I."[104] But despite his training and reputation as a Hispanist, Longfellow disappointed Sarmiento when he admitted that although he had read all the important Spanish writers, he was not at all familiar with Latin American literature. Sarmiento gave Longfellow works by Argentine writers and wrote to him later saying: "As a result of our conversation on South American literature when I had the pleasure of meeting you, I have been advised by my government that they are sending me some works of poetry and other books, which I will not neglect to pass on to you upon arrival."[105]

Sarmiento also gave Longfellow copies of his own works, and *Las escuelas* and the French edition of *Fa-*

[103] Longfellow, Journal for 1863-1869 (unpublished manuscript, Houghton Library, Harvard University), p. 84. See also Samuel Longfellow, *Life of Henry Wadsworth Longfellow With Extracts From his Journals and Correspondence* (Boston, 1896), II, 428.

[104] Addressee unknown; letter dated December 13, 1865, *Obras*, XXIX, 82.

[105] Letter of March 14, 1866, Longfellow Papers, Houghton Library, Harvard University.

cundo are to be found in the library of the Longfellow house in Cambridge. Longfellow was apparently much impressed with *Facundo,* because he thought of writing a long poem in Spanish based on it which he intended to call "Le Ruban Rouge" or "La Cinta Colorada," depending on whether he decided on a French or Spanish title.[106] Longfellow may have had a hand in the English translation of *Facundo.* In an undated letter, Mary Mann asked: "Is it too much of a favor for me to ask of you a translation of the two enclosed passages? The whole publication is a work of love, for no publisher will take any risk about it that will not *ensure* a return. So Hurd and Houghton have consented to publish it directly from the types, and without giving me *any* percentage for my trouble. I am very glad to get it done even so, for I am very sure it will prove interesting & give the public at least a good geography and history lesson."[107] I have not been able to discover which passages Mary Mann sent Longfellow, or whether he agreed to translate them.

Sarmiento also tried at one point to get Longfellow to translate something for him, the poem on Lincoln by Juana Manso which appeared in the second edition of *Vida de Lincoln.* Sarmiento had sent a copy of the first edition to Longfellow, and on March 14, 1866 he sent along the just-published second edition with this proposal:

> I enclose a copy of the 2nd. edition of the *Vida de Lincoln,* which has at the end some verses by Juana Manzo [sic] in Lincoln's memory.
>
> I hope you will find them appropriate. For me they

106 Correas, *Sarmiento and the United States,* p. 26.
107 Longfellow Papers, Houghton Library, Harvard University; probably early 1868.

have the merit of being the expression of the public opinion of my country; and, assuming you do not feel they disfavor the hero in any way, I would say that they express our feelings exactly.

I would consider it a great honor if you would agree to translate them into English and, if so, that you would then publish them in *The Atlantic Month* [sic] or another magazine. In the third edition of the *Vida de Lincoln* I will add the English translation, assured as I am that the name of Longfellow, and his approval of the verses, will have a most agreeable effect throughout South America. . . .

Fearing to have trespassed beyond the limits of your kindness I have the honor to remain. . . .[108]

Longfellow replied two weeks later:

Cambridge, March 30 1866

My Dear Sir,

I am extremely obliged to you for your letter and for the copy of the second edition of your excellent "Vida de Lincoln," which has reached me safely, and for which all North-Americans owe you grateful thanks. I should have written to you long ago to make my acknowledgments for this work as well as for "Civilisation et Barbarie," which is full of interest and information. The "Ruban Rouge" would be a good theme for a romance or an opera.

The poem by Manzo [sic] at the end of the "Vida de Lincoln" I like very much. It is simple, direct and forcible; qualities which I am afraid it would lose in translation. In reading it over the only stanza which easily and naturally translated itself is this;

[108] *Ibid.*

"Thou leavest to the nation for example
Thine own career as champion of the right.
Thy martyr-sepulchre to be a temple,
Thine apostolic word to be a light."
I hope you will pardon me for not having thanked
you sooner for your kind remembrance. The sole
reason has been my not knowing your address, whether
it was New York, or Washington, or where.

Hoping that when the warm weather comes, we
may have the pleasure of seeing you once more in
Cambridge, I remain, my Dear Sir, with great regard.

Yours truly
Henry W. Longfellow[109]

There is no evidence that the projected third edition of
the Lincoln book was ever printed, and Longfellow's
lack of interest in translating more than a few lines of
the Manso poem must have been the reason. Sarmiento
undoubtedly decided that without the added luster of
Longfellow's name there was no justification for another
edition.

Sarmiento remained in contact with Longfellow after
returning to Argentina. There is a letter of introduction
from Sarmiento to Longfellow in 1876 on behalf of an
Argentine friend about to visit the United States. Sarmiento also tells Longfellow that he has just attended a
centennial celebration at the American Legation in Buenos Aires. He congratulates him on the centennial and
says that he hopes the occasion has motivated Longfellow to "take his lyre down from the shelf."[110] Sarmiento
and Longfellow were apparently in contact as late as

[109] Letter of March 30, 1866, on display at the Sarmiento Museum,
Buenos Aires; incorrectly labeled "H. Goodfellow."
[110] Letter of July 10, 1876, Longfellow Papers, Houghton Library,
Harvard University.

1881, because there is a copy of *Ultima Thule* in the Sarmiento Museum in Buenos Aires with the following inscription: "Sr. D. F. Sarmiento with kind remembrance and regards of the Author, October 10, 1881."[111] Sarmiento also had an extensive relationship with another great American of this period, Henry Barnard. Barnard was Horace Mann's successor as a great leader in American education, and he naturally enjoyed the full measure of Mary Mann's interest and sympathy. Mary Mann put Sarmiento in contact with Barnard, and their relationship was to prosper sufficiently for Sarmiento to write to Barnard, just before leaving the United States in 1868, the following good-bye: "The common school system [will] carry the day at the opposed extremity of South America. You from here, and I from there, as San Martin and Bolivar of old, conquer the center."[112]

[111] It appears that this slim volume was brought to Argentina for Sarmiento by Mary Quincy Gould, wife of Benjamin Apthorp Gould, who had been in the United States for a visit and was rejoining her husband, then Director of the Cordoba Observatory. In his letter of December 24, 1882 to Mary Mann, Sarmiento wrote: "but we do not have Longfellow, the great poet who sent me his last poetry with Mrs. Gould, with us anymore" (*Obras*, xxxvii, 22). (Longfellow died on March 24, 1882.) On May 8, 1882, Sarmiento anonymously placed in the Argentine press an obituary for Longfellow which included the following remark: "Less than a year ago the wife of the astronomer, Gould, . . . brought from the United States, with his regards, one of the last poems of the great North American poet, with a dedication in beautiful handwriting to one of our public men on whose desk she was able to see the bust of the poet Longfellow" (*Obras*, xlv, 346). The small plaster bust of Longfellow mentioned here is now in the Sarmiento Museum.

For a more complete discussion of Sarmiento's relationship with Longfellow, see Michael Aaron Rockland, "Henry Wadsworth Longfellow and Domingo Faustino Sarmiento," *Journal of Inter-American Studies and World Affairs*, xii, No. 2 (April 1970), 271-279.

[112] Letter of July 21, 1868, Luiggi, "Letters, I," 210. Sarmiento's letters to Barnard are all in English, as Barnard, unlike Mary Mann and Longfellow, was not familiar with Spanish. Most of the letters were undoubtedly translated into English by Bartolito Mitre.

57

In her very first letter to him, Mary Mann told Sarmiento that "It will be a great pleasure to yourself as well as to our friend Dr. Barnard if you make his acquaintance during your residence in this country."[113] In her next letter she again mentioned Barnard, saying: "I have no doubt Mr. Barnard will be delighted to put into his Journal [*The American Journal of Education*] any account of educational matters there [in Argentina] which you will furnish him, and I shall write to him at once and ask him to call on you in New York. He will be all the more interested in you for your interest in his friend [Mann]."[114] Mary Mann then wrote to Barnard about Sarmiento. His diplomatic mission, she told Barnard, is "for the purpose of doing still more about education, and [he] wishes to know you, to whom I have referred him for every kind of information. He intends to see all the educational people while here and will undoubtedly seek you out in Hartford, but if you will call upon him in N.York at *58 W. 18th. street*, it would give him great gratification I know as it would hasten his acquaintance with you, and he is now occupied there. He is acquainted with your Journal."[115]

Sarmiento met Barnard for the first time at the Congress of the American Institute of Education in New Haven in August 1865, which he attended at Barnard's invitation. "I received with pleasure your kind invitation to attend the meeting of the American Institute of Education," Sarmiento wrote Barnard, "and I will be at the appointed time on board the steamboat to greet you for the first time. . . . I shall always be at your orders for any educational subject."[116] On August 30 Sarmiento

113 Letter of July 12, 1865, MMF.
114 Letter of July 22, 1865, MMF.
115 Luiggi, "Letters, I," 189.   116 *Ibid.*, 191.

wrote to Barnard asking if he would publish the speech Sarmiento had only partially delivered at the Congress in *The American Journal of Education*: "I enclose [for] you [a] copy of my article that was to be read at the meeting of the American Institute, and was left out for want of time. Will you be so kind as to have it inserted in your 'Journal.' I am unwillingly to throw it away after the time and expense incurred to prepare it. Besides, it will show to your readers that we are not altogether out of the world in education matters."[117] Barnard did indeed publish the speech. It appeared in the March 1866 issue under the title "The Dignity of the Schoolmaster's Work."[118]

During the next two years several other Sarmiento speeches or articles were published in Barnard's *Journal*, as well as articles by Mary Mann about Sarmiento or his various projects. Sarmiento and Barnard also collaborated on a number of educational projects. The following Barnard letter, which Sarmiento published in *Ambas Americas*, concerns the most serious of these joint undertakings:

St. John's College, Annapolis, Md.
March 21, 1867

I have received your generous letter of the 16th of this month and I am profoundly grateful for these demonstrations of interest in me and in my new work.

I have been able to disengage myself here so I will soon enter into my new work and I will send you then everything including the economics of this New Executive Department.

I am grateful for the newspapers and books on education in South America which, satisfying my desire,

117 *Ibid.*   118 XVI, 65-74.

you have kindly sent me. One of my first efforts will be to direct a complete study of the condition of education, systems, and institutions in the different countries of Europe and America. Can I count on you to take over the part on South America, at least to get me the statistics?

I hope to see you on Sunday, when I will be passing through New York.

Most sincerely yours,
Henry Barnard
Commissioner of the Office of Education of the United States[119]

Barnard had just been chosen as the first United States Commissioner of Education. A Department of Education was established by Congress in 1867, but a year later a subsequent bill abolished it and created in its place an "Office" and also reduced the Commissioner's salary. Sarmiento took almost as personally as did Barnard the 1868 bill limiting the importance of the Commissioner's position. As he later wrote to an Italian educator, "I attended [an] educational meeting . . . in Washington whose motive was the passage of a law creating a National Department of Education which *we proposed* to Congress. Passed and operating for one year, it was suppressed through the bad influence of Congressmen elected for other motives than the improvement of the people. I had the good fortune of being able to play a role in defending the Department through letters noting its advantages which I sent to Senator Sumner."[120]

These letters to Charles Sumner were Sarmiento's chief contribution during the controversy over the De-

---

[119] Retranslated into English from Sarmiento's Spanish translation, which appears in the facsimile edition of *Ambas Americas*, I, No. 1, 38.
[120] *Obras*, XLVII, 32, 33 (italics mine).

partment of Education. As he wrote to an Argentine friend, "My letters to Senator Sumner, . . . if they have the success which Barnard and Sumner predict for them, will have saved this institution in North America and made it productive of good in South America."[121] As with almost anyone else of consequence that Sarmiento knew in the United States, it was Mary Mann who put him in contact with Sumner. While he was visiting Washington, Mary Mann wrote to Sarmiento saying: "There is nothing in Washington life to soothe a perturbed spirit—but much to harrass the mind or the feelings. Mr. Sumner is an ark of refuge & a comfort to repose upon, & I hope you have found him there."[122]

Sumner was chairman of the Senate Education Committee which was hearing testimony on the proposed Department, and Sarmiento, undoubtedly with the encouragement of Barnard and Mary Mann, decided that letters from the Argentine Ambassador, who would be considered an "objective outsider," would be helpful.[123] Of his two letters to Sumner, both of which Mary Mann translated into English, one is particularly significant and is reproduced as an appendix to Mary Mann's translation of *Facundo*. In this letter Sarmiento argued against suppression of the Department, pointing out that in addition to its value to the United States (especially through bringing up the level of education in the South) it would present a shining example of public

[121] *Obras*, XLIX, 283.

[122] Undated, MMF. Mary Mann knew Washington life; Horace Mann served two terms as a Congressman.

[123] Sarmiento was also in contact with Representative (later President) Garfield, who was Chairman of the House Education Committee. A speech by Garfield on the subject of the National Department of Education was reproduced in the first number of *Ambas Americas* (see facsimile edn., pp. 13-26).

education to the rest of the world, especially South America.[124]

Sarmiento met or communicated with other prominent Americans during the period when he was in the United States as Ambassador, mostly through Mary Mann's efforts. George Ticknor, the Harvard Hispanist, admired Sarmiento's works, particularly *Recuerdos de provincia.* Sarmiento writings inscribed to Ticknor as late as 1874, when Sarmiento was completing his presidency, are in the Ticknor Collection in the Boston Public Library. Sarmiento mentions Ticknor in a long letter written from Boston to an Argentine friend: "The celebrated man of letters Ticknor has been seeking me for three days and today he writes asking for an appointment. You know very well that I do not need so much to make my head swell."[125] Sarmiento was also in contact during these years with Louis Agassiz, with Wendell Phillips, with the engraver John Sartain, with Frank Sanborn, and with the editor of the *Christian Examiner,* Joseph Allen.

The great majority of the people Sarmiento knew in the United States were New Englanders. This was not accidental. He had become enchanted with New England and its people during his brief trip in 1847, describing Boston at that time as "the Mecca of my pilgrimage" and ascribing a large share of the United States' accelerated development as compared to Europe and South America to the Puritan ethic. Later, when he was in the United States as Ambassador, he would speak of New England as "my personal country ever since I first

---

[124] Undated, but almost certainly of March 21, 1868. Sarmiento's letters to Sumner were sent to *The Massachusetts Teacher* by Mary Mann, who also wrote a short essay about their significance, and were published in the August and September 1868 issues of that periodical.

[125] Letter of October 5, 1865 to Aurelia Velez, *Obras,* XXIX, 67.

saw it."[126] It is clear that although the United States as a whole was his model, New England, and more specifically the Boston-Concord area, was the starting point for all those things he celebrated in the United States. "This is New England," he wrote, "the cradle of the modern republic, the school for all of America," and Boston he described for an Argentine newspaper as "the pioneer city of the modern world, the Zion of the ancient Puritans, the fatherland of Franklin, the citadel of liberty, the Academy of thought, . . . the laboratory of the sciences, and the headquarters from which the apostles of democracy go out to carry to the western states the practice and spirit of free institutions. Her schoolmasters and mistresses, her rectors and professors of schools and universities, her workers and manufacturers have received divine inspiration. *Euntes in mundum Universum.* Europe contemplates in New England the power which in the future will supplant her. In New England, Massachusetts, in Massachusetts, Boston."[127]

Sarmiento was not keen on the American South. The South, he felt, shared the barbarism or backwardness typical of Europe and South America. "The South with its slaves," Sarmiento wrote in the introduction to *Vida de Lincoln,* "was the geological level under the present one. It was an intermediary point between Europe and America and the point of communication between South and North America. Add to this that Florida was Spanish, Louisiana and Mississippi were French, and Texas hasn't finished being Mexican." In other words, continued European influence and the proximity of

[126] Letter of October 7, 1865 to Mary Mann, *BAAL,* III, No. 9 (1935), 77.

[127] *Obras,* XXXI, 179; article written for *El zonda* on October 9, 1865, *Obras,* XXIX, 71.

Latin Amerca were responsible for the South's inferior development as compared to the North.[128] The Southern states approximated South America in their development. As Sarmiento said in a speech not long after returning to Argentina, "When the top statesmen in the United States asked me to tell them something about my country, I answered, with sorrow, that our situation was the same as that of the Southern states."[129]

Although little about the South attracted him, Sarmiento did not confine his affections to New England. He also was fond of the Middle West, particularly Chicago, which he referred to as "The Queen of the West."[130] After returning from a trip to the Midwest in the summer of 1866, he wrote an article entitled "Hacia el Oeste" for an Argentine newspaper, in which he said:

> On the other side of the Alleghenies, the new world begins. . . . On this side of the Alleghenies there is history, there are centuries. On the other side, everything began yesterday. . . . At the beginning of this century a new sound was heard in the forests of those lands. . . . It was the axe of the squatter; and since then that noise hasn't stopped but has, instead, been mixed with all the other strange and discordant human sounds. . . . In New England and New York one sees surprising and admirable progress in industry, the arts, human knowledge, and machinery. But all of this is natural progress, a step beyond that attained in the rest of the world. In the West, yankee genius has more room to move about and expand, to try new things that would seem impossible in the older states. In the

[128] *Obras*, XXVII, 16.
[129] "Discurso a los maestros," *Obras* (1st edn.), XXI, 245.
[130] *Obras*, XXIX, 179.

West they try things which are superhuman, inconceivable, seemingly absurd.[131]

During Sarmiento's last trip through the Middle West, in June of 1868, he was awarded an honorary doctorate by the University of Michigan,[132] thereby realizing the boyhood dream recorded in *Recuerdos de provincia*. Like Benjamin Franklin, he had achieved the highest goal of the self-made man.

When Sarmiento returned to the East he had less than a month left in the United States. During the previous few months the news from his political supporters in Argentina had been increasingly good. "They write me from my country that I am the only candidate possible for the presidency," he wrote to Mary Mann. Having received no instructions from his government, Sarmiento was in something of a quandary about whether he could leave the United States and return to Argentina. He decided, however, that his election was so certain that he had best start back to South America at once. He went to Washington for his official good-byes, but "had to take leave of the President in writing, as I had no letters of recall. To Mr. Seward I said what was necessary to satisfy him about my not having resided in Washington."[133] Leaving the legation in the hands of young Mitre, he sailed from New York on July 23, 1868 aboard the *Merrimac*. As his ship passed out into the bay, he thought: "Farewell to the United States! I carry it with me as memory and model. It has the beauty of

---

131 *Obras*, XXIX, 172, 173, 182.

132 For a description of the events surrounding the awarding of Sarmiento's honorary doctorate, see Michael Aaron Rockland, "Sarmiento's Honorary Doctorate From the University of Michigan," *The Michigan Alumnus*, LXXVI, No. 4 (December 1969), 20-23, 34.

133 Letter of December 24, 1867, *BAAL*, III, No. 10 (1935), 230, 231; *Obras*, XLIX, 282.

the Hudson, Staten Island, Niagara, and Chicago. It has Mrs. Mann, Davidson, Emerson, Longfellow, and so many other noble people. The Republic as an institution. The future promise of the world. Farewell! Farewell! Farewell."[134]

On August 16, 1868, while the *Merrimac* was off the coast of Brazil, the Argentine Congress, to which the election had been thrown because none of the three candidates had a majority, gave Sarmiento 79 of 131 votes cast. He had thought this might happen. He had written to Barnard two days before leaving the United States, "I am almost sure that I have been elected President. My correspondence dates from a day after the election in Buenos Aires. I had 24 votes, against 4 lost; . . . if the majority were not decisive the Congress is to decide and then I have . . . 4/5 of the votes."[135] On August 17 the *Merrimac* put in at Bahia harbor. There the news had arrived of Sarmiento's election, and he was given a 21-gun salute by the *Warrior*, an American warship which had put in at that port for provisions or repairs. The ship's band struck up "Hail Columbia" as the *Merrimac* came alongside, and the Captain of the American ship came on board to present his compliments to Argentina's new President.[136]

After a short stop in Rio for talks with the Brazilian emperor, Sarmiento steamed on to Buenos Aires, where he arrived on August 29. He was greeted and acclaimed by the people and the government still in power. A critical newspaper had asked during the just-ended electoral campaign: "What will Sarmiento bring us from the United States if he is elected President?" and had

---

[134] *Ibid.*, 292. Aboard ship with Sarmiento was General Henry C. Worthington, the new United States Ambassador to Argentina.
[135] Letter of July 21, 1868, Luiggi, "Letters, I," 210.
[136] *Obras*, XLIX, 312-314.

answered: "Schools! Nothing more than schools."[137] The criticism was well taken, for the day after Sarmiento arrived in Buenos Aires he told a large delegation of teachers and students who came to call on him: "We need to make all the Republic a school." "Schools," he said, "are democracy."[138] He must have been reminded at that moment of his statement of long before, which we have already quoted: "An educated people would never elect a Rosas."

On October 12, 1868, Domingo Faustino Sarmiento was inaugurated as the second President of a united Argentina. He at once began to create institutions embodying the ideals which had so long inspired him. Naturally, it was to the field of education that he devoted his greatest energy, as he strove to overcome Argentina's educational deficits. In one of his first messages to Congress he proposed a public library system like the one he had admired so much in the United States. He built schools: when Sarmiento came to power there were thirty thousand children in school in all of Argentina. Six years later, when he retired from office, there were one hundred thousand. The fact that Argentina has the best educational system in South America today is largely due to his efforts.

His major achievement in the educational field was to set up a system of normal schools throughout Argentina. For this purpose, he imported sixty-five American schoolteachers, almost all of them young ladies from New England. The fantastic story of this nineteenth-century "Peace Corps" has been told definitively by Alice Houston Luiggi in her book *65 Valiants*.[139] As usual

---

[137] "Discurso a los maestros," *Obras* (1st edn.), XXI, 244.

[138] *Ibid.*, 247, 248.

[139] Mrs. Luiggi's book has been published in both languages: *Sesenta y cinco valientes* (Buenos Aires, 1959); and *65 Valiants* (Gainesville, Fla., 1965).

with any Sarmiento project which in any way concerned the United States, Mary Mann was intimately involved in this venture. Always surrounded by schoolteachers and engaged in educational projects with her sister Elizabeth, Mary Mann was just the person to handle recruitment for Sarmiento.

Another major accomplishment of Sarmiento's presidency in the area of education, as well as in science, was the creation of the National Observatory at Cordoba, the first astronomical observatory in the Southern Hemisphere. Here for the first time the southern skies were charted systematically. The work was entrusted to Benjamin Apthorp Gould, the Harvard astronomer, who went to Cordoba in 1870 at Sarmiento's invitation and remained there until 1885, when his work was completed and he returned to the United States.

These two projects illustrate the extent to which Sarmiento remained in contact with the United States and Americans throughout his term as president. Another American with whom he corresponded was his counterpart in the United States, President Grant. When Sarmiento founded the Argentine Military Academy he wrote to Grant to ask if Argentine officers might train at West Point, so that on their return their experience might benefit the Argentine Academy.[140] Grant replied that attendance by foreign military officers at West Point was prohibited by law, but that he intended to "request of Congress the necessary authority to permit young Argentine military officers to study at West Point."[141] When Sarmiento died, a newspaper mentioned that "He was

[140] National Archives of the United States, "Notes from the Argentine Legation," Vol. 2, Sarmiento to Grant, Buenos Aires, 12 February 1874.
[141] Letter of April 15, 1874, on display in the Sarmiento Museum in Buenos Aires.

in communication with General Grant who, when he was President, sent a message to President Sarmiento . . . recommending that, to govern well, he should not read critical newspapers."[142]

As President, Sarmiento rarely made a speech or introduced legislation without mentioning the United States or his American friends. Dedicating a hospital in 1873, he said: "Why should I not introduce you here to my friend, Mrs. Mann, who after 66 years of a busy life writes me every month, telling me of her achievements in the creation of asylums for the deaf and dumb."[143] When General Worthington, then United States Ambassador to Argentina, was about to return home, Sarmiento addressed these words to him: "We have begun to habituate ourselves to the idea that the United States is not just a friendly nation, as are the others, but our sister country and our tutor on the dangerous road which we must follow and along which she has made magnificent progress. We regard it as impossible that we could have differences with the United States."[144] But his admiration for the United States, which sometimes approached adulation, was not always helpful to the President with his Argentine constituency. An editorial in *La prensa*, now dean of Buenos Aires newspapers, described his constant references to the United States as "excessive."[145]

This was not the only criticism he heard as President, for there was a darker side to his administration. A ruinous war with Paraguay, which had begun during the

142 *El censor*, September 14, 1868, p. 1 (on display in the Sarmiento Museum in San Juan).

143 Correas, *Sarmiento and the United States*, p. 40.

144 National Archives of the United States, General Records of the State Department, "Diplomatic Dispatches from the Argentine Republic," Vol. 17, Worthington to Fish, 10 July 1869.

145 *La prensa*, June 9, 1870.

previous administration, continued throughout most of his. In 1871 a yellow fever epidemic all but decimated the population of Buenos Aires. There was a nearly successful attempt on the President's life as he rode through downtown Buenos Aires in his carriage. Constant crises led him to take strong measures, and his political enemies accused him of adopting many of the same tactics used by the personalist gaucho leaders he had sworn to destroy. They called him "Don Yo," and they said that he was "arbitrary," "tyrannical," "immature," and "a prima donna." Shortly before the end of his term of office a revolt broke out, led by, of all people, his former political colleague and comrade-in-arms, ex-President Mitre. "So who do you think is making these difficulties?" he had earlier written to Mary Mann. "The ex-President and his Ministers, the present Vice President, the Speaker of the *Cámara*, and a large part of the Congress which is left over from the past Administration."[146] Sarmiento appears to have become increasingly isolated during his administration; his letter to Mary Mann indicates that he felt even his Vice President had turned against him.

Part of his problem lay in being a prisoner of his own "civilization versus barbarism" thesis. He often dismissed rural and nativist elements out of hand as reactionary and, in so doing, alienated people who might otherwise have been with him. Sarmiento tended to forget that he was as much a son of San Juan as of Buenos Aires and that he had probably won the presidential election because he was the only candidate who appealed to elements in both country and city. He had unfortunately grown to have such faith in "progress," that is, in cities, machines, and organization, that he did not

[146] Letter of August 11, 1869, Luiggi, "Letters, II," 349.

sufficiently recognize the evils which these bring with them. In some ways his administration was typical of the bureaucracy which Jose Hernández's *Martin Fierro* (1872), the epic poem of gaucho life, meant to satirize. *Martin Fierro* and *Facundo*, the two most famous works of Argentine literature, are thesis and antithesis in the city-country dichotomy which has always been central to Argentine life.

Despite the mistakes he made and the difficulties he encountered, Sarmiento accomplished much during his administration—and he inspired even more. If there was disorder and turmoil, the candid observer would have to admit that there has been too much of this in almost every Argentine administration down to today. The difference betwen Sarmiento and other Argentine Presidents is that he was somehow able to rise above the immediate problems confronting him and to make real and lasting contributions to Argentina. When he left office in 1874, he left a united and progressive country, with a sure future if it could avoid the dissension which had plagued it in the past.

After 1874 Sarmiento became a John Quincy Adams-like figure in Argentine life, taking on one elective or appointive political post or cultural task after another as befitted the elder statesman he had become. He also continued writing, both as a journalist and as a historian and philosopher. In 1883 his last major work, the two volume *Conflicto y armonías de las razas en America*, was published.[147] This is a sociological treatise which attempts to explain why Latin America lagged behind other regions, particularly North America, in development. In *Conflicto*, Sarmiento pushes his civilization versus barbarism thesis to illogical and even dan-

147 *Obras*, XXXVII and XXXVIII.

gerous extremes. Whereas in *Facundo* and, as we shall discuss in part II of this essay, in *Travels* he had discarded such notions, in *Conflicto*, which he called his "Facundo grown old," Sarmiento finds the basic difference between North and South America in national origin and race. South America was settled by the Spaniards, with their monarchic, antidemocratic, and rigidly Catholic ideas, while the United States was settled by the Puritans, a people dedicated to hard work, education, and democracy. Also, he writes, "the Anglo-Saxons did not admit the indigenous races as associates or even as serfs in their society, whereas the Spanish colonizers absorbed into their own blood a prehistoric and servile race."[148] Sarmiento feels that the only solution to South America's problems is massive immigration from Europe and that the only way to catch up to the United States is to *be* the United States.

The dedication of *Conflicto* reads: "Dedicado a Mrs. Horace Mann en Boston Mass.," and it is followed by a letter to Mary Mann dated December 24, 1882 and occupying twenty printed pages. Before finishing the book, he had written to Mary Mann at one point to say that while writing of the Pilgrims, who he felt were responsible for the free institutions of the United States, he had been "so carried away by the grandeur of it, that I felt a glow like that a blacksmith feels as he bends over his forge."[149] Finishing the book, he wrote to her that "The 24th of the same month [December 1882] I finished the letter-prologue and dedication of the book with a melancholy note. Various friends of our group had already parted definitively. Remaining are you, Miss Peabody with her kindergarten, Gould with his tele-

148 *Obras* (1st edn.), XXXVIII, 415.
149 Quoted in Correas, *Sarmiento and the United States*, p. 43.

scope, and me offering my humble services as a historian."[150]

Mary Mann died in 1887. Sarmiento was informed of her death by her son, Benjamin Pickman Mann, who was also responsible for seeing through the press the novel his mother had begun many years before and finished only a few days before her death: *Juanita: A Romance of Real Life in Cuba Fifty Years Ago.*[151] When informed of Mary Mann's death, Sarmiento prepared a long obituary for *El nacional.*[152] Although there are many notable things in the obituary I might quote, these words, which he wrote two years before her death, are the most appropriate ones for closing our discussion of Sarmiento and Mary Mann: "I have a chapter in my life's story which I shall write someday and entitle, 'Sarmiento's Women.' . . . My mother is one of them. . . . My godmother was another. The third is Mary Mann, 80 years old today, who helped me through her friendship and enthusiasm—as I was in the educational field the successor to her Horace. She opened the door and found me a seat among the great men of the United States."[153]

In 1884, a year after *Conflicto* was published, the Argentine government commissioned the publication of the collected works of Sarmiento. The first volume was published in 1885, in Chile. The work was carried out under the supervision of Luis Montt, son of Sarmiento's friend, Manuel Montt. But after the publication of Volume VII, the work was transferred to Argentina and put under the supervision of Sarmiento's grand-

150 Quoted in Rafael Alberto Arrieta, "Horacio Mann, en el 150º aniversario de su nacimiento," *La prensa*, April 28, 1946, p. 1 of second section.

151 See note 69.   152 *Obras*, XLV, 340-342.

153 *Obras*, XLVI, 261.

son, Augusto Belin Sarmiento. Eventually, fifty-two volumes and an index were compiled, the last volume being published in 1903. Several Argentine commentators have written that if all of Sarmiento's work worthy of being in print were to be published, the *Obras completas* would be more than one hundred volumes.[154]

In his final years, his health failing, Sarmiento was spending a good deal of his time in Asuncion, Paraguay, where the climate was milder. He made his last speech there, and on that occasion did not neglect to mention the United States. "Chance," he said, "has been kind enough on this occasion to put me beside his Excellency, the Minister of the United States, who has chosen to honor this act with his presence; for it was in his country that I studied the reasons for that nation's extraordinary development, and the bases of its liberties, in order to apply them to our land."[155] He died in Asuncion on September 11, 1888 at 77 years of age, and an Argentine warship was sent to bring his body to Buenos Aires. The crypt of his tomb in La Recoleta Cemetery is lined with books. Ironically, not far away lie the remains of Facundo Quiroga, who also died on September 11, and some years on this day La Recoleta has been the scene of pitched battle between the teachers and students who have come to visit Sarmiento's grave and the Tacuara and other neofascist youths for whom Facundo Quiroga remains a hero.

[154] Augusto Belin Sarmiento writes: "Putting together all of the unpublished and published writings which are known, instead of fifty-two volumes there would have been more like one hundred" (prologue to the index of the *Obras completas* [which is really a fifty-third volume], p. vii). And Emilio Carilla feels that "Today, apart from the advantage of a more faithful and better done edition, the true *Obras* would run to not fifty-two but one hundred volumes" (*El Embajador Sarmiento*, p. 5).

[155] Correas, *Sarmiento and the United States*, p. 44.

There are many monuments to Sarmiento, but the ones which would have pleased him the most are that Argentina celebrates September 11 as Dia del Maestro, a day on which all schools are closed; that in 1943, at the Inter-Amercan Educational Conference in Panama, a declaration was approved establishing September 11 as Dia del Maestro throughout the Americas; and that at another international educational conference held in Mexico City in 1964 Sarmiento was declared "Maestro Universal de la Educación del Pueblo." These are fitting monuments to the man who while Ambassador to the United States went about the country introducing himself as an educator and who was later known in his own country as the "Schoolteacher President."

2. Sarmiento's *Travels*

Sarmiento's *Viajes* is made up of eleven letters, described by one Argentine scholar as "letter-reports,"[1] to various comrades, most of whom were Argentine, anti-Rosas exiles living in Chile and Uruguay. Originally appearing as two volumes in 1849 and 1851, *Viajes* is published in three volumes in modern editions. The first two, *De Valparaiso a Paris* and *España e Italia*, consist of five letters each. The third, *Estados Unidos* or *Travels in the United States in 1847*, is made up of a single extremely long letter addressed to Valentin Alsina, a lawyer and formerly a professor at Buenos Aires University, then exiled in Montevideo.[2]

The letter to Alsina is dated November 12, 1847, eight days after Sarmiento set sail from New Orleans for Havana on the *P. Soulé*, "a wretched and pestilent sailing vessel which . . . carried its cargo of pigs plus three or four moribund consumptives who embarked with us and bunked in extremely narrow, hot cabins filled with cobwebs" (p. 307). On November 12 he must have been three days away from Havana, since the first entry for Havana in his expense notebook is dated November 15.

But we should not simply take Sarmiento's word for it that he wrote a book-length letter of two hundred pages (at least four hundred handwritten pages, con-

[1] Noberto Rodriguez Bustamante, Introduction to *España e Italia*, p. 40.

[2] Alsina was the editor of the anti-Rosas Montevideo newspaper *Comercio del Plata*, whose previous editor had been assassinated by a Rosas agent. Sarmiento saw Alsina briefly early in his journey, when he stopped off in Montevideo to change ships before reembarking for Europe. Alsina would later serve as Governor of the Province of Buenos Aires; his son, Adolfo, was Vice President in the Sarmiento administration. Sarmiento held Alsina in high esteem, saying of him at one point: "*Salud*, Alsina! The Republic which has such sons is still not lost!" (*Obras*, III, 105).

76

sidering the size of his script) on November 12, 1847 on a pitching boat with his traveling companion, the practical joker Santiago Arcos, aboard.[3] Nor do I imagine that he finished the letter during the next two days, or while in Cuba (his time there was spent crossing the island on horseback), or that he ever posted it to Alsina. Although some of the ten shorter letters which make up the rest of the *Viajes* were published in newspapers in France, Spain, Uruguay, and Chile during the trip and before being incorporated into the *Viajes*,[4] there is no evidence of prepublication of any part of *Travels*. It is probable that the four-hundred-page letter to Alsina represented too much of an investment of time and energy to entrust to the mails. What seems more likely is that Sarmiento took notes during his trip through the United States, began to write aboard the *Soulé*, and did the major part of the writing on his return to Chile. The fact that Volume II of the first edition of *Viajes*, which includes *Estados Unidos*, was not published until 1851, two years after Volume I, supports this point of view.

What I am suggesting is that, rather than a letter to

[3] The chief actor in several of the most humorous scenes in *Travels* is Santiago Arcos, a wealthy Chilean who lived a soldier-of-fortune existence in Europe and America. He turned up in California during Gold Rush days, and he later took part in the Battle of Caseros against Rosas. Sarmiento met Arcos for the first time in New York City, when Arcos, in characteristic fashion, insinuated himself into a group which included Sarmiento by asking: "'Do any of you know Señor Sarmiento who should have just arrived from Europe?' This was Don Santiago Arcos, who, recognizing me, told me he had come from France in my pursuit, that from now on we would be inseparable until Chile, and that we were friends, very good friends of long standing, accompanying these words with that laugh of good will which has the power of disarming the most fastidious aloofness" (p. 215). Arcos' last letter to Sarmiento, written as he lay very ill in Paris in 1874, relates his answer to a man who had asked what President Sarmiento had accomplished: "He has made 100,000 citizens (the schools), who will in turn make 500,000" (letter of September 10, 1874, *Obras*, XLV, 306, 307).

[4] Preface to *De Valparaíso a París*, p. 46.

Alsina, *Travels* is a book dedicated to him. The letter
was the form or literary device Sarmiento found convenient for expressing his thoughts. In his Preface to the
Viajes, he tells the reader that "the letter is such an
elastic and malleable literary form as to lend itself to
all styles and admit all matters"; and, he continues, the
letter "adapts itself . . . well to the natural variety of
the journey."[5] It seems clear, therefore, given his sophistication about the form he adopted, that Sarmiento intended to make a book of his "letter" to Alsina from the
start.

The *Viajes* is regarded by Argentine scholars as one
of Sarmiento's chief works. Roy Bartholomew calls it
"the most literary of his books and one of the principal
works in the Spanish language in the nineteenth century."[6] Alberto Palcos describes it as "one of his brilliant
works for its style and judgments."[7] Ricardo Rojas puts
Viajes on the same level as *Facundo* and *Recuerdos de
provincia,* Sarmiento's most widely read books, saying
that all three are "brother books," with the "same point
of view and same importance."[8] Bartholomew supports
Rojas' idea: "When Sarmiento leaves [on his world trip]
he has already published *Facundo.* When he returns he
has not yet written *Recuerdos de provincia.* Between
these two treasures of our spiritual history is situated the
Viajes, equally valuable."[9]

Estados Unidos is the best part of the *Viajes,* both for
the quality of its insights and the originality of its
thought. Alberto Palcos feels that Sarmiento "dedicated

[5] *Ibid.*
[6] In the commentary on the inside cover of *España e Italia.*
[7] Introduction to *De Valparaíso a París,* p. 38.
[8] *El pensamiento vivo de Sarmiento,* p. 14.
[9] See note 6.

the best chapters of the *Viajes* to the United States."[10]
More significant, Sarmiento himself wrote to Luis
Montt in 1886, when Montt was compiling the first few
volumes of the *Obras completas* in Chile, asking that he
"give special attention to the part on the United States
. . . because you must know that *I place capital importance on my revelations on that country* [his italics]. . . .
My trip was like Marco Polo's; I discovered a world and
I adhered to it."[11]

We have already described in part 1 of this essay how
Sarmiento came to "adhere" to the United States during
his world tour, following his disillusionment with
France and with Europe in general as models for Argentina. The United States, as one Argentine historian
has eloquently written, became at this time and forever
after "his road to Damascus."[12]

At the same time as he was singling out the United
States as a model for his fellow exiles and revolutionaries
scattered about South America, Sarmiento was saying
much that was important and novel about the United
States. One of the main distinctions of his *Travels* is its
recognition, at this surprisingly early date, that the
United States was the coming great power. At a time
when the United States received little serious consideration in most European capitals, Sarmiento was insisting
that it already was or was at the point of becoming the
most important country in the world. "Today," he
writes in *Travels*, "nothing stops the Yankee!" (p. 50).

10 Alberto Palcos, Introduction to *De Valparaiso a París*, p. 32.

11 This letter is to be found on p. 8 of *Obras*, xxix. It is incorrectly
dated October 20, 1866, and for this reason it has been placed in this
volume of the *Obras*, which contains miscellaneous writings from Sarmiento's years as Ambassador. Its correct location is Volume v. The
letter must have been written on October 20, 1886, when Luis Montt
was compiling the first seven volumes of the *Obras completas* in Chile.

12 Antonio de la Torre, Introduction to *De Valparaíso a París*, p. 24.

And elsewhere he says, "The United States will certainly be and, in fact, is already, by reason of its power and prestige, the foremost nation of the world."[13] As one Argentine Sarmientista points out, "Don Domingo divined the colossal future of the United States at a time when it was all but ignored on the rest of the planet"; and another writes that, "At a time when Europe disparaged the United States and had little confidence in her future and her institutions, he declared that in twenty years . . . she would be the dominant nation in the world."[14] *Travels* largely addresses itself to the question of how this could be true of a nation that had been in existence only a little more than a half-century.

Like other writers who have tried to explain the uniqueness of the United States, such as Hector St. John de Crèvecoeur and Frederick Jackson Turner, Sarmiento divides his discussion between environmental and cultural factors, between natural and human resources. Early in *Travels*, after describing what lands and resources he would require if he were entrusted with the mission of creating an ideal republic, Sarmiento exclaims: " 'Land of Cockaigne!' a Frenchman would say. 'The Isle of Barataria!' a Spaniard would suggest. Imbeciles! It is the United States as God created it, and I would swear that, creating this part of the world, He knew full well that round about the nineteenth century the dregs of His poor humanity, trampled upon elsewhere, enslaved and dying of hunger so that the few can live a life of luxury, would come together here, develop

[13] From Sarmiento's "Memoria al Instituto Histórico de Francia" of 1853, quoted in Alberto Palcos' *The Pan-American Ideals of Sarmiento*, p. 10.

[14] Alberto Palcos in the Introduction to *De Valparaíso a París*, p. 40; Amaranto Abeledo in "En torno a los viajes de Sarmiento a los Estados Unidos," *Revista de educación* (Buenos Aires), II, New Series (March 1957), pp. 2, 3.

themselves without obstacle, grow great, and by their example avenge the human race for so many centuries of feudal domination and suffering" (p. 118). In the United States, he feels, "God has at last permitted the concentration in one organism, in one nation, of enough virgin land to permit society to expand infinitely without fear of poverty, with iron to complement human strength, coal to make the machines go, forests to provide materials for shipbuilding" (p. 179). "The American's greatest potential," he continues, "lies in his possession of the land which will be the nursery of his new family" (p. 163).

Nevertheless, Sarmiento is also quick to point out that "The Europeans attribute American prosperity to the advantages that a new country offers, with virgin lands easy to obtain; which would be a satisfactory enough explanation if South America, big as it is, did not have an even greater quantity of virgin lands, equally easy to obtain, and yet have backwardness, poverty, and greater ignorance, if such is possible, than exists among the European masses" (pp. 154-155). Abundant land and natural resources, though contributing factors, are not decisive. The land must still be distributed in such a way as to encourage the creation of individual and national wealth. In the United States, he writes, "There is a regular procedure for the distribution of these lands," and "The state is the faithful administrator of the abundant lands which belong to the Union." In South America, on the other hand, "The fatal error of the Spanish colonization . . . , the deep wound which has condemned present generations to inertia and backwardness, was in the system of land distribution" (pp. 163-164).

Sarmiento is, therefore, celebrating not so much the physical conditions which Americans encountered in their country as what they have done with them. Argentines and other South Americans, with an equally promising situation, have neglected to exploit it, while the most characteristic thing about Americans "is their ability to appropriate for their own use, generalize, popularize, conserve, and perfect all the practices, tools, methods, and aids which the most advanced civilization has put in the hands of men. . . . There are no unconquerable habits that retard for centuries the adoption of an obvious improvement, and, on the other hand, there is a predisposition to try anything" (p. 132). Sarmiento would seem to be saying that the reason for the superior development of the United States is to be found not so much in her lands and natural resources as in her people.

But it was not Sarmiento's view at this time (though it would come to be by the time he wrote *Conflicto y armonías de las razas en America*) that national origin, or race, that is, differences between Anglo-Saxons and Spaniards, was the key factor in explaining the disproportionate development of the United States as compared with South America. He does betray an attraction to Anglo-Saxon industriousness when he writes, "Why was it the Anglo-Saxon race that discovered this piece of the world which is so well suited to its industrial instincts, while South America, a land of gold and silver mines and gentle and submissive Indians, has fallen to the Spanish race—a region aptly suited to its proud laziness, its backwardness, and its industrial ineptitude?" (pp. 118-119). But he is just as quick to "establish one fact: that the aptitude of the Anglo-Saxon race is also no explanation for American development. Englishmen are the inhabitants of both sides of the Niagara River, but, nevertheless, there at the point where the English colony touches the American population, the eye perceives that they are two distinct peoples" (p. 155). Differing economic, political, and social development in the United States and Canada, he concludes, must result from factors other than the national origin of the settlers of the two countries.

In addition to discarding race or national origin as significant to the development of the nation, Sarmiento has a most interesting and unique thesis on the immigrant. "In the United States European immigration is a barbaric element. Who would have believed it! Except for natural exceptions, the European . . . comes from the neediest classes, is usually ignorant, and is not accustomed to the republican practices of the land. . . . And so it is that foreigners in the United States are the burden of scandal and the leaven of corruption annually introduced into the bloodstream of that nation which for so long has been educated in the practices of liberty." Sarmiento goes on to describe various accommodations which had been made for the benefit of the immigrant, including the easing of citizenship requirements in the Western states, and he adds: "Society in the United States is very well organized to counter this relaxation of rules in order to disseminate population over the country, and splendid results would long ago have been produced if it were not an interminable task while *i barbari* keep coming from Europe by the hundreds of thousands . . ." (pp. 191-192).

Sarmiento repeatedly belittles any contribution that the immigrant, a newcomer from decadent Europe, might be capable of making to the civilization of the United States. He feels that the Yankee is uniformly so much more highly educated and more advanced than the immigrant that *he* is the civilization-bringer, not the immigrant. He sees value in the melting pot being created in the United States, as when he writes that "the fragments of old societies are coming together . . . , mixing, and forming the newest, the youngest, and the most daring republic on the face of the earth" (p. 124). But he feels that whatever of value the immigrant brings, the Yankee can make something better of it, for "The American, far from barbarizing, as we have, the elements which European civilization handed him when he came as a settler, has worked to perfect them and even to improve upon them" (p. 139).

Sarmiento even casts aspersions on the reproductive powers of the immigrant. After discussing the practice of marrying early and producing large families in the United States, as well as the sharply rising population figures, he writes: "Immigration has something to do with these figures, but only to a limited extent. The immigrant is not a prolific animal until he has received the Yankee bath" (p. 137).

Unwilling to single out either environmental or cultural factors or natural or human resources as the explanation for America's extraordinary development, Sarmiento concludes that "these factors are interdependent: liberty and abundant land; iron and industrial genius; democracy and superior ships. Try to separate them one from the other in your mind. Say that liberty and public education have nothing to do with this unprecedented prosperity which is surely leading to undisputed supremacy. The fact is that in the European monarchies decrepitude, revolutions, poverty, ignorance, barbarism, and the degradation of the greatest number are always found together" (pp. 179-180).

What Sarmiento ultimately seems to think makes the United States different from other societies is the liberty and equality of opportunity which her citizens enjoy. "Can freedom of religion produce wealth?" he asks, and he answers his own question affirmatively, though he admits that "It is not easy to demonstrate the connection between liberty and the marvels of prosperity displayed by the United States" (p. 154). Liberty and equality create a climate for progress, he feels, by giving every citizen the confidence that all things are possible for him.

Sarmiento cites the free atmosphere characterizing railroads in the United States as an index to social and economic progress. "The railroads, as a means to wealth and civilization," he writes, "are common both to Europe and the United States, and since in both lands they date from just yesterday, through them you can study the spirit that pervades both societies." "In France," he continues, "everything pertaining to the railroad . . . is looked over carefully by the engineers before traffic is allowed to move. . . . The train does not leave the platform until four minutes after an army of guards have ascertained that all travelers are in their seats, the doors closed, the road clear, and no one closer than a yard to where the train will pass. Everything has been foreseen, calculated, and examined so that all can tranquilly sleep in their hermetically sealed jail." In the United States, on the other hand, "the rails are of wood with iron plates on top which often get loose, so the eye of the engineer is constantly fixed on the track in order to avert a disaster. . . . The train starts slowly from the station, and when it is already underway passengers jump aboard and fruit and newspaper vendors jump off. Everyone walks from one car to the other just for the fun of it and to feel free, even when the train is going at top speed." "The physical and moral consequences of

both systems," Sarmiento writes, "are all too perceptible":

> The European is a minor under the protective guardi-
> anship of the state. His ability to take care of him-
> self is judged to be inadequate. Warning signals, in-
> spection, insurance, every means to preserve his life
> is put at his disposal. . . . Everything but his right
> to take care of himself, his inclination, and his will.
> The Yankee stands on his own two feet, and if he
> wants to commit suicide no one will hinder him. If he
> wants to run after a train and dares to jump aboard,
> grabbing hold of a bar to save himself from the wheels,
> he does it. If a little urchin newsboy, in his eager-
> ness to sell one more paper, has allowed the train to
> pick up speed before jumping off, all will applaud his
> skill as he lands on his feet and walks away. Here is
> how nations' characters are formed and how liberty
> is applied. There may be a few more victims and
> accidents, but on the other hand there are free men
> and not disciplined prisoners whose lives are adminis-
> tered.   (pp. 156-158)

Equality on the trains also works for the progress of the
nation:

> In France there are three categories of railroad cars,
> In England four. One's nobility is measured by the
> money he can pay, and the managers, in order to make
> the man who pays little as miserable as possible, have
> lavished comforts and luxuries on the first-class cars
> and left thin, hard plank benches for those in the
> third-class cars. I do not know why they haven't placed
> pins on the seats to further mortify the poor. In the
> United States . . . the accommodations and the cush-

ions are excellent and the same throughout the train, and for that reason the price of the ticket is the same for everyone. I have found myself seated on the train with the governor of a state on one side and a man whose calloused hands indicated that he was a common woodcutter on the other. . . . democracy in the United States has distributed comfort and luxury equally in all of the railroad cars in order to inspire the poor. (pp. 160-161)

Liberty is manifested in the United States especially through the freedom of movement that the American enjoys. "The word 'passport' is unknown in the States," Sarmiento writes, "and the Yankee who has the pleasure of seeing one of these European documents in which the traveler's every movement is recorded shows it to his companions with gestures of horror and loathing." Even young boys and unmarried girls are free to go where and when they like: "The boy who wishes to take the train, steamship, or canalboat and the unmarried girl who leaves for a visit two hundred leagues away never encounter anyone who asks them with what object, with whose permission, they have left the paternal home. They are simply exercising their liberty and their right of free movement" (pp. 158-159).

Freedom of movement and of activity have both an educational and an economic role in American life. "The Yankee child," Sarmiento comments, "astonishes the European with his boldness, his crafty prudence, and his knowledge of life." He is already an entrepreneur: " 'How is your business going?' my traveling companion Arcos asked a clever boy who was giving us a guided tour of the books, periodicals, and pamphlets he was trying to get us to buy. 'It's going well. For three years

87

I have been earning my living by it and I already have three hundred dollars saved. This year I will put together the five hundred I need to form a partnership with Williams and get a bookstore with which to operate throughout the state.' This merchant was between nine and ten years old" (p. 159). Sarmiento speculates that these freedoms, coupled with the boldness which they encourage, are the reason Yankee clipper ships are outstripping the ships of other nations in the oceans.

Freedom is reinforced in the United States by the relative insignificance of the state. "Americans live without a government" (p. 152), Sarmiento says, and this is directly related to the enterprising and independent habits of Americans as compared with Europeans and South Americans, whose strong, highly centralized governments discourage initiative. "The civilization and power of the United States are equal to the sum of the civilization and power of the individuals who make it up," Sarmiento writes, "but that sum, represented by the national government, is not as our Latin ideas of government dictate." Here Sarmiento argues for federalism as opposed to centralism and also for the benefits to society which result when tasks are carried out by institutions independent of government. In the United States, he says, "Statistics, monuments—all is done by independent groups" (p. 280).

Power vested in society and in the individual rather than in the state is nowhere better illustrated than in the absence of a large, permanent military establishment. "Such is the idea of the negation of the personality of the state," Sarmiento reports, "that after a war the ships, guns, and cannons which served to make the national power effective are sold at public auction" (p. 280). Furthermore, the "permanent [American] army amounts to only 9,000 men. It is necessary to make a trip to special places to see anything of the army's equipment or of the soldiers themselves, and there are families and towns in the Union which have never seen a soldier" (p. 152).

The decentralized administration of the United States is to a large degree the product of the diversity inherent in Protestantism. "The sentiment of unity, centralization, and organization struggles at a disadvantage against local and individual energy, which is the basis of the political organization of that country and the product of the Protestant spirit" (p. 279). It is to this spirit that Sarmiento attributes the absence of a Department of Education in the United States, and he suggests that if the influence of an institution such as the Board of Education of Massachusetts were to be extended over the Union, "you would have to say that a radical revolution had taken place in the lives of these people" (p. 280).

But although Sarmiento celebrated liberty and democracy in the United States, he did not approve of everything in this nation's life. A republican, writing for his exiled fellow republicans scattered about Latin America, he was forced to admit that although the United States might be his road to Damascus, his conversion had not blinded him to its flaws. "The Republic exists!" he told his countrymen. "Only, upon looking at her closely, one finds that in many respects she doesn't correspond to the abstract idea we had of her." Unfortunately, he felt, whereas "the ugliest ulcers of the human species have disappeared in the United States, certain scars which European peoples still bear here have turned to cancer, while new illnesses arise for which there is no known remedy nor one sought" (p. 116). One of Sarmiento's main criticisms was of the tendency toward democratic excess, as, for example, in granting immediate rights to ignorant immigrants. "Just as the patriarchate existed in Rome and Venice," he tells his colleagues in exile, "here there is democracy. The Republic, the ideal government, will come later" (p. 117). There was much to emulate in the United States, but certain of its characteristics would be rejected by Argentines on founding their ideal Republic: "So, then, our Republic, with liberty and power, intelligence and beauty, that Republic of our dreams for the day the misguided tyrant falls, whose organization we have discussed with such sincerity while under the harsh spur of the inconveniences of exile—that Republic is a desideratum still, possible on this earth if there is a God who directs human destinies toward a good end . . ." (pp. 116-117).

Thus, despite his enthusiasm for almost all aspects of American life, Sarmiento does look upon it with a critical eye from time to time in *Travels*. One long section of the book is entitled "Avarice and Bad Faith." Here he develops an interesting theory: that the very liberty and democracy he celebrates in the United States is the mother of the fraud rampant in the country. "Avarice," he says, "is the legitimate daughter of equality, while fraud comes (strange as it may seem) from liberty itself." Sarmiento means that equality puts society's advantages within the reach of every citizen, while liberty provides the opportunity to pursue them. In static societies, fraud hardly exists, because the great mass of the people do not aspire to anything beyond their present misery. In the United States, on the other hand, the people are possessed by an "unbridled . . . passion" which is the result of "twenty million human beings . . . all at once, creating capital for themselves and for their sons . . ." (pp. 182-183).

Sarmiento also criticizes American manners, albeit good-naturedly. In describing the American at table, he writes: "But then, what incongruousness, what incest, what promiscuity in their dishes! The Yankee *pur sang* eats all his food, desserts, and fruit from the same plate, one at a time or all together. We saw one fellow from the Far West, an unsettled land like the Phoenician's Ophir, begin his meal with great quantities of fresh tomato sauce taken straight and scooped up on the tip of his knife! Sweet potatoes with vinegar! We were frozen with horror, and my traveling companion was filled with gastronomical indignation upon seeing these abominations. 'And will not heaven rain down fire upon them?' he asked. 'The sins of Sodom and Gomorrah must have been minor compared to the ones these Puritans commit every day'" (p. 148).

But countering democratic excesses, fraudulent practices, and crude manners, Sarmiento believed, were strong civilizing forces working throughout the United States. Applying his "civilization versus barbarism" thesis to the United States, he found that paralleling the individualism which in its extreme form expressed itself in selfishness and greed was an equally strong spirit of community. "As you see," he wrote, "these people carry about with them organically . . . certain constitutive principles of association. Political science becomes moral sentiment. . . . If you want to understand fully the road this people has followed, get together a group of Englishmen, Frenchmen, Chileans, or Argentines, not common people but all from the cultivated classes, and ask them without warning to constitute themselves as an association. They will not know what you are talking about . . ." (pp. 171-172). In the United States, however, "wherever ten Yankees come together, even if poor,

91

ragged, and unintelligent, b⊙re applying an axe to the base of a tree in order to construct a dwelling, they meet to arrange the bases of their association" (p. 175).

Sarmiento several times speaks of a passion for civic improvement as characteristic of Americans. He finds that the American has developed a special sentiment, a "political conscience": "It is something that has been getting itself ready for four centuries. It is the idea inherent in rejected doctrines held by defeated groups in Europe which now, with the Pilgrims, the Puritans, the Quakers, *habeas corpus*, the legislature, the jury, unoccupied lands, distance, isolation, untamed nature, independence, etc., is being developed, perfected, and established" (p. 174).

His reference to the Pilgrims and Puritans here is worth elaborating upon, especially because Sarmiento feels that the Pilgrim-Puritan influence is one of the major barriers in the United States (particularly in isolated areas) to the kind of barbarism which flourished in the pampas of Argentina. "Make room for a civilizing element," he writes, after derisively describing frontier fundamentalist and evangelical religion,

> the most active in keeping religious, political, and industrial life in the United States full of the old spirit of colonial days while at the same time keeping it open to all progress. I speak of the descendant of the old Pilgrims, the heir to their tradition of resignation through toughening manual labor and the originator of the great social and moral ideas which have made the American nationality: in short, the inhabitant of the New England states, of Maine, New Hampshire, Massachusetts, etc. This is the Brahmin race of the United States. Like the Brahmins coming down

from the Himalayas, the inhabitants of these old states have spread out toward the Western reaches of the Union and have educated by their example and methods the people who, without skill and science, are prospering on the newly cleared land. . . . The sons of that chosen portion of the human species are even today the mentors and the leaders of the new generations. More than a million families throughout the Union are believed to be descended from that noble stock. They have stamped upon the Yankee countenance that placid kindliness which is characteristic of the more educated class. They carry to the rest of the Union the manual aptitude which makes an American a walking workshop, the iron energy for struggling with and conquering difficulties, and the moral and intellectual aptitude which makes him equal, if not superior to the best of the human species has produced to date. These immigrants from the North discipline the new populations, injecting their spirit into the meetings which they call and preside over, into the schools, the books, the elections, and into the operations of all American institutions. . . . The barbarism produced by isolation in the forests and the weakening of republican practices by the immigrants is thus checked and lessened by the descendants of the Puritans and Pilgrims.   (pp. 197-199)

Sarmiento feels that by 1847 the Unitarians had inherited the mantle of the Pilgrims and Puritans and were the chief source of the progressive spirit pervading the United States: "the religious philosophy of the descendants of the Pilgrims trickles down through all levels of society, shortening the distances which separate sects, creating bridges which further unite them, and

93

finally absorbing them in Unitarianism. . . . This religious philosophy is rapidly being extended in the six New England states. Its center is Boston, the American Athens, and its propagators are the wisest men in America" (pp. 201-202).

Sarmiento mentions other civilizing influences in the United States. Education is, of course, a major one: "United States statistics show a figure for adult males which would indicate a total population of twenty million inhabitants, all of whom are educated [and] know how to read and write. . . . The American is a man . . . [who is] master of himself, with a spirit elevated by education and a sense of his own dignity. It is said that man is a rational being to the extent that he is able to acquire and exercise reasoning powers. From this point of view there is no country on earth which has more rational beings than the United States, even including countries which have a population ten times as great" (p. 154). Sarmiento is enthusiastic about the quantity and quality of newspapers, published books, and public libraries as barriers to barbarism, particularly on the frontier. The daily mail has a similar function: "The daily mail service works remarkably well. The post comes to the front doors of every faroff town and leaves there in some public document a topic of conversation and some news of what is happening in the nation. You know that it is impossible to barbarize wherever the post, like a daily rainfall, dissolves all indifference born of isolation" (p. 192). He also regards elections as civilizing institutions. "The election of the President exerts no small civilizing influence," he writes.

The American engages in fifty elections a year. Defeated in the election for the Council on Public Education, he throws himself into the campaign for sexton of his church. If he loses there, he waits with doubled passion the election for attorney, the election for mayor, the election for state representative, or that for governor. For a whole year he is filled with bad feelings about one and love for another candidate for the presidency, and he gets just as worked up over the congressional elections. At the time of a presidential election the Union is shaken to its very foundations. The squatters come out of their forests like shades evoked by a conjurer. The fate of every last tortoise of them is involved in the outcome. . . .

The election of the President is the only bond which unites all the far corners of the Union, the sole national concern that moves all of the people and all of the states at the same time. The electoral contest is, therefore, an awakener, a school, and a stimulant which revives a life otherwise made drowsy by isolation and hard work.   (pp. 193-194)

Because of these civilizing forces at work within it and because of its great virtues Sarmiento felt that the United States, although not perfect, was still the best available model for young and aspiring nations such as Argentina. "Let us be consoled by the fact . . . that these democrats are today the people who have made the most progress toward finding the political solution for which Christian people are groping, blundering along with monarchies as they are in Europe and overwhelmed by brutal despotism as we are in our own country." To evaluate the meaning of the United States, he felt, "one must first educate his judgment to overlook its apparent organic defects in order to be able to appreciate it for what it really is" (pp. 115-117).

In his eagerness to find a model for Argentina, however, Sarmiento may have been too ready to overlook the "organic defects" of the United States. We have already mentioned several of his criticisms, but others, which he should perhaps have made, are absent from *Travels*. Slavery, for example, the least defensible institution in American life, is not given the attention it merited, and Sarmiento also seems intent on excusing Americans for its persistence. In his brief discussion of slavery, he describes it as "the deep ulcer and the incurable fistula which threatens to corrupt the robust body of the Union" (p. 304). But it is the Union that concerns him, not the slaves. He is "afraid that this colossus of a civilization . . . may die in the convulsions which will attend the emancipation of the Negro race . . ." (p. 273). He does not criticize the Americans for slavery. "Why," he asks, "should the United States, which in practice has realized the greatest progress in regard to equality and humanity, be condemned to the strange fate of being the site of the last battles against the ancient injustice of man to man. . . .?" Notice that he says, "be condemned," as though slavery were beyond the power of Americans to eradicate, something fate had unfortunately visited upon them. "Should we throw the perpetuation of slavery in the face of the Yankees?" he asks. His answer is a decided "no," though he does name another culprit. "Slavery is a parasitical vegetation which English colonization has left glued to the leafy tree of American liberty" (pp. 304-305). Europe, the Old World, is to blame for slavery in the United States!

Sarmiento gives short shrift to another aspect of the United States which we might have expected to concern him: American expansionism, or what has come to be called "Yankee imperialism." Though American expansionism was not the overriding issue for Latin Americans during the past century that it is today (they still worried more about Spain and the other European nations), the Mexican War, which was in progress while Sarmiento was in the United States, did create an awareness of the danger inherent in the growing power of their northern neighbor. Though Sarmiento does not refer to the war, he does say at one point: "I do not mean to make Providence an accomplice in all American forward movement, since at another time this theory might be used to justify attempts at attracting politically or uniting with (or 'annexing' as the Americans say) Canada, Mexico, etc." But he follows this statement up with another in which he exclaims: "If that day comes, the union of free men will begin at the North Pole and, for lack of further land, end at the Isthmus of Panama" (p. 123). It would be imperialistic of the United States to "annex" Canada and Mexico, he feels, but on the other hand this would guarantee the freedom of those countries.

This ambivalence toward, if not advocacy of, an American manifest destiny expanded to include the hemisphere is very curious in a Latin American even in the nineteenth century and is an indication of the extent of Sarmiento's commitment to the United States during this period of his life. This attitude would become somewhat modified with time, but it appears that his enthusiasm in 1847 for the United States, his new-found model, sometimes precluded a realistic examination of its less salient qualities. Occasionally his admiration approaches naïveté. One scholar writes: "That Sarmiento saw the United States through rose-tinted spectacles admits of no doubt. His admiration . . . was often undiscriminating and at times somewhat ingenuous";

and another feels that Sarmiento's analysis was "at times blind to one entire side of the scene."[15]

However true this may be, *Travels* is a welcome corrective to other books on the United States by foreign visitors, many of which are as unkind as Sarmiento is generous. As the American Sarmientista Madaline Nichols writes, "Whether or not the United States is peculiarly sensitive to analysis, the writing of works of criticism of the country has opened up a most profitable market to foreign *literati*. Ever since the time of Dickens, they have come in apparently endless succession. The resultant works of such men are usually uncomplimentary to the country of their visit; their pecuniary success is *de scandale*. A notable exception to the general rule is presented by Domingo Faustino Sarmiento, even though he was one of the forerunners of this invading legion who have taken their pleasure in revealing North America to its citizens."[16] Another American schol-

---

[15] Percy Martin, "Sarmiento and New England," *Hispanic American Essays*, pp. 326, 327; Allison Williams Bunkley, *Life of Sarmiento*, p. 304.

[16] Sarmiento, *A Chronicle of Inter-American Friendship* (Washington, 1940), p. 33. In 1865, while Sarmiento was in the United States as Ambassador, Dickens was also in this country, on a lecture tour. Sarmiento went to Steinway Hall in New York to hear Dickens read from the Pickwick Papers. He was not favorably impressed:

> My ticket cost me four dollars, and in Boston they were paying as high as fifty to have the right to hear—Can you imagine?—reading!
>
> That's all it was. A man was going to read a book, a novel, which everyone in the world has read; and they are paying four, ten, twenty dollars to hear him. Dickens is going to pick up two hundred thousand dollars in fourth months for the labor of reading one hour each night and his patience in receiving cordial and respectful applause. On the side he will be taking some notes for another book on America which will earn him another hundred thousand.

Sarmiento regarded Dickens as typical of Europeans who looked down their noses at the United States. "The celebrated novelist Dickens," he writes, "visited the United States twenty years ago, and in his

ar, Irving Leonard, has expressed similar thoughts on *Travels*: "Few North Americans appreciate the fact that a century ago, when such Europeans as Dickens, Mrs. Trollope, DeTocqueville, and others were writing their critical and, occasionally, condescending impressions of the democratic ways and manners observed in the United States, there came among our great-grandfathers one of the most notable figures of Hispanic America who was a fanatic admirer of nearly all things Yankee. Lacking the aristocratic and somewhat snobbish prejudices of English and French critics, this great Spanish-American democrat saw in the land of Benjamin Franklin the bright hope of mankind and the promise of a better world."[17]

Sarmiento was a republican, as most of the nineteenth-century foreign writers on the United States, such as Dickens, Tocqueville, and Mrs. Trollope, were not. His tastes were egalitarian. When describing American manners he admits that "The Yankees are the most uncivil little animals under the sun," but in the next breath he hastens to disclaim this by saying

> At least that is what such competent judges as Captain Marryat, Miss [*sic*] Trollope, and other travelers have said about them. But then, if in England and France the coal miners, woodcutters, and tavernkeep-

writings [*American Notes*, 1842 and *Martin Chuzzlewit*, 1844] spoke of this country as if it were an English boy of twenty; which it was then, that is, a robust lad, bursting with health and showing his fists, perhaps not so well-bred—like any villager, but looking a great deal worse through the spectacles of an Englishman. Well, I can tell Dickens, since I was around these parts in those days too [in 1847]—even though I am not English and am very much an American—I can tell him the day and the hour when a youth enters upon the age of reason" ("Lecturas de Carlos Dickens," *Obras*, XXIX, 230).

17 "Sarmiento's Visits to North America," *Michigan Alumnus Quarterly Review*, XLIX (July 1943), 324.

ers were to sit down at the same table with artists, congressmen, bankers, and landowners, as is the case in the United States, the Europeans would form another opinion of their own culture. . . . Europeans make fun of these rude habits, which are more superficial than profound. . . . I do not mean to defend or excuse these characteristics. Still, after examining the chief nations of Christendom, I have come to the conclusion that the Americans are the only really cultured people that exist on this earth and the last word in modern civilization.   (pp. 150-151)

He goes on to say "Europeans and even South Americans complain about many defects in the character of the Yankees. For my own part, I celebrate these very defects. . . ." (pp. 152-153). However deplorable, these flaws were an indication of the advanced level of freedom and justice at which the United States had arrived in comparison with the rest of the world.

He was not, however, oblivious to the inherent dangers of such a society, some of them the same ones which had worried Tocqueville. There are, in fact, quite a number of parallels between Sarmiento and Tocqueville, perhaps in part the product of Sarmiento's familiarity with *Democracy in America*, required reading for Argentine intellectuals. In *Facundo* Sarmiento declared that "Tocqueville revealed to us for the first time the secret of North America," and he once inserted Tocqueville as an issue in a Chilean electoral campaign.[18] Like Tocqueville, Sarmiento feared the excesses to which de-

[18] Mary Mann's translation of *Facundo* (Collier edn.), p. 104. In the Chilean electoral campaign of 1841, which we have already discussed, Sarmiento urged the readers of his newspaper to study Tocqueville if they wanted to know what kind of government was needed in Chile See Alberto Palcos, "Sarmiento, Tocqueville, y la candidatura presidencial del General Bulnes," *La prensa*, August 6, 1961.

mocracy was prone. The prevalence of fraud, as we have already mentioned, he saw as quite possibly "the disagreeable fruit of the mating of liberty and democracy" (p. 182). Sarmiento, too, feared the tyranny of the majority, as when he writes of "*la ley* Lynch" and of the power of the citizens of a state to force the state government to repudiate a debt: "Demand payment? Before whom? Here you have the first rascal in the world who recognizes no judge on earth: the sovereign people. The President, the Congress, and the Supreme Court can do nothing against this class of rogue. Neither the government of the state itself nor the ashamed cultured class can do anything, because their power comes from the vote of the ignorant and indolent populace, and these will not accept having to contribute again toward repaying the contracted debt. In this way the affairs of Mississippi, Illinois, Indiana, Michigan, Arkansas, and several other states have been conducted. What a noise the London bankers make in the face of this terrible thievery!" (p. 186).

Sarmiento, like Tocqueville, is aware of the tendency of equality to produce uniformity. After describing the virtues of small-town, Jeffersonian life in the United States, Sarmiento says: "The picture of this uniform decency and general welfare, even if it satisfies the hearts of those who enjoy seeing a part of the human race partaking in equal shares of the joys and advantages of society, tires one at last with its monotonous uniformity" (p. 139). Sarmiento also predicts that sometime in the near future all American faiths will be amalgamated into Unitarianism, which he considers the religion of democracy. Although he can see great benefits in such a development, he also says: "I conclude all of this, my good friend, with something that would

101

freeze the good Yankees in horror to hear: which is that they are marching straight toward unity of belief and that one day not far off the Union will present to the world the spectacle of a universally devout people without apparent form to their religious beliefs" (p. 202).

It is of interest to compare Sarmiento and Tocqueville, for I believe *Travels* merits consideration along with *Democracy in America* as one of the most significant books written on the United States by foreign visitors during the first half of the nineteenth century (or at any time). An Argentine writer who shares my view states: "Sarmiento was without doubt one of the two most sagacious voyagers who contemplated the United States during the first half of the nineteenth century and expounded their ideas on it; the other was the Frenchman, Alexis de Tocqueville, whose visit took place some years before Sarmiento's." However, he continues,

> . . . their conclusions were diametrically opposed. The Frenchman arrived from Europe a skeptic on the possibility of realizing the ideal of democratic institutions and the capacity of nations for governing themselves in this way, so that his work, *Democracy in America*, presents the subject negatively. Sarmiento, on the other hand, does not try to give us an exclusively rational or intellectual view of the United States. He describes and becomes enthusiastic (carried along by his impetuousness and his enthusiasm for everything he saw); and he did not allow time to go by to order his impressions but instead just serves them up fresh, with absolute sincerity. . . . Describing errors and imperfections too, Sarmiento is able to immerse himself in the intimate spirit and life of the

northern nation . . . with a constructive good will which an American writer points to when he describes Sarmiento as "a positive Tocqueville."[19]

The American writer referred to here is Allison Williams Bunkley. The epithet "a positive Tocqueville" is not entirely accurate, because it implies that Tocqueville's views on the United States were essentially negative, which they were not. Bunkley qualifies his statement, however, by saying that "The Frenchman saw the underlying elements, those which . . . would be future dangers in both the democratic government and the Industrial Revolution. Sarmiento saw the optimism of the surface. De Tocqueville saw the pessimism of the underlying current. . . . One is an inspiration. The other is a warning."[20]

Like Tocqueville, Sarmiento is uncommonly prophetic on many aspects of American life. "Of the books written about the great Republic of the North in the middle of the nineteenth century, . . . Sarmiento's . . . stands out as a remarkable example of clairvoyance," comments one Argentine scholar, and another writes in a similar vein that "One is astonished by his penetration, his generalizations and inferences, and, above all, by his intuitions and prophecies . . . which even today are valid."[21]

But Sarmiento's insights into American life have proven to be less durable than Tocqueville's. No one would maintain today that Americans "live without a government" or that there are "families and towns in the Union which have never seen a soldier." Our trains

19 Alberto Girri, in the commentary on the inside cover of *Estados Unidos*.

20 *Life of Sarmiento*, p. 303.

21 Alberto Palcos in *The Pan-American Ideals of Sarmiento*, p. 12; Edmundo Correas in *Sarmiento and the United States*, p. 9.

today are much like the French ones Sarmiento describes: we have rules and regulations and on some public transport we even have classes. One does not think of the United States any longer as a place where people are particularly willing to take risks; insurance is one of our major industries. Sarmiento's analysis of the United States is postulated upon an ever-retreating horizon of virgin land and simple, essentially material problems; but as Frederick Jackson Turner and more recently John Kennedy with his New Frontier program have suggested, our frontier has become internal and our problems increasingly complex and abstract. Sarmiento, in short, describes a United States which largely does not exist any longer.

An Argentine scholar asks: "If Sarmiento had lived until the end of the nineteenth century and the beginning of the twentieth, would he have maintained to the same degree his admiration of the United States? The question is difficult to answer. Nevertheless, despite everything which might be urged to the contrary, I would say, 'No.' "[22] It is ironical that if Sarmiento were alive today he might in many ways prefer his own Argentina—where the frontier begins at the edge of Buenos Aires, where children still jump on and off moving trains and buses, and where there is hardly a red light in the cities to impede traffic—to the United States. He might also want to revise his "civilization versus barbarism" thesis, with its unqualified commitment to progress, if he were to see that "progress" has brought air pollution, nuclear weapons, and the other technology-related miseries of our times.

But if *Travels* cannot match *Democracy in America* in farsightedness, it is well to remember that Sarmiento's

[22] Emilio Carilla, *El Embajador Sarmiento*, p. 150.

book is, after all, essentially a travel book, while Tocqueville's is a work of political philosophy. Sarmiento's chief purpose was to describe the United States at a particular stage of its development, while Tocqueville's was to interpret the peculiar meaning and role of the United States in history. Where Sarmiento equals if not surpasses Tocqueville is in social and cultural commentary. There are passages in *Travels*, such as the long description of American mating practices, which have no equivalent in *Democracy in America*. And Sarmiento's social criticism, unlike Tocqueville's, is lightened by much splendid humor, not a little reminiscent of Mark Twain, even in translation.[23] The two books complement one another: Tocqueville's is an analysis of the American mind and American institutions, while Sarmiento's describes the American personality and the American way of life.

The excellence of the work of commentators on American civilization has always been measured using Tocqueville as a yardstick. A pamphlet on *American Studies in Asia*, for example, bemoans the fact that "there is no Asian Tocqueville."[24] But there is a Latin American Tocqueville, and Sarmiento is that man.[25]

---

[23] See, for example, Arcos' practical joking with the Presbyterian minister (p. 302); the passage describing the many ways that Americans choose to sit, none orthodox (pp. 149-150); and the long sequence where Sarmiento is stranded in the middle of the United States (pp. 283-292).

[24] Reuel Denney, *American Studies in Asia: A Brief Survey* (Wilmington, Del., 1964), p. 3.

[25] Chapter 24 of Bunkley's *Life of Sarmiento* is entitled "A South American De Tocqueville." Bunkley also writes that Sarmiento "would have liked to have been the De Tocqueville of Hispanic America" (p. 210). In *Facundo* Sarmiento wrote that "South America and the Argentine Republic above all has needed a Tocqueville" (*Obras*, VII, 6). However, Sarmiento probably meant that a Tocqueville was needed as a commentator on South America and Argentina rather than that a South American of Tocqueville's stature was needed as a commentator on the United States.

Or, rather, he *will* be as soon as Americans begin to take seriously what is thought and written about us by the great men of the southern regions of this hemisphere. Of these men, none have interested themselves in the United States on the scale and with the profundity that Sarmiento has. As more of his writings on the United States are available in English he will certainly become a major figure in American cultural history.

Notes on the Translation

Sarmiento's *Viajes* was originally published in Santiago, Chile in two volumes: *Viajes en Europa, Africa i America* (1849 and 1851). When Sarmiento's *Obras completas* was compiled, the two volumes of the *Viajes* were consolidated as Volume v (1886), by far the thickest volume of the *Obras*,[1] and the title was slightly modified to *Viajes por Europa, Africa y America 1845-1847*. In 1922, however, the *Viajes* were broken up into three volumes: *De Valparaiso a Paris* (Vol. I), *España e Italia* (Vol. II), and *Estados Unidos* (Vol. III). This 1922 edition was published in paperback as part of the "La Cultura Argentina" series edited by Jose Ingenieros and Julio Noé. In 1955, 1957, and 1959 Hachette of Buenos Aires also published the *Viajes* in three paperback volumes, edited by Gregorio Weinberg and with introductions by noted Sarmiento scholars.

Travels in the United States in 1847 is the English title I have given to *Estados Unidos*, the last volume of the three. I have relied primarily on the Hachette edition for the translation of *Travels*, although all earlier editions have also been consulted. The Hachette edition is in all respects true to the original edition, except for some helpful modernization of spelling.

As does Volume III of the Hachette edition, I have included that part of the *Diary of Expenses* pertaining to Sarmiento's time in the United States as an appendix to *Travels*, using the original *Diary* as my text. The *Diary*, the little notebook of expenses kept by Sarmiento during his trip, was discovered among his papers in the

1 The *Obras completas* (Santiago and Buenos Aires, 1885-1903) was republished by Editorial Luz del Dia between 1948 and 1956, Volume v appearing in 1949.

Sarmiento Museum in Buenos Aires in 1947 and published in facsimile by the museum in 1950. It contains,
in meticulous detail, all of Sarmiento's expenses and
purchases, from "baggage" and "boots" to "orgy" and
"oranges." The *Diary* reveals an element in Sarmiento's
character of which both his detractors and disciples
have heretofore been largely unaware. Prior to its publication, Sarmiento was usually described as a disorganized
and even erratic person, but present scholarship will
have to consider his consummate attention to detail in
the *Diary*, reminiscent of nothing so much as Thoreau's
bean-patch economics in *Walden*.

Travels in the United States in 1847 is the second
major Sarmiento work to appear in English—the first,
Facundo, or *Life in the Argentine Republic in the Days
of the Tyrants* as Mrs. Horace Mann entitled her English translation, having been published a century ago
in Boston (1868). Mary Peabody Mann also apparently
thought at one time of translating Sarmiento's *Viajes*
into English, but she was never to realize the project.

Sections of *Travels* were translated into English by
Stuart Edgar Grummon for Allison Williams Bunkley's
Sarmiento Anthology (Princeton, 1948), and Inés Muñoz
did an anthology of selections from the *Viajes* for the
Pan American Union, calling the book *Travels; A Selection* (Washington, 1963). The present translation is the
first in which *Travels in the United States in 1847* has
been treated as an integral book and offered to the
American reader as a "new" classic of our literature.

The major problem in this translation was in achieving a balance between three often conflicting interests:
presenting a readable English text; maintaining some
of the flavor of Spanish-Argentine idiomatic expression;

and communicating the atmosphere of mid-nineteenth-century America. Accomplishing all of these things simultaneously is difficult, and compromise has sometimes been the only solution. However, Sarmiento's complicated sentence structure has been reorganized (without tampering with his paragraphing; his paragraphs usually go from midthought to midthought) in order to approximate normal American English expression; an occasional familiar Spanish word, such as *simpático*, as well as a few typically Argentine words, such as *porteño*, have not been translated; and typical nineteenth-century American words, such as "emporium" (Sarmiento says "emporio"), instead of "market," have been employed.

Foreign words other than Spanish have been left untranslated. Also, it seemed to me that knowing what English Sarmiento had at his command or favored in 1847 would be of interest to even the most casual reader, and so Sarmiento's English vocabulary is signaled throughout *Travels* by the use of small caps. The Sarmiento Museum in Buenos Aires has in its possession the Spanish-English dictionary used by Sarmiento while in the United States, *Neuman and Barretti's Dictionary of the Spanish and English Languages* (Boston, 1847). On the title page Sarmiento has written in English: "How do you do Mr. Joseph/How do you do Mr. Migueño."

Sarmiento's few, erratically placed footnotes have normally been retained, and my own occasional notes are indicated by asterisks. *Travels* offers splendid opportunities to the scholar who likes to get his *sics* in, but this temptation has been resisted. *Sics* do not belong in a translation, and my own notes have been added only when something absolutely needed clarification or correction. I wanted this book to be, as much as possible, Sarmiento's.

The most frustrating problem was what to do with the words "Norteamerica" and "Norteamericano." We call our country either "the United States" or "America" and our citizens "Americans." Latin Americans usually call our country "North America" and our citizens "North Americans" because, they insist, they are Americans too; that is, for them, "the New World" and "America" are synonymous. It is possible for us to understand their feelings about this, but geographically, historically, and emotionally we could not be brought to call ourselves "North Americans" and our country "North Am rica," if for no other reason than that North America, for us, includes Canada and Mexico. Sometimes Latin Americans refer to us as "Estadounidenses," which does not help, because we do not call ourselves "United Statesians" (which is the only way to translate this word). Nor should we have to resort to this awkward term: citizens of the United States of Brazil are not called "Estadounidenses" or "United Statesians."

Politically, the problem has no solution, though the fact that all languages have different words for other nations and peoples should be a consoling thought (for example, Germany, *Deutschland, Alemania, Alemagne*). Perhaps the best thing for inter-American relations is simply to use the words "America" and "Americans" when speaking English and "Norteamerica" and "Norteamericanos" when speaking Spanish.

In translations of Latin American books for the American reader, the familiar names of his country and people should be employed. This is therefore my practice in almost every case where Sarmiento uses "Norteamerica" and "Norteamericanos." I occasionally use "North America" or "North Americans" for clarity, for example, in making comparisons between the two continents of the hemisphere and their peoples, or where this is necessary for capturing Sarmiento's expression or style more exactly. Of course, Sarmiento, like any Latin American who has spent some time in the United States and been infected by our way of describing our nation and people, sometimes slips and calls our country "America" and our people "Americanos." But this inconsistency only makes it easier to apply the policy I have adopted.

Travels in
the United States in 1847

By Domingo F. Sarmiento

I. A General Description

Señor don Valentín Alsina

November 12, 1847

I leave the United States, my dear friend, in that state of excitement caused by witnessing a truly new phenomenon, one which is filled with uncertainties, without plan, without unity, which bristles with crimes that illuminate with their sinister light acts of heroism and self-sacrifice, which is embellished by such fabulous ornaments as ancient forests, flowery prairies, cruel mountains, and human dwellings in whose peaceful environment virtue and innocence reign. I want you to know that I am departing at once sad, thoughtful, pleased, and deeply impressed, with half of my illusions broken or crumbled, while others struggle against reason to again conjure up that image in which we always enclose ideas when they refer to objects we have not seen, just as we assign certain features and a certain tone of voice to a friend we know only through letters. The United States is something without precedent, a kind of extravaganza which at first shocks and runs counter to one's previous ideas about it, but which is great and noble, occasionally sublime, never disappointing. It demonstrates such permanence and natural power that ridicule would bounce off its surface like a spent bullet off the tough hide of an alligator. That social body is not a deformed being, not a monster of known species, but as different a political animal as those fossil monsters whose bones are still being uncovered. To evaluate it, one must first educate his judgment to overlook its apparent organic defects in order to be able to appreciate it for what it really is. Of course, you will be running the risk that, having overcome your first feeling of strangeness, you will fall in love with it, decide that it is beautiful, and proclaim a new order of human affairs, just as Romanticism, after overthrowing the old idol of Franco-Roman poetry, tried to conceal its own monstrous qualities.

Educated as you and I are, my good friend, under the iron rod of the most awful tyrant,* and fighting him unceasingly in the name of right, of justice—in the name, in short, of the Republic—we have, as have so many others who wished to realize plans arrived at through conscience and human intelligence, taken heart on seeing in the midst of the leaden night which weighs upon South America that halo of light shining from the North. At last we have told ourselves, in order to endure the evils of the present: "The Republic exists, strong, invincible; her lamp is lit; and someday justice, equality, and law will come to us when the South reflects the light of the North." Ah, yes, the Republic exists! Only, upon looking at her closely, one finds that in many respects she doesn't correspond to the abstract idea we had of her. At the same time that the ugliest ulcers of the human species have disappeared in the United States, certain scars which European peoples still bear here have turned to cancer, while new illnesses arise for which there is no known remedy nor one sought. So, then, our Republic, with liberty and power, intelligence and beauty, that Republic of our dreams for the day the misguided tyrant falls, whose organization we have discussed with such sincerity while under the harsh spur of the inconveniences of exile—that Republic is a desideratum still, possible on this earth if

* Juan Manuel Rosas.

116

there is a God who directs human destinies toward a good end and if justice is a sentiment inherent to our nature, an organic part of it and the goal of its education.

If I were not afraid, then, that the citation would give an incorrect impression, I would repeat, in giving you my ideas on the United States, the words that Voltaire puts into Brutus' mouth:

Et je cherche ici Rome, et ne la trouve plus!

Just as the patriarchate existed in Rome and Venice, here there is democracy. The Republic, the ideal government, will come later. Let us be consoled by the fact, however, that these democrats are today the people who have made the most progress toward finding the political solution for which Christian peoples are groping, blundering along with monarchies as they are in Europe and overwhelmed by brutal despotism as we are in our country.

Do not expect me to give you an orderly description of the United States, even though I have visited all of her great cities and crossed or followed the borders of twenty-one of her richest states. I have another purpose. At the heights of civilization which the noblest part of the human species has reached, definite physical conditions, for which there are no permanent substitutes, are necessary for a nation to be or to have the potential for being powerful. If God were to put me in charge of designing a great Republic, our Republic, for example, I would not accept such an important responsibility unless I were granted at least these conditions: unlimited territory, so that there might someday be a population of two hundred million inhabitants; a wide frontage on the seas, with coasts indented with gulfs and bays; a varied surface, but one which would not present obsta-

117

cles too great for the development of the railroads and canals that will cross the nation in all directions; and, as I will never consent to do without railroads, there must be so much coal and iron that in the Year of Grace 4751 the mines will still be as active as on the first day. An abundance of trees, for construction, would be the only obstacle to the easy clearing of the land I could tolerate. I would take personal charge of exploiting the navigable rivers which must cross the country in every direction converting themselves into lakes where there is a nice view, flowing into all the seas, linking all the climates together so that the produce of the poles will come directly to the tropical regions and vice versa. Then, for my future designs, I would ask for an abundance everywhere of marbles, granites, porphyries, and other building stones, without which nations cannot leave their eternal mark on a forgetful earth.

"Land of Cockaigne!" a Frenchman would say. "The Isle of Barataria!" a Spaniard would suggest. Imbeciles! It is the United States as God created it, and I would swear that, creating this part of the world, He knew full well that round about the nineteenth century the dregs of His poor humanity, trampled upon elsewhere, enslaved and dying of hunger so that the few can live a life of luxury, would come together here, develop themselves without obstacle, grow great, and by their example avenge the human race for so many centuries of feudal domination and suffering. How is it that the Romans did not discover this land which is so eminently suited for industry (in which they did not engage), for the pacific invasion of colonists, and for the ample well-being of the individual? Why was it the Anglo-Saxon race that discovered this piece of the world which is so well suited to its industrial instincts, while South America,

118

a land of gold and silver mines and gentle and submissive Indians, has fallen to the Spanish race—a region aptly suited to its proud laziness, its backwardness, and its industrial ineptitude? Is there not order and premeditation in all of these cases? Is there not Providence? Oh, my friend, God must be the explanation for these things!

I forgot to request for my Republic, and I do so here in order to get it on record, that I be given as neighbors nations of Spanish stock, Mexico, for example, and Cuba there on the horizon, an isthmus, etc.

I am not the first, by the way, to be impressed by the character of the United States. A traveling companion* wrote to one of his friends in Europe:

I have never heard of a place where God has surpassed Himself as He has here. Without doubt He must have been in good spirits when He sketched degrees o to 6 longitude, east and west of Washington. This is beautiful and finely drawn! Every river is six miles wide, every lake is at least four hundred miles in circumference; everywhere there are immense forests of trees in perfect harmony with the landscape. Not a single hill or island is arid; vegetation is everywhere, just as in your Pyrenees mountains.

With respect to the general geography of this country, I will give you a few quick ideas. Imagine a rectangular area of land of around two and a half million square miles, bathed by different seas to the south, east, and west. To the north a river which springs from a chain of lakes as large as the Caspian Sea acts as a boundary and offers a means of communication from the deepest interior to the Atlantic Coast. The mouth of the Saint

* Santiago Arcos.

119

Lawrence, which is the name of that terminal river, is outside the United States; but to the south, at about the height of Montreal, begins Lake Champlain, which is no wider than a river. Lake Champlain almost meets the headwaters of the Hudson, thereby offering the New York emporium communication with the Lakes and with upper and lower Canada.

Since the rectangle we have traced is just a little smaller than Europe, it needs, in theory, some interior artery by means of which life can penetrate to and circulate in the interior. To fill this requirement, the Mississippi, the greatest river on earth, flows southward from the vicinity of Lake Erie for fifteen hundred navigable miles, including in its volume the waters of the Ohio, the Arkansas, the Illinois, the Missouri, the Tennessee, the Wabash, and many others which flow into it alternately from east and west, and carrying the products of the most remote plantations on its mixed currents to the Gulf of Mexico. The notable thing about the distribution of waters in North America is that some come together in a great receptacle and then go on to the east united in the Saint Lawrence; others flow toward the south and combine in the Mississippi; while there are no rivers independent of these two great systems other than the Hudson, the Potomac, and the Susquehanna.

The Yankees would have been less than intelligent if they had not completed by canals Providence's obvious plan to provide easy water transportation to New York and New Orleans for the merchandise of Canada, thereby creating an internal navigation system covering a distance greater than that between America and Europe. Also, since an American nation must live by exporting its raw materials, its cereals, and its furs, it must of necessity look to the Atlantic. Its most important concern should be that all routes of communication come together at the mouths and orifices of a great hydra whose simple structure consists of nothing more than an intestinal tube and mouths. But suppose it evolves to a higher form of life and goes through transformations in which it develops different systems such as the circulatory, nervous, and digestive. Life becomes more complicated, and now the mouth exists for the animal instead of the animal existing for the mouth. As its internal life becomes more complicated, secretory vessels are needed where food is better handled, which is the same as saying (the analogy is becoming tiresome) that with an excess of population and the development of wealth, national industries are born. The nation, without diminishing exports and imports, at last acquires an internal life which it must satisfy by itself and for itself. China in Asia and Germany and France in Europe present examples of this interior life which feeds powerful industries and leads to a greater accumulation of wealth. As one can imagine, when this happens in the United States the seaboard cities will not be the only centers of wealth. In order to make the extremes of the Union reasonably accessible to each other, there will be in the middle of the nation new industrial centers to distribute the products of the national labor to its extremities. Now look at the map of the United States and see if you can find an appropriate spot for such a center, a place which also is very accessible and which has an abundance of materials for manufacturing such as iron, wood, coal, etc. If you cannot find it right away, I will show you. In western Pennsylvania the Ohio, Allegheny, and Monongahela Rivers come together on their way to the Mississippi (that great artery which, as we have seen, controls and distributes the internal activities of the country).

At the confluence of these rivers is situated Pittsburgh. Pittsburgh is further connected by artificial canals and railroads with Baltimore on Chesapeake Bay and Philadelphia, New York, and Boston to the north. If one were to remove a little of the surface of the ground on which Pittsburgh was founded, a shelf of coal which extends for fourteen thousand square miles would be discovered. This is an area which is just a little smaller than England. In all of the country roundabout, even on the banks of the rivers, landowners can open a mineshaft under their very hearths to extract this substance, this factory food. In Marietta we left our steamboat, crossed two city streets, and, without further ceremony, entered a bituminous coal mine. Coal was being brought out from the inside of a hill in hand carts and dumped directly onto the decks of boats which were moored at the riverbank to receive it. From there, in caravans of shapeless rafts which are abandoned to the river currents, the coal makes its way without benefit of oar or sail to New Orleans, where it competes favorably with firewood cut in the immediate vicinity, whose price depends on the wages of the woodcutter. So much for coal. As for iron, it is found everywhere in equal abundance. Thanks to these enviable advantages Pittsburgh is rising up in the middle of the American forests, wrapped in a dense mantle of thick, foul-smelling smoke which has already earned it the name "The Yankee Birmingham." And it will be the future Yankee London because of the quantity of its factories and the cotton which comes upstream from New Orleans to be printed or woven by machines which almost always surpass their European counterparts. As an indication of what Pittsburgh may become, I recall that at the end of the last century the territory adjacent to it was still dominated by savages. In 1800 it already had forty-five thousand inhabitants, and by 1845 the population had reached two million.

Since the population of the United States advances toward the Pacific at a rate of seven hundred miles of frontier per year, it will be necessary later to have an industrial center even further into the interior. To that end nature has arranged that where the Missouri—which runs for twelve hundred miles—empties into the Mississippi, and not far from the point where the Ohio flows into that river on the opposite bank, there is another coal deposit, which, as far as is known, covers some sixty thousand square miles.

I do not mean to make Providence an accomplice in all American forward movement, since at another time this theory might be used to justify attempts at attracting politically or uniting with (or "annexing" as the Americans say) Canada, Mexico, etc. If that day comes, the union of free men will begin at the North Pole and, for lack of further land, end at the Isthmus of Panama.

When this comes about, the Great Lakes will be the center of a gigantic union, while Michigan, surrounded like a peninsula by the lake of the same name, Lake Huron, the Saint Clair River, and the base of Lake Erie, will be able to exploit the enormous coal deposits in the center of the state. In anticipation of that event, and because of the infallible Yankee instinct for sensing places which will produce wealth, the city of Buffalo is rising on the banks of that sweet-water sea, Lake Erie. This city, without ever having been a village, had thirty thousand inhabitants a year ago, and it probably has

123

fifty thousand today if it is making progress in the Yankee style. There is a railroad which, as a matter of course, crosses the five degrees of longitude from Albany daily, spilling into the streets of Buffalo a torrent of people who have come up the Hudson after crossing from Europe. They come to find a piece of forest land in this middle territory on which to establish a new family, like the tribes of Shem and Japheth that went out from ancient Babel to divide the uninhabited land among themselves. There is an equal confusion of tongues among these new arrivals, but the land soon puts its stamp upon them. Just as water, by rubbing the uneven surfaces of different stones together, produces pebbles which look like brothers, so the fragments of old societies are coming together in the flood of immigrants, mixing, and forming the newest, the youngest, and the most daring republic on the face of the earth. Oh, how much real truth there is in the moral mysteries of our race! How many intimate and inevitable relations are illustrated by physical things! The liberty which has emigrated to the North gives to him who goes there wings to fly. Human torrents are pouring into the primitive forests, and word passes silently overhead on iron strings to spread the news far and wide of man's occupation of the soil that has been reserved for him. The venerable spirit of investigation prepares to examine areas of knowledge which have been untouched from the beginning of time and to give them some physical form. Franklin, as you know, was the first to take the terrible thunderbolt into his hands and explain it to an astounded world. After Franklin's discovery (I mean "discovery" in the practical sense: the lightning rod which he gave to humanity), Volta, Oersted, Alexander, Ampère, and Aragó wrote about and made elaborate attempts to produce the telegraph, but it was Morse, an American, who made a successful experiment with thirty thousand dollars the United States Congress appropriated for his expenses. Is it not singular that the privilege has been granted to the United States of inventing the lightning rod and ether (thereby saving mankind from two great afflictions) and of giving lightning speed to man's activities through Fulton's steamboat and Morse's telegraph? When I left France there were experimental telegraph lines of this kind from Rouen to Paris and from Paris to Lille at the service of the government only. When I left the United States there was a circuit from New York which linked Washington, Baltimore, and Philadelphia and returned to New York, a total of 455 miles; another which linked New York, New Haven, Hartford, Springfield, Boston and returned to New York, a total of 452 miles; and a line from New York to Albany (150 miles), with branch lines from there to Buffalo (250 miles), to Rochester (252 miles), and to Montreal (205 miles). Stagecoaches covering 142,295 miles daily carry mail throughout the country, and there are 853 miles of artificial canals. The United States is surrounded by 3,600 miles of sea and in the north by 1,200 miles of lakes. New York serves as port for an internal navigational system of rivers, canals, and lakes covering some 3,000 miles, while New Orleans serves as another port for some 20,000 miles of internal waterways composed of the navigable rivers that unite in the Mississippi and which, together with the Saint Lawrence and the Great Lakes, make up a marvelous system of interior waterways.

Nature composed the features of the land in the Union, but without the American's profound ability in public works the task would have remained incomplete.

From Philadelphia to St. Louis, as from Buenos Aires to Mendoza, a great national highway crosses the land. In that direction canals are not possible, since the water flows south and east. From Lake Erie, however, there is a navigable canal uniting with the Ohio between Cincinnati and Pittsburgh which brings the produce of the extreme north, that is, from Lake Superior and Canada, to New Orleans at the lowest rates. At the eastern end of Lake Erie begins another canal which, after sending out a branch to Lake Ontario, connects with the Hudson near Troy, thereby linking by water Chicago (which is fourteen degrees to the west), New York, and Quebec. Another canal beginning at Pittsburgh skirts the Allegheny Mountains and puts Philadelphia on the Atlantic in contact with New Orleans on the Gulf of Mexico, making a waterway across the continent of more than a thousand leagues. It would be too much of a task to list all the railroad lines which supplement the water routes or connect with them, giving each state, city, and village cheap, rapid, frequent, and convenient transportation fitting everyone's pocketbook and appropriate for any kind of merchandise. Tocqueville has said that the railroads have lowered transportation costs by a fourth. The canals have almost abolished freight costs or brought them to the point where they are hardly to be considered; and yet such is the quantity of goods shipped that the canals bring in millions in revenue for the country each year.

From the general description of the United States, its "architecture" (meaning the physical attributes of the country that God has created and man has utilized and improved upon), I shall pass on immediately to a consideration of the village, which is the center of political life, just as the family is the center of domestic life. Examples to the contrary notwithstanding, the essence of the United States is to be found in its small towns. This cannot be said of any other country. The French or Chilean village is the negation of France and Chile, and no one would accept either its customs, dress, or ideas as representative of the national civilization. The American village, on the other hand, is a small edition of the whole country, in its civil government, its press, its schools, its banks, its town hall, its census, its spirit, and its appearance. From the midst of the primitive forest stagecoaches or railroad cars emerge and come upon a small cleared place, in the center of which ten or twelve houses have been raised. These houses are built of machine-made bricks held together by mortar and laid in very straight lines, which give their sides the smoothness of geometrical figures. They are two stories tall, topped by roofs of painted wood. Doors and windows are painted white and are fastened by patent locks, and green shutters give life to and vary the symmetry of the architecture. I am concerning myself with such details because they characterize a people and give rise to a whole train of reflections. The first thought which struck my mind when I saw this display of wealth and comfort was the difference between the productive power of nations. Chile, for example (and what applies to Chile is applicable to all of Spanish America), has a million and a half inhabitants. In what proportion are the houses— those that merit the name—to the population? Now in the United States, everyone, except the PIONEERS who still live in the deepest forest and the transients who stay in great hotels, lives in houses like those I have described, with all of the most modern equipment known to civilization. This suggests an economic principle which I shall quickly describe. Suppose that twenty million Americans occupy a million homes. Can you imagine the amount of capital invested to satisfy this need alone? Manufacturers of machine-made bricks have made fortunes with their products. Manufacturers of patent locks sell them for amounts a hundred times greater than in any other part of the world, while serving a smaller number of men. The manufacture of the cast-iron stoves in domestic use in all of the villages would be enough to occupy the factories of London. And the value of the houses in which Americans live in the "poorest" (though that word simply does not apply) towns, would be equal to the value of all the territory and real estate in any of our countries.

The kitchen, which is more or less spacious depending on the size of the family, has an economical cast-iron stove which comes with a complete set of pots and pans and culinary utensils, all produced by one factory specializing in these products. In some interior compartment of the house are kept plows which are of French invention and are the most powerful agricultural implements known: their shares open furrows a foot and a half wide, while a movable knife cuts the weeds. Only the slightest effort of the farmer is necessary to avoid tree-trunks. The light, wooden part of the plow is almost always painted red, and the harnesses which are thrown over the horses are from a harness shop and are always polished and have brass ornaments and yellow buckles to adjust them. The axes of the farm are also patented and of the best-known make, for the axe is to the Yankee what the trunk is to the elephant, his toothpick and his finger—what the knife is to us and the razor to the Spaniard. A four-wheeled carriage, light as a beetle's leg and always varnished and shined up as if it had just come from the factory, with polished, complete harnesses which are nicer than the ones on the Paris *fiacres*, provides transportation for the family. There is one machine for shelling corn and another for hulling wheat. Every agricultural and domestic task is a spur to the inventive genius of the manufacturer. The land next to the house, which serves as a flower garden, is separated from the street or public road by an attractive white picket fence. Do not forget that I am describing a poor town which still has no more than a dozen houses, is surrounded by formidable forests, and is separated by hundreds of leagues from the big cities. My village also has various public establishments: a brewery, a bakery, and various taverns or eating places, every establishment with its sign in gold letters, beautifully done by a professional. This is an important point. Signs in the United States are works of art and an indisputable example of the progress of the country. I have been amused all over Spain and South America looking at signs (where there were any) with uneven and broken-backed letters, their spelling errors advertising the blessed ignorance of the artist or amateur who made them.

The American is a classical man of letters when it comes to signs, and a crooked or fat letter or a mistake in spelling would be enough to insure a deserted counter for the shopkeeper. There are at least two hotels in the town for the lodging of travelers. There is also a printer who puts out a small daily paper, a bank, and a church. The post office daily receives regional or city newspapers for which the townspeople have subscriptions, and letters, packages, and travelers arrive and depart from it every day. Mail is carried to even the most distant points in four-wheeled vehicles with accommodations for passengers. The streets, which are progressively laid out as the population increases, are, as in the large cities, some twenty-seven yards wide. They include sidewalks on each side that are six yards wide and are shaded by trees planted for this purpose. The center of the street, until it is paved, is a mudhole in which all the town's pigs root. These animals occupy such a high place in the domestic economy that their meat competes in importance with wheat.

Since, as they say, "As the nest, so the bird," I will say a word about the villager. If he is a tavernkeeper, a storekeeper, or belongs to some other sedentary profession, his daily costume will consist of the following articles: patent-leather boots, pants and coat of black cloth, a black satin waistcoat, a tie of twilled silk, a small cloth cap, and, hanging from a black cord, a gold charm in the shape of a pencil or a key. At the end of this cord, and deep in his pocket, is the most curious item of the Yankee's dress. If you want to study the transformations the watch has gone through from its invention down to our own time, ask any Yankee you meet what time it is. You will see fossil watches, mastodon watches, haunted watches, watches which are the home of vermin, and inflated watches three stories high with drawbridges and secret stairways which you descend with a lantern in order to wind up. The model for Dulcamara's watch in *The Elixir of Love* emigrated with the first Puritans, and its descendants are citizens and are enlisted in the terrible ranks of those nativists who profess the most exalted Americanism. Every boat that comes from Europe brings hundreds of these immigrant watches, which are sold at the best prices in New York, Boston, New Orleans, and Baltimore from twelve reales* on up, thereby satisfying this national demand for watches. The

* The real was worth approximately 12 1/2 cents.

Yankee keeps a notebook in his pocket and, on going to bed, roughly sketches out in hieroglyphics his plans for the next day. Do not think that I am exaggerating about this widespread distribution of civilized ways in the towns as well as in the cities and among men of all classes. I choose at random the smallest towns whose description I have at hand. "Bennington has a town hall, a church, two academies, a bank, and nearly three hundred inhabitants."

"Norwich, on the right bank of the Connecticut,* has several churches, a bank, and seven hundred inhabitants."

"Haverhill has a town hall, a bank, a church, an academy, and sixty houses, etc."

Westward, where civilization diminishes, and in the FAR WEST, where it is almost nonexistent because of the sparseness of the population, things are of course different. Comfort is reduced to what is strictly necessary, and houses are LOG HOUSES, put up in twenty-four hours and consisting of logs placed one on top of another which meet at the corners and are joined by notching. But even in these remote plantations there is an appearance of perfect equality among the population in their dress, in their manners, and even in their intelligence. The merchant, the doctor, the SHERIFF, the farmer—all look the same. The farmer is the head of a family, and he is the owner of two hundred or two thousand acres of land—it doesn't matter which for our purpose. His farm implements (his ENGINES) are all alike, that is, all of the best quality. If a religious meeting is to be held in the vicinity, from the depths of the forest, down the

* Sarmiento is, of course, in error. Norwich is at the origin of the Thames, which flows some twenty miles to the east of the Connecticut.

mountains, filling every road, the country folk will come on horseback in long cavalcades, with the men in black trousers and jackets and the girls in dresses of the prettiest styles and most graceful forms. Once, aboard a steamboat on a long trip, my attention was from time to time drawn to a person who was perfectly dressed and who was notable for his natural good manners. It was not without surprise that I saw him, one morning as we drew nearer to a city, get a drum from his stateroom, tune it, and begin to play a tattoo to invite the young men of the place to join up in the army. He was a drummer! At times his watchchain fell on the drum and momentarily hindered the action of the drumsticks. Equality is thus absolute in customs and forms. Gradations of civilization are not expressed as among ourselves by different kinds of clothing. Americans do not wear jackets or ponchos, but have a dress common to all and a universal roughness of manner which gives an impression of equality in education.

But even this is not the thing most characteristic of the Americans. What is most characteristic of them is their ability to appropriate for their own use, generalize, popularize, conserve, and perfect all the practices, tools, methods, and aids which the most advanced civilization has put in the hands of men. In this, the United States is unique on this earth. There are no unconquerable habits that retard for centuries the adoption of an obvious improvement, and, on the other hand, there is a predisposition to try anything. An advertisement in one newspaper for a new kind of plow, for example, is carried in every paper in the Union the next day. The day after that they are talking about it on every plantation, and the blacksmiths and manufacturers in two hundred places are at the same time considering putting out the new model. Soon the new machines are put on sale, and a year later they are in use all over the Union. You would have to wait a century for something like this to happen in Spain, or in France, or in our own part of America.

Salvá's dictionary—the Academy's is not always accurate any more—defines the word "civilization" as "that degree of culture which nations or persons acquire when they pass from primitivism to the beauty, elegance, and sweetness of voice and manner appropriate to cultivated people." I would call this "civility." For neither an affected way of speaking nor extremely delicate manners represent moral and physical perfection or the abilities which a civilized man develops in order to subject nature to his desires.

After the villages of the United States, the attention of the traveler is drawn to the activity on the thoroughfares which unite them, whether on the macadam roads, the railroads, or the navigable rivers. If God were suddenly to call the world to judgment, He would surprise two-thirds of the population of the United States on the road like ants. So the same things I have said about building apply to travel. Since everyone travels, there is no impossible or unprofitable enterprise in the field of transportation. The 120 leagues from Albany to Buffalo are covered by train in twenty-four hours for $12. And for $15, a fare which includes four sumptuous and delicious meals daily, a steamboat voyage of 2,200 miles can be made in ten days between Cincinnati and New Orleans on the Ohio and the Mississippi. As the steamboats and trains pass through primitive forests, thoughtful passengers peer into dark and lonely encircling bowers, fearing to catch a glimpse of the last of the savage tribes which no more than ten years ago regarded these places as their ancestral hunting grounds.

The great number of travelers makes for cheap rates, and cheap rates in turn tempt those who have no precise object in mind to go somewhere. The Yankee leaves his house to take a bit of air or to go for a walk and ends up making a round-trip voyage of fifty leagues in a steamboat or train before returning to his normal occupations. When the sharp eye of industry discovers a good stretch of land for a railroad, the ground is cleared along the route and the felled trees are covered with a thin iron plate and used as the tracks. At first the train travels slowly, trying to keep its balance as it rocks from side to side on the precarious track. Passengers pour in from everywhere, and with the profits that they provide a true railroad is then constructed. Such a train is never completely safe, in order not to be too costly, but this does not increase the rate of accidents by much. The cars are always comfortable and spacious, and if their cushions are not as luxurious as the ones in first-class coaches in France, neither are they so stupidly hard as those in the second-class coaches in England. Since there is only one class in United States society—Man—there is no need for three or four classes of coaches as is the case in Europe. But where American luxury and grandeur is unrivaled on this earth is in the steamboats on the northern rivers. The boats which navigate the Mediterranean look like sewers or nutshells compared to them! They are three-story floating palaces, with galleries and promenade decks. Gold shines from the capitals and architraves of a thousand columns which, as on the *Isaac Newton*, for example, flank gigantic chambers large enough to hold the entire Senate and House of

Representatives. Artistically hung damask draperies disguise staterooms for five hundred passengers, and there are colossal dining rooms with numberless tables of polished mahogany and porcelain and silver service for a thousand diners. The *Isaac Newton*, with a capacity of 2,000 passengers, has 750 beds, 200 private staterooms, is 341 feet in length and 85 in width, and in addition can take on 1,450 tons of cargo.

The *Hendrick* is 341 feet long and 72 feet wide, has 150 separate staterooms and 600 beds with feather mattresses; it has ACCOMMODATIONS for 2,000 passengers and can take them 144 miles for a dollar. A New Yorker goes to Troy or Albany on the night boat, speaks with his agent the following morning, and is back in New York that evening ready to take up his affairs again. During ten or twelve working hours he has covered 100 leagues. The South American who has just got off the boat from Europe, where he has been ecstatically admiring what he regarded as the ultimate in man's power and industrial progress, is astonished to see those colossal American constructions and transportation facilities and wonders if Europe really does lead the world in civilization. I have seen French, English, and Sardinian sailors express unfeigned astonishment at finding their nations so small and so backward compared with this gigantic country.

On the Hudson River steamboats there is a *sancta sanctorum* where no profane eye can penetrate, a mysterious abode whose delights can at best only be guessed at from the traces of perfume which escape whenever the door is opened momentarily. The Americans have developed customs which have no parallel and which are unprecedented on this earth. The unmarried woman, or "man of feminine sex," is as free as a butterfly until

135

the moment she seals herself in the domestic cocoon in order to fulfill through marriage her social functions. Before this act she travels alone, wanders about the streets of the city, carries on several chaste and public love affairs under the indifferent eyes of her parents, receives visits from persons who have not been presented to her family, and returns home from a dance at two o'clock in the morning accompanied by the young man with whom she has waltzed or polkaed exclusively all night. Her good Puritan parents tease her at times about her loves, of which they have heard rumors, and she, clever thing, enjoys brushing off their conjectures and giving the lie to the evidence.

After two or three years of FLIRTING* (that's the American verb), dances, walks, trips, and coquetries, this girl one day at lunch reluctantly asks her parents if they know a tall, blond young man, machinist by trade, who at certain periods has come to see her every day. Her parents have been waiting for a year to hear this. The upshot of the matter is that a connection is agreed upon of which the parents are being told at the last moment but which they knew about all along from their informants. The marriage accomplished, the young couple jump on the next train and leave to display their happiness through woods, towns, cities, and hotels. In the coaches you can always see these charming young couples of twenty years of age embracing, reposing each in the bosom of the other, and wearing such affectionate expressions as to infect all travelers around them, even the most obstinate bachelors, with the idea of getting married immediately. No better propaganda for marriage exists than these public demonstrations of conjugal bliss.

* Sarmiento says *flirtear*, which would be the infinitive of the Spanish verb "to flirt," if there were such a verb.

Owing to this, the Yankee never arrives at the age of twenty-five without having a large family. And here is the explanation for the amazing propagation of the species which is going on in that fortunate land. In 1790, the population was recorded as almost four million; in 1800, five million; 1810, seven million; 1820, nine million; 1830, twelve million; 1840, seventeen million; and in 1850 it will be twenty-three million. Immigration has something to do with these figures, but only to a limited extent. The immigrant is not a prolific animal until he has received the Yankee bath.

Returning then to the thousands of newlyweds who go about inflaming and enlivening the atmosphere with their breaths of spring, it is interesting to note that the steamboats on the Hudson and other principal rivers have special compartments fitted out for them. They are called bridal suites. In these chambers stained-glass windows let in a discreet light which contains all the soft colors of the rainbow. Rose-colored lamps burn at night, and day and night the perfume of flowers, sweet-smelling waters, and burning incense sharpen the thirst for pleasure which consumes the chosen inhabitants. The factories of Paris have not created damasks and muslins costly enough for the flowing folds that hang from gilded canopies and envelop the lawful saturnalia of the bridal suite. After having seen Niagara Falls, bathed in the hot springs at Saratoga, breezed through one hundred cities, and covered a thousand leagues of countryside, the newlyweds return after fifteen days, exhausted, in wonder at everything, and happy, to the blessed boredom of the domestic hearth. The wife has said good-bye forever to the world, whose pleasures she had enjoyed for so long in complete liberty, good-bye to the cool green forests, witnesses of her love, and good-bye to the waterfalls, the roads, and the rivers. From now on, the closed domestic asylum will be her perpetual prison, ROASTBEEF her eternal confessor, a swarm of blond and frolicsome little ones her constant torment, and an uncivil but GOOD NATURED husband, sweaty during the day and snoring at night, her accomplice and solace. I attribute to these ambulant amours, in which American FLIRTING* ends, the mania for travel which distinguishes the Yankee and makes him a born traveler. The rage to travel is increasing by leaps and bounds every year. The revenue from all public works, railroads, bridges, and canals in all of the states in 1844, compared with the previous year, showed an increase of $4,000,000, which means that the value of these projects increased by $80,000,000 in that year alone, computing interest at 5 percent. The American knows by heart all the various distances between points of his country. When a city comes into view, there is, in the coaches and steamboats, a general movement of hands into pockets, of unfolding of topographical maps of the environs, and of fingers describing the point in question. One New York house alone has in ten years sold a million and a half atlases and maps to the public. I am sure that no firm in Paris has produced as many for sale all over the world. Each state has its own geological map showing the composition of its soil and the exploitable minerals that it contains. Each county has its own topographical map in ten different editions of all sizes and prices. No sooner had the first cannon shot been fired on the Mexican frontier than the Union was flooded with millions of maps of Mexico on which the Yankee traced the movements of the army, gave battle, advanced, took the capital, and there set up camp until late news arrived by telegraph giving him the true posi-

---

* This time Sarmiento invents a new Spanish noun: *el flirteo.*

tion of the armies. Then he set them going again with his finger on the map and by the force of his conjectures and calculations put the American troops "at this very moment" back in Mexico City again. The Mexicans could take lessons from any Yankee woodcutter on the topography, products, and resources of the country which, without knowing anything about it, they inhabit.

But let us go on for awhile with our description of the thoroughfares. On the lakes and on the Hudson and longer rivers the steamboats put in to shore at designated places to renew their supply of firewood, an operation which takes less time than taking on new passengers or changing mules at a Spanish posting station. Coming out of an ancient forest and along scarcely passable ways you can see a family of ladies in their dancing dresses accompanied by men dressed in the eternal black coat. These are varied occasionally by a man in an overcoat or now and then by an old man in a Puritan-style velvet cloak, with white hair down to his shoulders like Franklin and a round, low-crowned hat. These people's carriages are of the same construction and have the same varnished and polished finish as those which are driven about the streets of Washington. Their horses, in shiny harnesses, are of English stock that has not lost any of its slender beauty or Arabic qualities on emigrating to the New World. The American, far from barbarizing, as we have, the elements which European civilization handed him when he came as a settler, has worked to perfect them and even to improve upon them. The picture of this uniform decency and general welfare, even if it satisfies the hearts of those who enjoy seeing a part of the human race partaking in equal shares of the joys and advantages of society, tires one at last with its monotonous uniformity. Of course, the picture is sometimes tarnished by the appearance of a slovenly rustic in a faded and dirty frock coat or tattered dress coat who reminds the traveler of some of those disagreeable-looking Spanish or South American beggars. But then again, the romantic clothing worn in the region surrounding Naples doesn't improve the view either. Nor do the mantillas of the lower-class women of Seville, nor the vestments embroidered in gold which the Jewish women of Algiers and Oran wear. France herself, which has all the world under the despotic reign of her styles, amuses the traveler with the traditional hair-arrangements of her countrywomen, a different one for each province. Around Bordeaux, ladies' coifs reach the frightful height of two feet above the head, like those combs made from the shell of an entire tortoise which the ladies of Buenos Aires at one time wore with great pride. Taking all this, plus the fur robes and spurs worn by the Chileans, into consideration, I suspect that provincialism everywhere manifests itself in grossness.

A country girl in the United States is distinguished from her city cousins only by her rosy cheeks, her round, plump face, and her frank and simple smile. Aside from this and a little less style and ease in the way she wears her shawl, she and all American women belong to the same class, and their good looks honor the human race.

On this trip we are making through the United States, my good friend, whether we stroll around the galleries or decks of steamboats or go by the slowest train, we finally come to the—I won't say *gates* of a city (a European term which suggests the prison walls which surround their cities)—but to a disembarking point. From here we go with three hundred other travelers to take up quarters in one of the magnificent hotels whose coaches-and-four and uniformed servants wait for us at the arrival point, unless we want to follow the crowd on foot with our bags in our hands. As the steamboat in which I was descending the Mississippi came around one of the bends which are so typical of that great mass of water, we saw on the horizon the dome of Saint Charles', a comforting indication of the proximity of New Orleans after seven hundred leagues of nothing but water and forest. It was set high above steplike clumps of trees in autumn colors and bordering it were emerald sugar plantations. And although the appearance of the surrounding area does not favor the comparison, the sight of that faraway dome brought to mind the dome of Saint Peter's in Rome, which you can see from all points of the compass as if it were the only thing there. From twenty leagues it appears much more colossal than one would imagine looking at it from close by. At last I was going to see in the United States a basilica designed along classic lines and on a scale dignified enough for religion. Someone asked us if we had hotel arrangements and suggested the Saint Charles as the best appointed. "From the dome," he added, "you will at sunrise be able to see the great panorama of the city, the river, the lake, and the surrounding countryside." The Saint Charles, which lifted its proud head above the surrounding hills and woods, the Saint Charles, which had called up my memory of Saint Peter's in Rome, was no more than a hotel!

Here is the sovereign people who build palaces to shelter their heads for a night! Here is the religion which is dedicated to man as man, and here the marvels of art are lavished on the glorification of the masses! Nero had his Domus Aurea, but the Roman plebeians had only the catacombs to shelter themselves!

Our admiration did not diminish on drawing near

141

the base of that superb palace which many European princes would envy; with the exception of the Capitol in Washington, no civil or religious monument in the United States is superior in size or good taste. Above a substructure of granite which is devoted to wine cellars and storehouses rises a base of white marble (FREE-STONE) supporting twelve fluted columns of composite order, six of which, projecting forward from the rest of the building, support a lovely pediment. The wings which extend the facade on both sides hold between the base and the architrave of the columns four floors, whose windows do not interfere with the classic style. Under the portico formed by the pediment a Jupiter-size statue of George Washington guards the entrance, which leads to the spacious marble rotunda beneath the great dome. In this grand area are distributed tables covered with periodicals from all over the country and European ones a fortnight old.

The hotel's offices are in the front of the building. Superb staircases twist upwards on themselves like brass serpents, giving access to all of the upper regions of the hotel and leading to the very dome which, encircled by a gallery of Corinthian columns, crowns the monument. An orderly array of servants stands ready to satisfy the slightest whim of the traveler. In the winter a fireplace large enough to burn a ton of coal comforts the traveler as he registers his name in the great book always kept open for this purpose, and he is then shown his rooms and his luggage is brought up. A powerful gas lighting system, with more than a thousand jets distributed throughout the building, provides brilliant illumination. In the left wing, extending to the back of the building, is the dining room, a chamber surrounded by columns, illuminated by colossal brass chandeliers, and wide enough to contain three parallel mahogany tables that run the length of the room, a distance of a little less than half a block. Seven hundred diners gather round these tables in winter, the busy season in New Orleans. The private parts of the building are just as luxurious as these colossal public areas. My traveling companion, dominated by philosophical concerns, had in previous conversations shown little more than indifference for the advantages of this or any other system of government, but on walking about the internal passageways which communicate with hundreds of rooms decorated in degrees of luxury to correspond with the demands of the diverse pocketbooks of the guests and which, according to him, extended for fantastic distances, he said to me: "I am converted. Through the intercession of Saint Charles I now believe in the Republic, in democracy, in everything. I pardon the Puritans, even that one who was eating tomato sauce straight, with the tip of his knife, and before the soup. Everything should be pardoned a people who raise up monuments to the dining room and crown their kitchens with domes like this one!"

Even though the Saint Charles is the Saint Peter's of hotels and cost $700,000 to build, it still is not the largest or the best-constructed of the popular palaces. Every large city in the United States boasts of two or three monstrous hotels that compete among themselves in offering luxury and comfort to the public at the lowest prices. The Hotel Astor is a magnificent granite building occupying with its great mass one side of Washington Square in New York. More money has been put into the Astor than into any church in that city. After visiting the United States and seeing the results they have obtained there through natural means, I have come to

143

the conclusion that if you want to know if a machine, an invention, or a social doctrine is useful and can be applied or developed in the future, you must test it on the touchstone of Yankee knowhow. Hotels have an extremely important role in the domestic life of nations. Static nations, like Spain and its derivative countries, do not need hotels; the domestic hearth is enough for them. But in dynamic societies, with an active life and a future, the hotel will be more important than any other kind of public construction. A hundred years ago the hotel was barely known in Paris and unheard of in the rest of Europe. Forty years ago Fourier based his social theory on the phalanx, which offered living quarters for as many as two thousand people who were able to provide comforts for themselves which families isolated in private homes could not enjoy. The proof that Fourier was not wrong is in the American hotel, which by simply following man's desire for convenience has already reached the monumental form and size of the phalansteries. Since the Christian church is divided into sects in the United States, where there were cathedrals before, now there are chapels. Where the importance of the individual reaches the heights it has in American democracy, the temple's power diminishes in proportion to the multiplication of sects, and the hotel inherits the dome of the ancient tabernacle and takes on the aspect of the baths of emperors. Religious architecture continues to wither and fade away while popular architecture exhausts itself inventing peculiar forms, dimensions, and methods. The American bank, a construction as solid as a strongbox, has an Ionic facade, or if not Ionic, Egyptian. Why do the Yankees insist upon these two heavy orders for their strongboxes? Above all American monuments a lightning rod has been placed, and it is already common architectural usage to put atop domes or cupolas, as a finishing touch, the statue of Franklin holding a lightning rod. We already have, then, a Mercury charged with protecting the domestic hearth or a Saint Barbara to intercede against lightning bolts! If the Americans have not, then, created a new kind of architecture, they have at least developed national applications, forms, and a character influenced by their political and social institutions, which is what occurred with all the architectures that have come down to us from antiquity. An odd confusion reigns today in Europe over the application of the fine arts. The reestablishment and renovation of the Gothic church has accompanied the romantic movement in literature. The pantheon built by the French Republic has remained unfinished, as if it is waiting for better times to fulfill its object. The temple of glory built by Napoleon, the most Greek, most Olympian construction that the Romans or French ever saw, is now the Church of Magdalene, whose pleasant, smiling architecture seems to be ridiculing the tears of that repentant Loreta of Jerusalem, while the images of the Virgin and the saints have gone to the museums in Rome, London, Dresden, and Florence, to stand shoulder to shoulder and be confused with the statues of the pagan gods and the nudes of profane painting. In the United States it is the public architecture which has appropriated for itself the use of symbols of worship, if you will forgive the term. The bank is Ionic. The hotel is often Corinthian and always monumental. And even the inventor of lightning rods now has his elevated post and architectural function. This tendency has been extended to the very capitals of Roman columns, shaping them in the image of an ear of corn, symbol of American agriculture.

145

As for the internal arrangement of the large hotel, nothing could be more usual than the good order common to these establishments. At the entrance, a portico containing the administrative offices; a register in which the entering guest inscribes his name and the clerk notes "560" or "227" in the margin. This is the number of the chamber assigned to the guest as well as that of his bell, which, like all those in the hotel, is connected by sealed wires to the same office. In the vestibule, for the information of the traveler, signs are posted advertising goings-on in the city. Theatrical presentations, meetings, sermons for the day, steamship departures, train schedules, etc., are all posted. Adjoining the vestibule there is a reading room containing the principal newspapers of the Union and the latest numbers from Europe. A smoking room and four or five conversation and reception salons complete this part of the public conveniences of the hotel. Thermal baths are available to the guests at any hour. The ladies also have their own gracefully and luxuriously decorated reception and entertainment rooms. Two or three pianos are part of the hotel's equipment. At half past seven in the morning the insupportable vibrations of a Chinese gong passing through all the corridors inform the guest that it is time to get up. At eight, a new and more alarming vibration announces that breakfast is served. A mob of "monastics" answers the call by charging down each of the corridors toward the immense "refectory." Here the life of these people, who are as serious when they laugh as when they eat, begins to show itself. Where every man is equal to the last individual in society, there is no protection for the weak, for the same reason that there is no hierarchy to separate off the powerful. How one would fear for

146

the women in this solemn act of popular sovereignty if the hotel regulations did not come to their rescue.

"Art. 1: No one may take a seat at the common table until the ladies, with their husbands or kinsmen, have occupied the head and adjacent sides of the table.

"Art. 2: Guests are requested not to smoke or chew tobacco at the table.

"Art. 3: At the sound of the bell, gentlemen may sit down in the remaining seats."

These laws being well known, the gastronomical crowd automatically lines up behind the seats with both hands placed on the back of the chair and all eyes fixed on the servant who is about to give the desired signal with the bell. As this functionary takes the sonorous instrument in his hand the double line stirs. The slightest hint of the coming sound and bodies undulate like stalks of wheat in the gentlest breeze. The bell is raised in the attitude of sounding, and there is a great scraping of chairs across the floor which accompanies, if it does not precede, the harsh jingling. Instantly begins a racket of plates, knives, and forks colliding with each other which goes on for five minutes, letting all the world know for half a league around that eating is going on at a hotel. It is impossible to follow with the eye the events of the meal in the midst of all this uproar, despite the activity and skill of fifty or one hundred servants who try to give a certain style to the uncovering of dishes and the pouring of tea and coffee. The American has two minutes set aside for lunch, five for dinner, ten for a smoke or to chew tobacco, and the rest of the day for staring at the newspaper you are reading, the only one that interests him because it belongs to someone else.

A strong breakfast, LUNCH at eleven o'clock, dinner,

and tea are the four regular meals in that unfolding society, although the rules do not prohibit breakfast at five o'clock for those who are leaving on a steamboat or the early cars, nor is anyone who arrives at the hotel at any hour of the day or night ever denied a snack. But then, what incongruousness, what incest, what promiscuity in their dishes! The Yankee *pur sang* eats all his food, desserts, and fruit from the same plate, one at a time or all together. We saw one fellow from the FAR WEST, an unsettled land like the Phoenicians' Ophir, begin his meal with great quantities of fresh tomato sauce taken straight and scooped up on the tip of his knife! Sweet potatoes with vinegar! We were frozen with horror, and my traveling companion was filled with gastronomical indignation upon seeing these abominations. "And will not heaven rain down fire upon them?" he asked. "The sins of Sodom and Gomorrah must have been minor compared to the ones these Puritans commit every day."

In the reading rooms, four or five parasites support themselves heavily on your shoulders to read the same tiny bit of print you are reading. If you are going downstairs or want to pass through a doorway, no matter how little traffic there is, the man behind you will push you in order to hang onto something. If you are tranquilly smoking your cigar, a passerby will take it out of your mouth in order to light his own, and if you cannot at that moment take it back, he will personally see to sticking it into your mouth. If you have a book in your hands and close it for a moment to look about, the man next to you will help himself to it and read two chapters. If the buttons on your overcoat have deer, horse, or boars' heads in relief, everyone who spies them will come up to you and go over them one by one, turning you about

148

from left to right to better examine the walking museum. Finally, if in the North you wear a full beard (which means you are a Frenchman or a Pole), at every step you will be surrounded by a circle of men who will look at you with infantile interest, calling to their friends and acquaintances to step up and satisfy their curiosity in person.

All of these liberties, it should be understood, you can take in turn with the other fellow without anyone complaining about it or showing the least sign of disagreeableness. But where the national genius and instincts really reveal themselves is in the attitudes assumed by the Yankees in society. This needs some explanation. Among a people who advance their frontier a hundred leagues each year, set up states in six months, transport themselves from one end of the Union to the other in a matter of hours, and emigrate to Oregon, the feet would naturally enjoy the same esteemed position as the head among those who think and the chest among those who sing. In the United States you will see evidence everywhere of the religious cult which has grown up around that nation's noble and worthy instruments of its wealth: its feet. While conversing with you, the Yankee of careful breeding lifts one foot knee high, takes off his shoe in order to caress the foot, and listens to the complaints that his overworked toes make. Any four individuals seated around a marble table will infallibly have their eight feet on top of it unless they can get seats upholstered in velvet, which, because of its softness, the Yankees prefer to marble. In the Fremont* Hotel in Boston I have seen seven Yankee DANDIES in friendly discussion seated like this: two with their feet on the table; one with his feet on the cushion of an adjacent chair; another

* "Tremont" is intended.

with a leg hooked around the arm of his own chair; another with both heels dug into the edge of the cushion of his chair so that his chin rested on his knees; still another embracing or "legging" the back of his chair in the way that is usually only reserved for the arm (this posture, impossible for all other peoples of the world, I have tried without incident, and I recommend it to you if you wish to give yourself cramps in punishment for some indiscretion); another one, finally, if we do not already have the seven, in some other absurd position. I do not remember if I have seen Americans seated on the backs of their chairs with their feet on the cushion, but I am sure that I never saw one of them proud of sitting in the natural way. Lying down is the height of elegance, and the initiated reserve this sign of good taste for when ladies are present or when a LOCOFOCO listens to a WHIG SPEECH. The Secretary of the Chilean Legation, upon arriving in Washington, had some business to transact with a Congressman. Going to the Capitol during a session, he inquired the location of the man's seat and found Mr. N. stretched out, his legs extended on his neighbor's seat, snoring loudly. The Chilean had to wake him, but once their business was over the Congressman turned over on his other side, doubtless to await the end of an interminable speech by some orator of the opposition. Americans profess the admirable and conciliatory principle of not discussing religion or politics with anyone except those who are of their own sect or persuasion. This system is based on an obvious understanding of human nature. The Yankee orator strives to confirm his followers in their beliefs rather than to convert his opponents, who meanwhile are dozing or thinking of their businesses. To sum up, the Yankees are the most uncivil little animals under the sun. At least, that is what such competent judges as Captain Marryat, Miss* Trollope, and other travelers have said about them. But then, if in England and France the coal miners, woodcutters, and tavernkeepers were to sit down at the same table with artists, congressmen, bankers, and landowners, as is the case in the United States, the Europeans would form another opinion of their own culture. In civilized countries, good manners have their limit. The English lord is uncivil out of pride and contempt for his inferiors, while the masses are uncivil out of brutality and ignorance. In the United States, civilization holds sway over such great numbers that, slowly, improvement is coming about. The influence of the gross masses on the individual forces him to accept the customs of the majority and creates, finally, a kind of national consensus which may turn into pride and chauvinism. Europeans make fun of these rude habits, which are more superficial than profound, and the Americans, for the sake of argument, become obstinate and justify them as going hand in hand with liberty and the American way of life. I do not mean to defend or excuse these characteristics. Still, after examining the chief nations of Christendom, I have come to the conclusion that the Americans are the only really cultured people that exist on this earth and the last word in modern civilization.

Everybody in the United States carries a watch; in France, not a tenth of the people have one. The great majority of Americans wear dress coats and the garments which go with them, all clean and of good quality. In France, four-fifths of the nation dresses in nankin blouses.

The Yankees have efficient kitchens, Durand plows, and coaches. They live in clean, comfortable houses.

* *Mrs.* Trollope.

The day-laborer earns a dollar a day. The Americans have railroads, artificial canals, and navigable rivers in greater number and covering greater distances than those of all of Europe together. Comparative statistics for railroads in 1845 were as follows: England, 1,800 miles; Germany, 1,339; France, 560; the United States, 4,000. This means there are 86 miles of railroad for each million inhabitants in England, 16 miles for each million in France, but 222 miles for each million in the United States. The United States' telegraph system is today the only one in the world which is at the disposal of the people, providing instant communication between one extreme of the Union and the other.

The only country in the world where the ability to read is universal, where writing is practiced by all in their daily lives, where 2,000 periodicals satisfy public curiosity, and where education, like welfare, is everywhere available to all those who want it is the United States. Is there any country in the world which can compare with it in these respects? In France there are 270,000 voters; that is, among 36 million individuals in the oldest civilized nation, only 270,000, according to the law, are not considered beasts. Reason is not recognized as the important factor in governing.

In the United States, every man has a natural right to a role in political affairs, and he exercises it. On the other hand, France has a king, 400,000 soldiers, fortifications in Paris which have cost 2 billion francs, and a people dying of hunger. Americans live without a government, and their permanent army amounts to only 9,000 men. It is necessary to make a trip to special places to see anything of the army's equipment or of the soldiers themselves, and there are families and towns in the Union which have never seen a soldier. Europeans and even South Americans complain about many defects in the character of the Yankees. For my own part, I celebrate these very defects, attributing them to the human race, our century, inherited problems, and the imperfection of intelligence. A people made up of all the peoples of the world, with thought and speech free as air, without tutors, without an army, and without bastilles is the product of all its human antecedents, European and Christian. Their defects therefore are those of the human race in a given period in its development. But as a nation, the United States is the latest result of human logic. It does not have kings, or nobles, or privileged classes, or men born into power, or human machines born to obey. Is not this in agreement with the ideas of justice and equality which Christianity accepts in theory? Well-being is more generally distributed among this people than in any other nation. The population increases at a speed unknown among other nations. Production increases at an astonishing rate. Do freedom of action and lack of government enter into this, as the Europeans believe? It is said that the ease in occupying new lands is the cause of so much prosperity. But then why in South America, where it is just as easy if not easier to take up new land, are population and wealth not increasing? There are cities and even capitals so undynamic that not even one hundred new houses have been put up in the last ten years. No census has yet been taken of the mental capacity of the inhabitants of any South American nation. The population is considered only in terms of the number of inhabitants, and from this total strength and value are computed. Perhaps for war—looking at man as a machine for destruction—this statistical method may have its value, but a peculiarity of the United States makes even this calculation invalid. In killing, one Yankee is worth many men of other nationalities; therefore, the destructive force of the nation can be considered as equal to two hundred million. The rifle is the national weapon, target shooting the children's diversion in the wooded states, and hunting squirrels in trees, picking them off by hitting their paws, so as not to injure the pelt, an amazing skill that all acquire.

United States statistics show a figure for adult males which would indicate a total population of twenty million inhabitants, all of whom are educated, know how to read and write, and enjoy political rights, with exceptions so few that they cannot even be said to qualify the generalization. The American is a man with a home or the certainty of having one, a man beyond the clutch of hunger or desperation, a man with hopes for the future as bright as the imagination can invent, a man with political sentiments and needs. He is, in short, master of himself, with a spirit elevated by education and a sense of his own dignity. It is said that man is a rational being to the extent that he is able to acquire and exercise reasoning powers. From this point of view there is no country on earth which has more rational beings than the United States, even including countries which have a population ten times as great.

It is not easy to demonstrate the connection between liberty and the marvels of prosperity displayed by the United States. Can freedom of religion produce wealth? Yes, but how does the right to attend this or that church and hold to this or that belief develop forces of production? In the eyes of each religious sect the others do not exist, so their isolated freedom does not affect the nation's economy. The Europeans attribute American prosperity to the advantages that a new country offers, with virgin lands easy to obtain; which would be a satisfactory enough explanation if South America, big as it is, did not have an even greater quantity of virgin lands, equally easy to obtain, and yet have backwardness, poverty, and greater ignorance, if such is possible, than exists among the European masses. Besides, being a new country does not mean anything if action is wanting.

Many times I will return to this intellectual and moral census in attempting to explain America's surprising social phenomena. For the moment I just want to establish one fact: that the aptitude of the Anglo-Saxon race is also no explanation for American development. Englishmen are the inhabitants of both sides of the Niagara River, but, nevertheless, there at the point where the English colony touches the American population the eye perceives that they are two distinct peoples. An English traveler, after describing various examples of industry and progress on the American side of the falls, added:

I am again under the jurisdiction of the laws of the English government, and, therefore, I do not feel like a foreigner now. Although in general the Americans are civil and pleasant, nevertheless an Englishman who is a stranger among them is annoyed and disgusted by their boasts of prowess in the last war and of their superiority over all the other nations, accepting as they do as an unquestionable fact that they surpass all other nations in virtue, knowledge, bravery, liberty, government, and every other characteristic. Nonetheless, no matter how much this attitude merits criticism, I cannot but admire the energy and spirit of enterprise they show in everything, and I deplore the apathy of the English government with respect to improving the provinces. One glance at the

155

banks of the Niagara is enough to show on which side the government is more effective. On the United States' side they are putting up great cities, there are numerous ports with breakwaters protecting the bays, and stagecoaches run up and down the roads. There is a great deal of commercial activity represented by wagons, carts, horses, and men moving in all directions. On the Canadian side, separated by just a stretch of river, there is an old settlement on what looks like improved land, and yet there are only two or three stores, one or two taverns, a port as God left it (without any public works protecting it), one or two little boats anchored, and a rickety wharf.

Another traveler, after giving examples of the growing industry on the American side, said of the Canadian side: "The country we crossed was very far along toward harvest without there being any sign of preparation to gather it in. Wherever we stopped to change horses we were assaulted by bands of children selling apples, and for the first time on this side we saw some beggars." Not long ago a great group of Americans went to Canada to live, only to turn around and go back to the United States. The railroads, as a means to wealth and civilization, are common both to Europe and the United States, and since in both lands they date from just yesterday, through them you can study the spirit that pervades both societies. In France, everything pertaining to the railroad, including the leveling of the roadbed, is looked over carefully by the engineers before traffic is allowed to move. Wooden fences guard both sides of the track. Double lines of cast-iron rails make for easy travel in both directions. If a local road crosses the tracks, strong gates guard the crossing, scrupulously closing a quarter of an hour before the cars are to pass in order to avoid accidents. At intervals along the entire road sentinels are posted to keep the tracks clear and give warning with different colored flags if there is danger or an obstacle which may hold up the train. The train does not leave the platform until four minutes after an army of guards have ascertained that all travelers are in their seats, the doors closed, the road clear, and no one closer than a yard to where the train will pass. Everything has been foreseen, calculated, and examined so that all can tranquilly sleep in their hermetically sealed jail. Let us now look at what happens in the United States. The railroad crosses leagues of primitive forests where there are still no human settlements. Since the company lacks funds, the rails are of wood with iron plates on top which often get loose, so the eye of the engineer is constantly fixed on the track in order to avert a disaster. One track serves for going and coming, with sidings at intervals where the up train can wait while the down train goes by on the other side. There is not a soul to warn of accidents. The railroad passes through the towns, and the children are seen in the doorways of their houses or on the tracks, enjoying themselves. The railroad, besides being a thoroughfare, is also a local road, and the traveler will see people who move aside just enough to let the train by and then get back on the track again to continue their journey. Where local roads cross the railroad there are no gates but simply a sign which says: "Attention To Bell Near Tracks," hieroglyphics which let the teamster know that there will be two of him if he is imprudent enough to cross the tracks at the moment when the train is passing. The train starts slowly from the station, and when it is already underway passengers jump aboard and fruit and newspaper vendors jump off. Everyone walks

157

from one car to the other just for the fun of it and to feel free, even when the train is going at top speed. Cows like to rest themselves right on the tracks, and so the American locomotive is preceded by a cowcatcher which has the charitable mission of pushing these indiscreet creatures to one side so that they are not pulverized by the wheels. More than once a boy has gone to sleep on the tracks only to be bounced four yards by a cowcatcher which saved his life even though it broke or dislocated a limb. The physical and moral consequences of both systems are all too perceptible. Europe, with its ancient science and riches accumulated for centuries, has not been able to open half the railroads which are now giving movement to the United States. The European is a minor under the protective guardianship of the state. His ability to take care of himself is judged to be inadequate. Warning signals, inspection, insurance, every means to preserve his life is put at his disposal. Everything but his reason, his discernment, his daring, his liberty. Everything but his right to take care of himself, his inclination, and his will. The Yankee stands on his own two feet, and if he wants to commit suicide no one will hinder him. If he wants to run after a train and dares to jump aboard, grabbing hold of a bar to save himself from the wheels, he does it. If a little urchin newsboy, in his eagerness to sell one more paper, has allowed the train to pick up speed before jumping off, all will applaud his skill as he lands on his feet and walks away. Here is how nations' characters are formed and how liberty is applied. There may be a few more victims and accidents, but on the other hand there are free men and not disciplined prisoners whose lives are administered. The word "passport" is unknown in the States, and the Yankee who has the pleasure of seeing one of these European documents in which the traveler's every movement is recorded shows it to his companions with gestures of horror and loathing. The boy who wishes to take a train, steamship, or canalboat and the unmarried girl who leaves for a visit two hundred leagues away never encounter anyone who asks them with what object, with whose permission, they have left the paternal home. They are simply exercising their liberty and their right of free movement. Because of this, the Yankee child astonishes the European with his boldness, his crafty prudence, and his knowledge of life at ten years of age. "How is your business going?" my traveling companion Arcos asked a clever boy who was giving us a guided tour of the books, periodicals, and pamphlets he was trying to get us to buy. "It's going well. For three years I have been earning my living by it and I already have three hundred dollars saved. This year I will put together the five hundred I need to form a partnership with Williams and get a bookstore with which to operate throughout the state." This merchant was between nine and ten years old. "Are you a landowner?" we asked a strapping youth who was traveling to the FAR WEST. "Yes. I'm going to buy lands. I have six hundred dollars!"

Alongside the railroad runs the telegraph line; though sometimes, to shorten the distance, it leaves the normal routes and carries the most important news 200 leagues through the thickest forest. When in 1847 the first trials were being made in France between Rouen and Paris, the press announced the existence of 1,635 miles of telegraph lines already existing in the United States. When I arrived there were 3,000 miles, and while I was crossing the country between New York and New Orleans an association was formed and a line strung from the first of those two cities to Montreal, in lower Canada, where I had been fifteen days before. Today there are probably 10,000 miles, and within very few years the telegraph lines will measure the same 80,000 miles that the mail covers. In France the telegraph is for the government's use; it is a state matter. In the United States it is simply an active and energetic business, the administration accepting any message which will be paid for. Can ideas come to a more damaging state than this, where the liberals and republicans in France consent to such a monopoly and to doing without the most expedient means of communication? In Harrisburg, with a population of 4,500 souls, the electrical telegraph had so much daily traffic as to keep the fellow who served it running, while at the same time in France they had not even been able to accomplish a miserable experiment. I make these comparisons to show the different atmosphere in which the people are educated and the moral and physical energy which is released. In France there are three categories of railroad cars, in England four. One's nobility is measured by the money he can pay, and the managers, in order to make the man who pays little as miserable as possible, have lavished comforts and luxuries on the first-class cars and left thin, hard plank benches for those in the third-class cars. I do not know why they haven't placed pins on the seats to further mortify the poor. In the United States the railroad car is a room fifty-five feet long and of ample width, with seats that have movable backs, so that if you turn two seats the other way a circle of conversation of four people is formed. There is an aisle down the middle of the cars to facilitate movement, and, since the cars are open at both ends, fresh air comes in from all sides and the curious can walk from the first to the last car while the train is going. The accommodations and the cushions are excellent and the same throughout the train, and for that reason the price of the ticket is the same for everyone. I have found myself seated on the train with the governor of a state on one side and a man whose calloused hands indicated that he was a common woodcutter on the other. Thus, by the respect accorded every man, the sentiment of equality is diffused throughout society. The aristocracy of Venice established equality by insisting upon the austere gondolas in order not to offend the pride of impoverished nobles, while democracy in the United States has distributed comfort and luxury equally in all of the railroad cars in order to inspire and honor the poor. These two facts are enough to measure the liberty and the spirit of both nations. The *Times* once said that if France had abolished the passport liberty would have been advanced more than it has been in half a century of revolutions and advanced social theories, and the proof is in the United States.

This, then, is a superficial examination of the spectacle of liberty in North America. In the middle of the cities men are reared in a "savage state," if you will. Women of all social stations loiter about the streets and byways flirting from the age of twelve to fifteen, marry whom they choose, travel, and then are entombed in the new home to rear the family. The child attends school from an early age and familiarizes himself with the books and the ideas of men. By fifteen years of age he is indeed a man, and from then on he is independent. He has not seen soldiers, and he knows nothing of *gendarmes*. The confusion of the streets entertains him, exalts him, and educates him. His passions are allowed to develop in their full flower and vigor. He has

161

a profession, and he gets married at twenty, sure of himself and of his future. The general progress of the Union makes him optimistic and advances his own affairs. And then how many grandiose dreams agitate his mind, how many roads open in all directions for him to try! Is he an artisan? Then a great association, a factory, will cover the States with the products of his art. Or perhaps he is interested in bringing a European invention into the country, or in improving machines already in use, or perhaps he will invent something. Today, nothing stops the Yankee! For a long time I have believed that the United States' role was, and would be for many years, one of adopting and utilizing progress in human intelligence made in other countries. European science would invent and America would popularize the efficient kitchen, the Durand plow, the locomotive, the telegraph. Nothing more natural than to think this way, and yet nothing less correct. The statistics collected in the last ten years show that a good measure of the inventions and improvements adopted in England are of American origin. The Americans have modified the steam engine, improved the keel of ships, and perfected the railroad car to the point where articles are exported to Europe itself. In Russia and in other places, American businessmen and their products are always preferred for their reliability. The Yankee wooden bridge, which at times is used to cross rivers twelve city blocks wide and supports trains filled with agricultural products on a shaky-looking frame and base, is nevertheless the fruit of the most profound study of the laws of gravity, of repercussion, elasticity, and the equilibrium of the combined forces. Yankee cleverness already has reduced the bridge to a science and puts these structures up everywhere to stand the test of torrents, hurricanes, and enormous weights. Half the farming implements in the world are inventions of the American's genius, and the steam mill as well as the keg in which flour is packed are products of his factories and his ability to produce tremendous results with very limited means.

But the American's greatest potential for development lies in his possession of the land which will be the nursery of his new family. In the midst of the most advanced civilization the Sons of Noah are dividing the wilderness lands and the Nimrods are laying the foundation for a new Babylonia. The Yankees leave behind those societies which expand in the ordinary fashion, by adding one new house to the hometown or new grazing fields to the ancestral farm.

The state is the faithful administrator of the abundant lands which belong to the Union, and in the sale of property to each man neither the intervention of speculators nor fluctuations in prices that close the door to small fortunes are permitted. The land costs a dollar an acre—the most important fact for the future landowner. There is a regular procedure for the distribution of these lands, whose beauty only God could have created.

The state sends its engineers to mark out the saleable lands using a heavenly meridian as basis for their calculations. If at one hundred leagues to the south or north it is necessary to measure another portion of land, the engineers will look for the same meridian, so that one day, perhaps within two centuries, the lines which divide the entire continent into zones will appear complete and without interruption as if all were just a small piece of land. This rectilinear agricultural measurement is something distinctly American. Land in the Province of Buenos Aires, that great pampa which is smooth as a table, was carved by the genius of Rivadavia* into shapes including parallelograms, triangles, and other forms convenient for recording on the map which the Department of Topography put out every ten years. By comparing the various editions one can easily study the movement of property by finding the average size of properties. The great properties are subdivided among their inheritors, and the small ones are always being put together because of the requirements of cattle-raising.

The fatal error of the Spanish colonization of South America, the deep wound which has condemned present generations to inertia and backwardness, was in the system of land distribution. In Chile, great concessions of land, measuring from one hill to another and from the side of a river to the banks of an arroyo, were given to the conquistadors. The captains established earldoms for themselves, while their soldiers, fathers of the share-cropper, that worker without land who multiplies without increasing the number of his buildings, sheltered themselves in the shade of their improvised roofs. The passion to occupy lands in the name of the king drove men to dominion over entire districts, which put great distances between landowners so that after three centuries the intervening land still has not been cleared. The city, for this reason, has been suppressed in this vast design, and the few villages which have been created since the conquest have been *decreed* by presidents. I know of at least five villages which were created in Chile in this official and contrived manner. But see how the American, recently called in the nineteenth century to conquer his piece of the world, does it. There the

---

* Bernardino Rivadavia, first President of Argentina after it gained its independence from Spain.

164

government has been careful to set aside land for all the coming generations. The young men aspiring to property each year crowd around the auction rooms in which public lands are sold, and, with the numbers of their lots in hand, they leave to take possession of their property, expecting to receive their titles later on from the offices in Washington. The most energetic Yankees, the misanthropes, the rustics, the SQUATTERS, in short, work in a manner which is more romantic, more poetic, and more primitive. Armed with their rifles, they immerse themselves in the virgin wilderness. For a pastime they kill the squirrels that unceasingly romp among the branches of the trees. A well-aimed bullet heads up into the sky to connect with an eagle which soars with majestic wings over the dark green surface formed by the boughs of the trees. The axe is the faithful companion of such a man, though he uses it for nothing more than to flex his muscles by throwing cedars and oaks to the ground. During his vagabond excursions this independent farmer looks for fertile land, a picturesque spot, something beside a navigable river; and when he has made up his mind, as in the most primitive times in the world's history, he says, "This is mine!" and without further ado takes possession of the land in name of the kings of the world: Work and Good Will. If one day the surveyor of the state's lands should arrive at the border of the land which he has laid out as his own, the auction will only serve to tell him what he owes for the land he has under cultivation, which will be the same sum as the adjacent uncultivated lands are going for. It is not unusual for this indomitable and unsociable character, overtaken by populations advancing through the wilderness, to sell his place and move away with his family, his oxen, and his horses searching for the desired

165

solitude of the forests. The Yankee is a born proprietor. If he does not have anything and never has had anything he does not say that he *is* poor but that he is poor right now, or that he has been unlucky, or that times are bad. And then, in his imagination he sees the primitive, dark, solitary, isolated forests and in the midst of them the mansion he means to have on the bank of some unknown river, with smoke rising from the chimney and oxen returning home with slow step to his property as the sun goes down. From that moment he talks of nothing else but going out to occupy and settle new lands. His evenings are spent over the map, computing the stages of the journey, tracing a route for his wagon. And in the newspaper he does not look for anything except announcements of sales of state lands, or word of the new city that is being built on the shores of Lake Superior.

Alexander the Great, upon destroying Tyre, had to give world commerce a new distribution center for the spices of the Orient, one from which they could be sent at once to the Mediterranean coasts. The founding of Alexandria was an example of Alexander's renowned cleverness, even though the commercial routes were known and the Isthmus of Suez the indispensable trading ground between the waters of the India, Europe, and Africa of those days. This work is accomplished every day by American Alexanders, who wander through the wilds looking for points that a profound study of the future indicates will be centers of commerce. The Yankee, an inventor of cities, professes a speculative science which leads him by deduction to the divination of a site where a future city must flourish. With the map extended in the shade of the forests, his sharp eye measures distances of time and space. He intuits the course which the public road will later have to take and he finds on his map the intersections which it will be necessary to make. He anticipates the invading march of the population which is advancing through the wilderness and calculates how much time both the people coming from the north and those coming from the south will take to draw near to the point at the confluence of two navigable rivers that he has chosen for study. Then, with a sure hand, he traces the route of the railroads which will link the commercial system of the lakes with his presumed metropolis, the canals which can be fed by rivers and arroyos that are at hand, and the thousands of leagues of waterways which go out in all directions like radii from the city he imagines. If, after settling these matters, he finds a shelf of coal or iron mines, he draws up a city plan, gives the city a name, and returns to the settlements to announce by means of the thousand echoes of journalism the discovery he has made of the site of a famous city of the future, the crossing point of one hundred commercial routes. The public reads the announcement, opens the map to check the precision of the calculations, and, if things look promising, comes rushing to buy lots, wondering which ones will be waterfront property, which ones will be close to Washington or Franklin Square. And in one year a Babel rises up in the middle of the forest, with all impatiently awaiting the day when the great destiny foretold for the city by topographical science will be realized. Communications are inaugurated. The newspaper of the place keeps everyone informed of society's progress. Agriculture gets underway. Temples, hotels, docks, and banks rise up. The port fills with ships, and the city really begins to extend its relations and to feel the urgency of linking itself by railroad or

167

canal with other great centers. One hundred cities on the Great Lakes, on the Mississippi, and in other remote places have originated in this intelligent and planned way, and almost all of them justify by their astonishing progress the certainty and the profundity of the economic and social studies which served as their genesis.

I know two classes of human beings who still retain the heroic spirit of the first days of man in the midst of contemporary moderation. They are the prisoners of Toulon and Bicêtre and immigrants to the United States. All the rest of the human species has become weak through civilization. These freedmen copy in their audacity the exploits of Francisco Pizarro or those of the Argonauts. They show courage, perseverance, endurance, slyness, and the violation of all moral law, of every principle of honor and of justice. Elsewhere, nothing has changed, except that a certain grandness of soul and a certain intelligence regarding the means used are lacking which shows human genius badly employed, the Alexander perverted and occupied in killing a few transients instead of razing nations. The panorama has changed as has the meaning of war and conquest.

In the United States iron characters, distributed to only one percent of the people in the rest of the world, abandon themselves to their heroic instincts and establish themselves and multiply. The Yankee spirit feels imprisoned in the cities. It needs to see from the door of its house the vast and shady colonnade formed by ancient oaks in the forests.

Why has the colonizing spirit died among ourselves, the descendants of the greatest colonizers? From Columbus down to a short time ago, without doubt the founding of a Spanish city was merely a stepping-stone to the invasion of more distant points. When Mendoza was defending himself against the Araucan Indians in the south he sent a detachment of sixty lancers to the east under the command of Captain Jofre, who crossed the Andes and founded two cities in the lonely wilderness on the banks of rivers they discovered: San Juan and Mendoza.

I will tell you how Americans get these herculean enterprises going, and you will see whether our South American conquistadors deserve our scorn for the means they used and for their reasons for embarking upon their great feats. Do you know how much conflict and foolishness both parties were involved in over the question of the Oregon border? Everything would have remained peaceful after the Americans and English had agreed on the matter, but the Yankee spirit, like the condor when there is blood, smelled good lands, rivers, forests, and ports in the argument. And now discussion has been resumed in the newspapers on the possibility of controlling the China trade from Oregon. They are talking about the possibility of laying a railroad from the Atlantic to the Pacific, an eight-day trip, taking bread which is still hot from the oven in Cincinnati and sending it to Oregon, and of a thousand other topics which are unlikely and absurd for anyone but a Yankee, accustomed as he is to think nothing impossible that can be imagined and, of course, having a mind which is trained to conceive of projects. When everything is set and the route to a remote Eldorado laid out, the best time of year for the trip, the exact day, and the point of departure are announced by emigrants who invite all the adventurers in the Union to accompany them on their glorious journey. On the day of the *rendez-vous*, lines of wagons arrive from all points on the horizon loaded with women, children, chickens, pots, plows, axes, chairs, and every kind

169

of household goods. Accompanying them are poor-looking livestock including fly-covered oxen and lame and defective mules and horses, who make up the working force of the expedition. And leading this great band are the tanned, expressive, and serious faces of the Yankees, who are dressed in greatcoats, frock coats, or threadbare dress coats, with rifles which serve them as batons and with the tranquil look of the Puritan and farmer.*

. . . .

When one reads a narrative of adventures like these he without doubt feels proud to belong to the human race. None of the great passions which have influenced history are in play here to fanaticize the spirit: neither the desperation of the remnants of the Grand Army,** nor the love of country of the ten thousand Spartans trapped between the barbarians, nor the thirst for gold, glory, and blood of the Spanish conquistadors. Men of

---

* At this point Sarmiento quotes at length from Joel Palmer, *Journal of Travels Over the Rocky Mountains to the Mouth of the Columbia River Made During the Years 1845 and 1846* (Cincinnati, Ohio, 1847). Sarmiento writes: "If I am to give you an exact idea of these emigrations and of the Yankee spirit, I shall need from this moment to dedicate myself to describing the daily incidents of one of the hundreds of astonishing marches through the desert made by these Sons of Noah without soldiers, without protection, without help from the state, and without authorization by the Union from which they part without a backward glance." The long passages from Palmer have been excised because they are of no particular interest to the American reader of Sarmiento and were translated into Spanish by Sarmiento because such materials would not have been readily available to Argentines. Palmer was an explorer who later became important in politics in the Oregon Territory. His book was "for a decade an important guidebook to overland immigrants for information concerning equipment for the journey and such details of the route as the location of suitable camping places, springs, and grassy oases. It remains the most complete record of pioneering along the old Oregon trail" (*Dictionary of American Biography*, ed. Dumas Malone [New York, 1935], VII, 146).
** Sarmiento is undoubtedly referring to Jose de San Martín's Army of the Andes.

that temper were given public lands by their nations to enrich themselves, they had families to help them, and they had animals to do the rough work. Americans cross six hundred leagues of wilderness for an ideal. They, who are the castoffs of the North American people, want to see the Union's stars exhibited in the Pacific firmament, want to see these markets snatched from England. They sacrifice themselves for the future of the nation. The Yankee knows that the first generation in the new lands fertilizes the earth with its sweat for the benefit of future generations. And when some hundreds of families had arrived in Oregon and formed a community, the leaders, leaving aside the axes with which they had been slowly clearing away the forests in order to be able to work the land and lay out their property, met in a deliberative assembly "with the object of establishing the principles of civil and religious liberty as the basis of all laws and constitutions which may in the future be adopted."[1]*

As you see, these people carry about with them organically, like a political conscience, certain constitutive principles of association. Political science becomes moral sentiment, perfecting the man, the people, even the mob. The municipality is converted into a phenomenon dependent upon spontaneous association. There is liberty of conscience and of thought. There is trial by jury. If you want to understand fully the road this people has followed, get together a group of Englishmen, Frenchmen, Chileans, or Argentines, not common people but all from the cultivated classes, and ask them without warn-

[1] Organic Law of Oregon, authorized July 5, 1845.
* At this point Sarmiento quotes at length from *The Organic and Other General Laws of Oregon, 1843-1872* (published by the State of Oregon, 1874), pp. 46-51. The same passages are reproduced in Palmer, *Journal of Travels*, pp. 179-189.

171

ing to constitute themselves as an association. They will not know what you are talking about and will not be able, like the Oregon adventurers, to establish with any kind of precision the foundations upon which the government of a new society must rest, a society which, because of the distance and the wilds separating it from the Union, is, in point of fact, unconnected to the motherland.[2] Some years later, from these diverse elements a territory will be formed; and from the territory a state to add a new star to the constellation of the North American states, with the same laws, practices, civil and political institutions, and, above all, with the same national character and stamped with the seal of energy of the colossus.

There is something going on in the United States which, even though it is related to fundamental principles inherent in the human species, has not until now been precisely defined. Languages have even lacked adequate words to describe it. If I tried to get it down on two pages I would provide you with the table of contents or the outline of a great book. What is morality? The code of precepts which one man's contact with another has given us after six thousand years so that men may live in peace without doing each other harm, can love one another, and can try to do good. The morality which through our fathers unites us to God is, even after Confucius, Socrates, and Franklin, still to be divined or stumbled upon. Where it is imperfect with regard to human intercourse—that is, with regard to those apart from us, the neighbor, the foreigner, and the enemy, classifications which distinguish three degrees of sepa-

[2] The President of the United States in the Message of 1848 asked that the inhabitants of Oregon be invited to enter into relations with the Union and that their common authority be recognized as a territory.

ration—revelation complements it. Legally we are not bound to our neighbors; the foreigner is the material from which slaves have always been made; and with the enemy all human concern ceases and death is dramatically meted out to him as quickly as possible, without remorse. When a man is called "enemy" he stops being part of our species. Neither law nor religion has been able to this day to do anything to counteract the effects of this classification.

But morality refers to the actions of individuals only. What is that other part of the life of man called, in which he is a member of a herd, of a hive, of a flock— that is, what of man in his capacity as a gregarious animal? Ask the Czar of Russia, a Lord in Parliament, Rousseau, Rosas, Franklin, and each one will describe a beautiful political system, with precepts, rules, rights, and responsibilities which serve as a code for individuals in their relations with the masses, with society. Some will make out that the *one* who governs will do what he wishes for the common good, others will maintain that the lords should have the right to exercise sovereign will, and there will not fail to be those who insist that every individual has the right to meddle in the activities of all, even though this right will depend on the quantity of possessions he has accumulated or the state of his reason. Human politics, thus, has not made as much progress as morality, and this science may be the most backward of all branches of thought, even though it deals with the oldest, most durable, and most important phenomenon: the society in which we live. The human species in general is lacking a sense, if you will. To the *conscience* which regulates the moral actions of individuals it is necessary to add that sense which, equally important, controls the rights and obligations involved in associa-

173

tion, the larger morality which applies to millions of men and exists among families, cities, states, nations, and humanity in its entirety. The city of Athens must have acquired this sense, as did the Roman patricians later. But the former has inflicted a wound on morality which has not healed down to today, that is, through their classification of "the enemy"; and the latter were destroyed and scattered by the *plebe*, who had, while in their shadow, acquired the same values as the patricians, and by the *foreigners*, who, from being conquered enemies, had risen to form part of the Roman Senate.

Forgive me for this pedantic tirade, but without it I cannot explain my idea: the people of the United States have acquired this sense, this political conscience, or whatever it should be called. As you would imagine, Bancroft deals with how they acquired it in his *History of the United States*. It is something that has been getting itself ready for four centuries. It is the idea inherent in rejected doctrines held by defeated groups in Europe which now, with the Pilgrims, the Puritans, the Quakers, *habeas corpus*, the legislature, the JURY, unoccupied lands, distance, isolation, untamed nature, independence, etc., is being developed, perfected, and established. In England, there are political and religious liberties for the lords and the merchants; in France, for those who write or govern. The people, the great mass —poor, disinherited—are still not aware of their membership in society. They will be governed monarchically, oligarchically, theocratically, or however the landowners, lawyers, military men, and literary men wish—because they will not do anything about it.

The Yankee will be a republican till the last day because of the perfection his political sense has attained; it is as clear and fixed as his sense of what is moral. It is by dogma, without which revelation would be useless, that morals are acquired, whereas there has never been any revelation to guide men's relations in society. If one part of the Union defends and maintains slavery it is because in that part the imprisoned, hunted, weak, and ignorant foreigner of color is in the category of *enemy*, and therefore morality cannot help him. But in all of the other states, among all classes or, rather, among the only class which makes up society, the *political* sense, which should be inherent in man, just like reason and conscience, is very mature. From this rises the phenomenon that wherever ten Yankees come together, even if poor, ragged, and unintelligent, before applying an axe to the base of a tree in order to construct a dwelling, they meet to arrange the bases of their association. One day pacts will no longer need to be written down, because everything will simply be understood. And these pacts are, as with the Organic Law of Oregon, a series of dogmas, a decalogue. Each man will believe what he wants to, will choose his own leaders, will say and write what he thinks, will be judged by a jury, and will have the right to bail for other than capital crimes.

Of course, we can only philosophize about this, whereas there is a better-defined area more susceptible to study. A man cannot arrive at the fullness of his moral and intellectual development but through education, and society fulfills the father through the education of his son. The provision of free schools is simultaneous with and at times even anticipates the founding of a town. Society needs a voice of its own, just as each individual needs one to express his ideas, opinions, and desires. There are *meetings* and a chamber of representatives converts all desires into law. A daily press occupies itself with expressing the interests, passions, and ideas

175

of the various groups. Since society, though born in the depths of the forest, is the daughter and heir of all progress, it will of course aspire to have as soon as possible daily mail, roads, ports, railroads, telegraphs, etc., and bit by bit it will have the plow, wearing apparel, perfected kitchen utensils, all patented, the last word in human ingenuity for one and for all.

These details, which may seem trivial, nevertheless constitute a unique phenomenon in the history of the world. I have just come from going about Europe, from admiring her monuments, prostrating myself in front of her science, and I am still astonished by the wonders of her arts. But I have seen her millions of peasants, proletarians, and mean workmen, and I have seen how degraded and unworthy of being counted as men they are. The crust of filth which covers their bodies and the rags and tatters in which they are dressed do not sufficiently reveal the darkness of their spirits; and with regard to politics and social organization that darkness is enough to obscure the minds of the wise men, of the bankers, and of the nobles. Imagine twenty million men who know quite a bit, who daily read what is necessary to exercise their reason and public and political passions, who have food to eat and clothing to wear, who in poverty maintain reasonable hopes which can be realized in a happy future, who lodge on their trips in comfortable and spacious hotels, who travel seated on soft cushions, who carry a wallet and geographic map in their pockets, who fly through the air on wings of steam, who are daily aware of everything that is going on in the world, who debate without end public issues which excite them passionately, who sit down as legislators and architects of national prosperity. Imagine this accumulation of activity, of joys, of forces, of progress working

176

at the same time almost without exception on twenty million people and you will feel what I have felt on seeing this society upon whose buildings and village squares the sun seems to shine brighter and whose members demonstrate in their projects, enterprises, and works a virility which leaves the rest of the human species far behind. The Americans today are the only ones who can be compared with the ancient Romans, with the difference that the former conquer nature through their own labor, while the latter became powerful by taking in warfare that which had been created by others. But there is the same virile superiority, the same persistence, the same strategy, the same preoccupation with a future of power and of grandeur.

The American boat is the best, the cheapest, and the largest in the world. If on a stormy day you should spot a ship running swiftly before the tempest, its sails, topgallants, upper studs, and lower studs bellied out by the wind, the French, Spanish, or English captain of your ship, who has reefed in even his mainsail, will tell you its nationality. He will inform you, gnashing his teeth angrily, that it is a Yankee boat. He knows it by its size, its audacity, and more than anything by the way it almost grazes his ship without raising its flag to salute him.

In European ports and docks your eyes will be greeted by a special section where colossal frigates which seem to belong to another world and another kind of men are moored. These are the Yankee clipper ships. Originally they were ordinary boats enlarged to carry a greater number of bales of cotton, but they have become a separate class of naval construction. Fifteen Hudson River steamboats, placed stem to stern, would make a wooden street a mile long. If on a stormy day in Le Havre or Liverpool you see a ship heading out to sea, it is a Yankee ship whose departure was scheduled for that day. The honor and glory of the stars in its flag prohibit it from postponing departure until the wind abates as do ships of other nations. Which ships are those which pursue the whale in the polar seas? Almost always they are American. Within that lonely hull, that SQUATTER of the waters, you find a small crew, all of whose members abstain from liquor because they belong to the Temperance Society. These men are toughened by hardship, and they rob danger and death of a small fortune with which to establish themselves in the States when they return, to buy some land to work and to put up a house in which, around a cast-iron stove, they will relate their sea adventures to their children. Last year, Queen Victoria was passing through Falmouth Bay on her sumptuous yacht, accompanied by Prince Albert. All the ships were turned out in their best to honor the royal visitors. Atop the mainmast of an American frigate a Yankee sailor could be seen standing on one foot, swaying with the ship as it rolled at anchor, and holding aloft his hat in greeting, a symbolic representation of the American Navy. The Queen got sick looking at him. There was an English sailor whose national pride made him want to imitate the American, but the Queen forbade him by her terrified expression. Would he have done it? He did not, and that is enough. It would have been an imitation of someone else's audacity, and anyone can do that. But only the genius of a people gives rise to an idea and provides the courage to execute it.

I linger over this matter of the American Navy because the ship is for the Yankee his means of international communication, the extension of his nation which puts him in contact with all others on earth. And in this time of universal movement, the nation which has the fastest and most economically built ships—and consequently the ones with the lowest freight rates—is king of the universe. In the Mediterranean, in the Indian Ocean, in the Pacific they are replacing, suppressing, and outdistancing, day after day, every other navy and all other commerce. Oh kings of the earth, you who have insulted the human species for so many centuries, who have trod upon reason and the political ideas of revolutionary peoples, know you that within twenty years the name of the American Republic will be for you what that of the Romans was for the barbarian kings. The theories and utopias of your philosophers, discredited by tradition, by law, and by truth, even though they are backed by half a million bayonets in order to justify the ridiculous, will also have to face this bright and triumphant truth.

When there are hundreds of states in the Union and hundreds of millions of well-educated, well-dressed, and well-fed inhabitants, with what will you oppose the sovereign will of this great Republic in the affairs of the world? Your guardians of beggary? But you are forgetting that the American ships will blockade you on all seas and in all ports. God has at last permitted the concentration in one organism, in one nation, of enough virgin land to permit society to expand infinitely without fear of poverty, with iron to complement human strength, coal to make the machines go, forests to provide materials for shipbuilding, public education to develop the productive forces of all individuals in the nation, religious liberty to attract whole groups of people to join the society, political liberty which looks with horror at despotism and special privilege. In short, He has created the Republic, strong and ascendant like a new star in the heavens. And all of these factors are interdependent: liberty and abundant land; iron and industrial genius; democracy and superior ships. Try to separate them one from the other in your mind. Say that liberty and public education have nothing to do with this unprecedented prosperity which is surely leading to undisputed supremacy. The fact is that in the European monarchies decrepitude, revolutions, poverty, ignorance, barbarism, and the degradation of the greatest number are always found together. Spit at heaven by thinking about the advantages of monarchy if you want to! The soil will become sterile under your feet, and the Republic will send its grains to feed you. The ignorance of the masses is the foundation of your thrones, and it is only amidst ruins that the crowns which ornament your heads shine like flowers. Half a million soldiers keep the jealousy and envy of one sovereign for another in balance, while the Republic, placed by Providence in a favorable land, like some great beehive, saves these immense sums of money, which are then applied to creating the prosperity which is indicated by an increase in power and strength. Your science and your studies only serve to enhance the Republic's splendor. *Sic vos non vobis*: you may invent electric telegraphs, but the Union will be the one to speed up communications. *Sic vos non vobis*: you may manufacture rails, but they will carry American products and commerce. Franklin had the audacity to present himself at the gaudiest court in the world dressed in hobnailed laborer's shoes and coarse clothes, and someday you will have to hide your scepters, crowns, and golden trinkets to present yourselves before the Republic, for fear that, as with comedians or jesters, it may show you the door.

Oh, my dear friend, how it excites me to think that

the moment is coming when the sufferings of centuries and of millions of men, as well as the violations of sacred principles by superstitions elevated to the level of theory and science, will confront a reality which will destroy them. The hegemony of the Republic, when it is strong and rich by hundreds of millions, is not far off. The progress of the American population indicates that this is so. It increases by hundreds while the other nations increase by one. The figures and the proportions are soon going to come into balance. And these figures, do they not express what a people accustomed to liberty, hard work, and cooperation carry about with them in the way of productive forces and physical and moral energy?

Avarice and Bad Faith

I imagine you must be quite tired of following me on these excursions, so, after discussing something more of the life of the nation, I will leave ideas and make for the most out-of-the-way places in the Union. From now on I will use for your convenience headings at natural dividing points to announce the subjects I will treat. Undoubtedly you will have comprehended that the one above proclaims that I am going to speak about the moral character of this nation. Those two words sum up, in effect, the reproach which they make, or, I should say, the stain which soils the moral character of the Yankee. One's enthusiasm for democratic institutions grows cold upon seeing the breaches in individual honesty which exist among the Yankees, and there is not a half-civilized people which may not feel itself superior to them at least in this respect. This is just the reverse of the situation in the great ancient and modern nations such as

181

Rome and England, where the state was a notorious bandit while the individuals who made it up practiced the most austere virtues.

As a government, the United States is irreproachable in its public acts, while the individuals which make up the country suffer from repugnant vices to which other nations are believed to be less subject. Does this come from some peculiarity of the Anglo-Saxon race? Is it the product of the amalgamation of so many different peoples? Will this be the disagreeable fruit of the mating of liberty and democracy?

Do not be astonished if I say that it is to this last reason, more than to any other, that I attribute the lack of morality which afflicts this people. Avarice is the legitimate daughter of equality, while fraud comes (strange as it may seem) from liberty itself. It is the human species of our times which is shown here, unmasked, just as it is, and it will be this way for several centuries more, or while the profound revolution in which the Yankees are taking the lead continues changing human destiny.

The world is changing, and so is morality. Do not be shocked! As with the application of steam to locomotion, of electricity to the transmission of the word, the United States has preceded all the world in adding a principle to human morality in relation to democracy. Franklin! All the ancient and modern moralists have followed in the path of a morality which took for granted, as fatal and necessary, the existence of a great mass of sufferers, of poverty, and of degradation, providing as compensation the charity of the rich and the resignation of the poor. From the inflexible caste systems of the Indians and Egyptians down to the slavery and common proletariat of Europe, all the moral systems have failed right

182

here. Franklin was the first to say: welfare and virtue; be virtuous in order to be fruitful and be fruitful in order to be virtuous. How close Moses came to these principles in his moral doctrines when he said: "Honor your parents that you may live long in the promised land." All modern laws are based on this new moral principle: Open the doors of society wide, for everyone, to well-being and riches.

That is how all the world is going, and God only knows the pains it will cost to get accustomed to the pleasures of life, to awaken the intelligence of those millions of human beings who for so many thousands of years have served to warm with their entrails the feet of nobles returning from the hunt. "What is capital?" ask today's economists. Capital represents the work of past generations bequeathed to present ones. Those people have capital who, like aristocrats, have inherited the fruit of the labor of past centuries or who have acquired it in this and the last century through discoveries in industrial sciences or in commercial speculations. Those who have capital are very few in relation to the great mass of poor. You have here, in my opinion, the origin of the unbridled American passion. Twenty million human beings are, all at once, creating capital for themselves and for their sons in a nation which was born yesterday on virgin soil, human beings to whom the past centuries have left no inheritance other than primitive forests, unexplored rivers, and uncultivated lands. Awaken in France or in England, for example, those twenty million poor people who, working twenty hours a day, would revolt to secure a salary barely large enough to keep them from dying of hunger, without aspiring to a better future, without even daring to dream about such things, as if these were pretensions improper to their station! Put the Chilean *rotos** into the world of high finance with the fixed idea of quickly making a fortune of fifty million pesos, and you will then see revealed the infernal passions which are sleeping in the spirit of the people. The Chilean *roto* will ask ten reales for the object he will sell us for one real if we offer it and still be satisfied. A Chilean thinks the people of his country are honorable because he is one of them and because of his scorn for the miserable *rotos*, but, nonetheless, the *rotos* form the great majority of the population. This explains the phenomenon which attracts one's attention to the United States. All the energy of the nation is devoted to the great enterprise of the present generations, to accumulating capital and to possessing the greatest amount of property in order to establish oneself in life. The French Revolution took another road, although it headed for the same goal: the unfolding of the moral energy of the nation. The marshal's baton was placed in the mouths of the cannons of the enemy and anyone could achieve military glory who was willing to go after it. You know the feats accomplished by that nation.

The American fights with nature and endures hardships in order to arrive at the supreme good which his social position makes him covet: comfort. And if morality gets in the way when he is about to reach his goal, is there anything strange in putting it aside in order to pass by or in giving it a push if it persists in interfering? The American is the people, the mass, a humanity which is not very moral yet and whose various gradations of development are concealed beneath a common appearance. "Who is this man?" you will ask in every part of

* *Rotos* means "broken ones," signifying the lowest class.

the world, and his external physiognomy will respond: he is a *roto*, a peasant, a beggar, a clergyman, a merchant. In the United States all men are to the eye one man, the American. Thus liberty and equality produce moral defects which are not so apparent in other places where the greater part of the people has no chance to exhibit them. What a tumult there would be if those people were suddenly bitten by the same tarantula!

The manner in which the United States is organized contributes to making these defects even more obvious. Such is the sense of life which is felt in the United States, the confidence in the future, the faith in the results which will come from work, and so large the sphere of activity, that credit depends more on the simple existence of the individual than on guarantees of collateral. A man who works will infallibly get ahead. Statistics on how wealth is accumulated demonstrate it. Besides, every man who works has credit. For example, a man going up the Mississippi in a steamboat proposes to buy four thousand casks of flour. The seller states his price and, after he finds out who the buyer's banker is, they come to an agreement. The seller writes to New York to this banker requesting a report on the solvency of the individual. The answer comes back: "He has $4,000,* his credit is good." Four months from the date the transaction was begun it is concluded in London, where the flour has been sold and where the money has been given to the seller's banker. When the time arrives for the termination of the contract, the seller knows what price flour is bringing in London and he also already knows that he can always rely on the solvency of his debtor.

* Sarmiento pays "4,000 pesos." Throughout *Travels* he uses dollars and pesos interchangeably, and in fact, the peso in 1847 was worth almost exactly a dollar. Wherever he uses "pesos" in describing costs in the United States, "dollars" has been substituted.

How many mistakes does a Yankee make before earning his fortune? Here we have bankruptcies; there they have only frustrated businesses, which hinder activity without paralyzing it.

When a state is an investor, it can get away with anything. A state negotiates in England for funds to open railroads. It gets them, and it goes through with the project. But since this is a new Western state with little population and little wealth, little money is realized in tolls for many years. The debtor state sincerely promises to pay, postponing from day to day, but, through necessity, it is lying. It gets angry with those who have lent it money, and, finally, one bad-humored day it presents itself at the door of its persistent creditor and announces in his very whiskers, in front of the whole world, that it repudiates the debt, that is, that it will not pay. Demand payment? Before whom? Here you have the first rascal in the world who recognizes no judge on earth: the sovereign people. The President, the Congress, and the Supreme Court can do nothing against this class of rogue. Neither the government of the state itself nor the ashamed cultured class can do anything, because their power comes from the vote of the ignorant and indolent populace, and these will not accept having to contribute again toward repaying the contracted debt. In this way the affairs of Mississippi, Illinois, Indiana, Michigan, Arkansas, and several other states have been conducted. What a noise the London bankers make in the face of this terrible thievery! And what is the remedy?

At this point the coin flips over. The newspapers of Europe cause universal execration to rain down like fire on Sodom and Gomorrah, and the fraudulent states laugh with insolence at such bravado. But in the states

186

which have not participated in the crime a reaction begins in the name of national dignity and the stained honor of the Union, and the delinquent states begin to take the matter seriously. A circle is drawn around them from which public opinion thunders criticism. The best people in these states which have *repudiated* their debts feel the disgrace of what is happening, but what can they do against the majority, which refuses to budge? A newspaper timidly takes up the question, publishing, as if by accident, a critical article. But of course it points out that, given the circumstances in which the state finds itself and the insolence of the English, the state has behaved correctly and has given the English a severe lesson so that in the future they will have more respect for the dignity of a sovereign (crooked) state. Soon, happily, circumstances begin to change: prosperity arrives. Would it not be convenient TO REPEAL the *repudiation*? Or, at least, to reconsider the matter, to arbitrate, etc.?

Now the sovereign people listens without getting angry. The following day notions of honor and sentiments of generosity creep into the discussion until at last public opinion begins to form, the reprobation shouted outside the state finds echoes within it, an ashamed look begins to appear on faces, energetic voices are raised among the minority in the legislature, and then everyone jumps on the bandwagon. The criminal state retraces its footsteps and enters into negotiations with the defrauded bankers, and at last the debt of capital is recognized as legitimate and the state offers to pay 60 percent of the interest. Another state, which has not been able to finish a canal in which capital was invested, asks that it be given the necessary funds to bring the project to a conclusion and promises to pay back everything. Still a third state remains inert in spite of the universal clamor which has been raised, because it is very poor, very isolated, and (do not be astonished) most crude.

This last needs some explanation.

Moral Geography

Previously I have said something of the physical geography of the United States, which, if it is not the basis of that country's prosperity, is its principal servant, in the same way that a man's fingers are the faithful executors of his thoughts. There is also a moral geography in that country, whose key features I should point out. Already knowledgeable about the land, you will now come to know something of the civilizing currents which carry to the far corners of the Union improvement, light, and moral progress.

You are familiar with the history and geography of the first thirteen states in the American Union. During two centuries the great political and religious ideas which England successively brought forth from its bosom were deposited there. Bancroft has made an inventory of those ideas, placing each of them in the locale where it was first introduced by, for example, the Pilgrims in New England, the Quakers in Pennsylvania, and the Catholics in Maryland. This colonization was less a matter of men who moved from one country to another than of political and religious ideas which required air and space in which to breathe and expand. Their fruit has been the American Republic, which came along very much before the French Revolution. The Declaration of the Rights of Man made by the Congress of the United States in 1776 is the first page in the history of the modern world, and all political revolutions which follow it on this earth will be a commentary on those simple, common-sense statements.

The Declaration of Independence was like the command to "Be fruitful and multiply" that God gave to the Hebrews. From that moment ideas and men began moving into the interior of the country. The Republic began giving birth to *territories* that were later converted into *states,* like a polyp putting out new tentacles from its body. Study the history of the South American republics from their independence on, and you will see what a difference there is. Chile subdivides its old provinces, but without increasing either the amount of populated territory or the number of cities. The old United Provinces of the River Plate are seen to dismember their territory and form with the fragments rickety and absurd states, while the provinces which still carry the Argentine name are depopulating themselves day after day, their old infant cities being extinguished like lights being turned off. In 1790, Maine, for example, had 96,000 inhabitants; in 1800, 151,000; in 1810, 228,705; in 1830, 400,000; and in 1840, 501,793. In 1790 New York had 340,120 inhabitants; in 1800, 586,766; in 1810, 959,949; in 1820, 1,372,812; in 1830, 1,918,608; and in 1840, 2,428,921.

But in addition to concentration, there is also expansion. Mississippi appeared on the scene in 1800 with 8,850 inhabitants, and by 1840 it already counted 375,651 souls. Arkansas was not heard from until 1820, when it presented a population of 14,273, but by 1840 it had nearly 100,000. Indiana had 4,762 in 1810, but thirty years later it had 685,866. Finally, Ohio, which in 1800 had a registered population of 40,365, had by 1840 grown by a million and a half. You would be as-

189

tonished by this flood of men which the first settlers in a wilderness watch arriving and establishing themselves around them. The man who pointed this out to me was not old, and yet he had seen the birth, development, and growth of one of the great states. Where do these men come from, since today there are no Deucalions throwing rocks over their shoulders to produce them? European immigration is only the second most important source of these waves of people, even though its sum may be considerable. It is the older or adult states which beget these men who keep appearing. The INDIAN HATER goes first, scattering the members of that extraordinary, instinctive race; persecuting the savage is his only creed, exterminating the indigenous peoples is his only desire. No one has commanded it. He goes to the forest with only his rifle and his dogs to hunt the savages, putting them to flight and making them abandon the hunting grounds of their fathers. Afterwards come the SQUATTERS, who are misanthropes looking for solitude in which to dwell, danger for excitement, and the work of felling trees for relaxation. The PIONEERS follow at a distance, opening the forests, sowing the earth, and spreading themselves over a great area. Immediately the capitalist impresarios are there, with immigrants as their laborers, founding cities and towns as the terrain counsels. At once the proprietary class, machinery, and industry arrive from the old states, and youth immigrates to make its fortune.

In this expansion of the American population civilization has well-marked levels, almost disappearing at the extremes of the Union—in the West because of the distance between inhabitants and the primitiveness of rural life, and in the South because of the presence of slaves and of Spanish and French traditions. Half a century would be enough for the incurable barbarism of the Argentine plains to establish itself in the far points of the Union were it not for the ebb and flow of vital elements of regeneration which dominate the country, keeping everything moving and insuring that the most distant and most isolated places are kept from stagnating and degenerating.

In the United States, European immigration is a barbaric element. Who would have believed it! Except for natural exceptions, the European—Irishman or German, Frenchman or Spaniard—comes from the neediest classes, is usually ignorant, and is not accustomed to the republican practices of the land. How can it be assured that the immigrant will at once understand that complicated mechanism of municipal, state, and national institutions, and, more important, that he will become like the Yankee in his love for every one of these, linking his existence and his very being to them in such a way that he would fear for his life or conscience if he neglected these institutions and what they represent? How can he become accustomed to the MEETING, in which at every moment he is urged to express HIS SENTIMENTS? And once these are expressed, once he has voted a series of AND TO BE FURTHER RESOLVED's, how can he experience that relief of a great weight having been lifted which the American feels when he has terminated an argument or demolished the opposition's point of view? And so it is that foreigners in the United States are the burden of scandal and the leaven of corruption annually introduced into the bloodstream of that nation which for so long has been educated in the practices of liberty. The Whigs, who are the more nationalistic party, have tried many times to put restrictions on immigration and also to prolong by many years the study an immigrant must engage in before obtaining his political rights. The Nativist Party, which today is extinct, tried to create a kind of fanatical nationalism very much like—although with different aims—our own *Americanismo*. But this dissipated in the new states when the first dark clouds of prejudice began to appear. The older states can disregard the foreigners because they are already densely populated and offer little incentive to the newcomer. But this, through necessity, is not the case in the Western states, where citizenship is practically bought at public auction and where the years necessary for establishing residence have been energetically lowered and requisites excused.

Society in the United States is very well organized to counter this relaxation of rules in order to disseminate population over the country, and splendid results would long ago have been produced if it were not an interminable task while *i barbari* keep coming from Europe by the hundreds of thousands and while there are lands by the thousands of millions of acres to be cleared. The forces of unification, purification, and improvement are so important that, if you will permit me, I will go on describing them.

The daily mail service works remarkably well. The post comes to the front doors of every faroff town and leaves there in some public document a topic of conversation and some news of what is happening in the nation. You know that it is impossible to barbarize wherever the post, like a daily rainfall, dissolves all indifference born of isolation. Do not forget that the postal system in the United States covers 134,000 miles, in some places assisted by the telegraph.

I am omitting the civilizing and catalytic influence of the periodical press.

Trial by jury calls men from the fields at any time to come together and decide criminal cases, and this judge, the common man, listens to the prosecution and the defense, weighs the arguments, considers the laws, gains experience in this role, and judges with total security of conscience. The tradition of the jury has created the horrible civil crime known as Lynch Law, which is unpunishable. Just as Jesus said, "Wheresoever three shall be gathered in my name, I will be with you," LYNCH'S LAW says to the Yankee of the forests, "Wherever seven men meet in the name of the people, justice will be in your hands." Be careful in the FAR WEST or in the slave states of angering men when there are seven of them together, or you may be strung up by those judges, who are more terrible and arbitrary than the invisible judges of the secret courts of ancient Germany. The law permits it, and those grim consciences will remain free of any remorse, feeling no more and no less than the member of the Spanish Inquisition who, having used all his tricks to get his victim to the blaze, watches him burn. Religion and democracy fall into crimes when their principles and objects are exaggerated.

The election of the President exerts no small civilizing influence. The American engages in fifty elections a year. Defeated in the election for the Council on Public Education, he throws himself into the campaign for sexton of his church. If he loses there, he waits with doubled passion the election for ATTORNEY, the election for mayor, the election for state representative, or that for governor. For a whole year he is filled with bad feelings about one and love for another candidate for the presidency, and he gets just as worked up over the congressional elections. At the time of a presidential election the Union is shaken to its very foundations. The

193

SQUATTERS come out of their forests like shades evoked by a conjurer. The fate of every last tortoise of them is involved in the outcome. There is the danger of not surviving the triumph of the Whig candidate, who is regarded as the reactionary one. If the election returns banish his hopes, the American clenches his fists and re- treats to his dwelling, swearing to make up his losses in the election for pastor of his faith.

The election of the President is the only bond which unites all the far corners of the Union, the sole national concern that moves all of the people and all of the states at the same time. The electoral contest is, therefore, an awakener, a school, and a stimulant which revives a life otherwise made drowsy by isolation and hard work.

But what really stirs up Americans are their religious sentiments. A lukewarm Catholic from one of our coun- tries would without doubt be astounded to see the grand and elevated scale on which religion is carried on in the midst of extreme liberty. Of course the Bible is all over the Union, from the LOGHOUSE in the forest up to and including the hotels of the big cities, the effects of its daily reading working for good and for ill. I say "for ill" too, because an attachment to the letter of its text produces disastrous consequences in narrow minds. As you know, in New England the laws of Moses gov- erned for a long time—such was and still is the belief in the immaculate perfection of every sentence and every verse in the Bible. On board a boat the marvels of chloroform were being discussed. A doctor asserted that this drug can be used for childbirth without danger. "And would you use it on your wife?" inquired a Puri- tan who was present. "Why not?" "Well, I wouldn't," replied his interlocutor seriously. "That depends on how much confidence a man has in its value." "No, Sir,

Genesis says: 'Woman shall bring forth children in pain,' and would you oppose the word of God?" As you can see, the question of chloroform was considered only from the point of view of conscience, and its benefits measured only with the Bible as yardstick. The Yankee's nasal accent, which is more pronounced in the interior, comes from daily reading of the Bible. But in spite of these minor objections, Bible reading does, nevertheless, produce great results. Moral precepts and evangelical phrases do seem to stick in the reader's mind, and the minister's sermon is then a commentary on subjects with which the listener is already familiar and about which his undeveloped mind begs for clarification. The rain of words falls, therefore, on porous and parched terrain—not as with our common preachers, who throw their words to the wind in the public plazas, not infrequently seasoning them with gross words, so that they fall like threats on the brutal souls of the people. Controversies between the sects insure greater interest and timeliness in Bible reading, and a man's whole life is not long enough to penetrate the great catalogue of mysteries enclosed in his sacred book. Sixty-seven theological schools disseminate religious knowledge throughout the Union, whereas there are barely ten schools devoted to the study of law (although they produce more than twenty thousand lawyers). In the United States the number of original works on theology is three times greater than those on scientific investigation. This national peculiarity will make these people something apart in the modern world.

To keep the sacred fires alive, there are thousands of itinerant ministers always on the move in even the most remote settlements, devoting their entire lives to missionary work. Tough and energetic men who agitate

195

wherever they go, they inspire minds to the contemplation of the eternal verities. Theirs are truly spiritual exercises, like those used by the Catholics, but even more spiritual; for without intimidating the country people with the penalties of hell, the minister or ministers who have come to an open-air religious MEETING or one held in a large improvised shed stir their dull minds by presenting the image of God in inconceivably grandiose terms. And when the stimulant has produced its effect, they send the women into the forest in one direction and the men in another, to meditate alone and commune with themselves on their own insignificance, helplessness, and moral imperfection.

The effects of this moral cure are strange and inexplicable. The women become delirious and twist and writhe on the ground, foaming at the mouth. The men cry and clench their fists. At last, a religious hymn, sung all together, slowly begins to sweeten these holy afflictions. Reason recovers its dominion, consciences are quieted and made tranquil, and a deep melancholy inhabits every face, mixed with symptoms of moral goodness as if feelings of piousness had been strengthened by that spiritual catharsis. Worldly people who have witnessed these scenes in the country attribute the singular effects of the word to the excitement which elevated ideas produce in the minds of persons who, because of the monotony of their isolated lives, pass whole months without experiencing any emotion either of pleasure or pain. These events are dramas involving God and his children whose scenes awaken the audience, causing it to take the most active part in the production. Perhaps the brain has movements and turnings as do the other organs of the human body. In any case, the inhabitant of the FAR-WEST is nothing like the coarse shepherd or peasant of our country, because he is abundantly prepared to hear the holy word by his reading of the Bible and by the theological commentaries of the divines. But the important thing to me in all this is that because of religious exercises, theological disputes, and itinerant pastors, this great mass of humanity lives in constant ferment, and the intelligence of the most far-away settlers is kept alert and active, its pores open to absorb all culture. It is like a cask, which, no matter what kind of liquid it contains, is always ready and able to serve; whereas if it were to be left vacant the staves would warp, the hoops would become loose, and, with the passing of time and changes in the weather, it would become forever useless.

But make room for a civilizing element, the most active in keeping religious, political, and industrial life in the United States full of the old spirit of colonial days while at the same time keeping it open to all progress. I speak of the descendant of the old Pilgrims, the heir to their tradition of resignation through toughening manual labor and the originator of the great social and moral ideas which have made the American nationality: in short, the inhabitant of the New England states, of Maine, New Hampshire, Massachusetts, etc. This is the Brahmin race of the United States. Like the Brahmins coming down from the Himalayas, the inhabitants of these old states have spread out toward the Western reaches of the Union and have educated by their example and methods the people who, without skill and science, are prospering on the newly cleared land. You will remember that the Pilgrims were a hundred and fifty wise men, thinkers, fanatics, enthusiasts, and politicians who emigrated and were tested by all the calamities which can befall mankind. You will recall, no doubt, how they

197

did not permit a servant to embark with them as the boat was departing the shores of Europe, being resolved that they would work the earth with their own hands and not recognize social inequalities in the new homeland they were seeking in America. You will also remember how all of them sat down under an oak on the spot where Boston is today, and, after giving thanks to the God of Israel for their safe arrival, discussed the laws which would be established for the glory of Jehovah and for their personal liberty. And, finally, you will remember how these men, in that moment, decided to establish schools, obligating each father, guardian, or protector of children to give them an elementary education for the spirit and manual tasks for the sustenance of the body. The sons of that chosen portion of the human species are even today the mentors and the leaders of the new generations. More than a million families throughout the Union are believed to be descended from that noble stock. They have stamped upon the Yankee countenance that placid kindliness which is characteristic of the more educated class. They carry to the rest of the Union the manual aptitude which makes an American a walking workshop, the iron energy for struggling with and conquering difficulties, and the moral and intellectual aptitude which makes him equal if not superior to the best the human species has produced to date. These immigrants from the North discipline the new populations, injecting their spirit into the MEETINGS which they call and preside over, into the schools, the books, the elections, and into the operation of all American institutions. The great colonial and railroad enterprises, the banks, and the corporations are founded and developed by them. The barbarism produced by isolation in the forests and the weakening of republican practices by the immigrants is thus checked and lessened by the descendants of the Puritans and Pilgrims. There is, therefore, an ebb and flow between these two contrary forces. More than anywhere in the world, there is rapid expansion and the mixing and juxtaposition of peoples in the Union. Someday it will be homogeneous, though both the original American and the new one, both traditional and progressive elements, will have their place. Is anything like this happening in the rest of the world in such a perceptible and consistent way?

Perhaps you have imagined that these instruments of national maturation and sophistication, the heirs of the ancient beliefs of the Pilgrims, maintain unchanging ideas and constitute a special sect. But in religion the United States is as varied as the customs and the surface of this earth. In no other part of the world can one say with greater accuracy that God is conceived in the image and figure of man. Americans have the elevated ideas about the essence of God which the Hebrews transmitted to us through Christianity. But the religious sects and their practices are adapted to the popular intelligence, descending to a species of what we would call fetishism if idols or manitos were employed as symbols. Theism is elevated to pure philosophy, without losing its profoundly religious character and even without parting from the great moral formulas of Christianity. As in all profoundly religious nations, there are today, at this moment in the United States, saints, prophets, envoys of God, visible descension and ascension of the Holy Spirit, and communion between heaven and earth. There are new religions being born and promising to take over the earth. The Mormons date from yesterday, and their inspired ones and bishops are working miracles. In witness of this, during my stay in the United States an unbeliever discovered that the dim light emanating from the face and limbs of a saint was due to a rubdown he had been given with phosphorus. The venerable holy man, undaunted, said that all miracles had been brought about in this fashion. The faith and fervor of the believers did not suffer in the least from this incident, and today there are more than 150,000 Mormons.

There are dancing religions, and their faithful, after hearing the minister's sermon, throw themselves into dancing until, inspired, they begin to twitch in a frenetic and indescribable fashion. At this point the subject, who is exhausted and half-mad, is thought to be illuminated. As I have seen the Reine Pomaré, Rigolette, and other celebrities at their dances and deviltries in the bal Mabille in Paris, I was not overly impressed by these manifestations of the Holy Spirit. Above these lower religious groups in the United States tower more respectable Christian sects such as the Baptists, Methodists, Presbyterians, Congregationalists, Christians, Episcopalians, Lutherans, Dutch Reformed, Roman Catholics, Friends, Universalists, Unitarians, and other groups, among whom I would include the pure Deists; for the religious spirit in that country is so tolerant that the negation of all religion, what we call irreligion, forms a sect apart against which no voice is raised. As an example of the comparative numerical strength of the various religions, note that the Baptists have (according to the figures for 1840) 1,130 churches and 4,907 clergymen; the Episcopalians, 950, served by 849; the Catholics, 912, with 545 priests; the Unitarians, 200, with 174 ministers; with the rest appearing in the list in descending order.

I have said "tolerant" in the genuine sense in which Americans use this word. The religious sects in the United States form true associations and religious bodies even though they live intermingled in the cities and rural areas. The doctor, the notary, the butcher, the apothecary, and even the boatman have to be of the same faiths as those who use their services. There is a silent war of proselytism going on, but tolerance is demonstrated by the impassiveness with which a Methodist will listen to a Catholic contradicting his dogmas and vice versa. In the United States, Catholics who dogmatically profess religious intolerance are like those tigers without claws and teeth we are accustomed to keep as pets. To this day a Catholic has never been known to bite anyone in the United States, where religious liberty reigns supreme over the breadth of the land, saving souls every year from the deceiving tricks of the devil.

This religious chaos, these one hundred contradictory truths, are in their turn being elaborated upon, slowly to be certain, but surely and increasingly. While the Mormon barbarism progresses, the religious philosophy of the descendants of the Pilgrims trickles down through all levels of society, shortening the distances which separate sects, creating bridges which further unite them, and finally absorbing them in Unitarianism. This is a new pantheistic sect which accepts all dissidences and recognizes all baptisms. Through its means grace has been transmitted and man elevated. It has divested itself of all narrow religious dogmas and will draw together Jews, Mohammedans, and Christians in one single embrace. Miracles and mysteries are ignored as things which do not harmonize with the organic form God has given to the human spirit, and they are classified as mere figures of speech. Christian morality as the expression and rule of human life, as an attainable common ground for all nations, is the only acceptable dogma for Unitarians, while virtue and humanity are the only religion and the only faith they prescribe for believers.

This religious philosophy is rapidly being extended in the six New England states. Its center is Boston, the American Athens, and its propagators are the wisest men in America.

As you see, the spirit of the Puritans has been active for two centuries, and it goes on providing pacific and conciliative solutions to problems, always working for progress without ceasing to struggle against present conditions, changing them gradually rather than doing away with them violently (as the philosophy born of Catholicism in the eighteenth century attempted to do, accomplishing so little). If you remember the religious spirit in Franklin's writings, you will note that these manifestations have antecedents in the philosophy of good sense preached by that great and practical man.

I conclude all of this, my good friend, with something that would freeze the good Yankees in horror to hear: which is that they are marching straight toward unity of belief and that one day not far off the Union will present to the world the spectacle of a universally devout people without apparent form to their religious beliefs. They will, without renouncing Christianity, have a philosopher, just as the Chinese have the grand figure of the moralist Confucius, and they will have a religion without worship. With the help of reason Confucius gave the world the axiom: "Do not do to others what you would not wish others to do to you," adding to it this sublime corollary: "Sacrifice yourself for the people."

If this happens, and it should, how great and productive for the species will be the experiment made among that portion of the human race. It will give man dignity through equality of rights, moral elevation through the disappearance of the religious sects which now divide him, energy for his physical being, and it will make him eminently civilized by allowing him to appropriate for his use and welfare all progress in human intelligence. The principle of religious tolerance is American. It is written in all their constitutions and has already become a common axiom. In the United States for the first time the word was spoken which may stop the torrents of blood which humanity has shed and which have continued to flow from the earliest times down to today. Catholics, Puritans, Quakers, Calvinists—all these variations of one faith came to the North American colonies, to juxtapose themselves without mixing, the hatreds which the struggle in Europe had engendered still living among them. The Pilgrim fathers were the most exclusive people, "because they had crossed the world," says Bancroft, "in order to enjoy the privilege of living by themselves." Religious war and persecution had already come between these poor remnants of a common shipwreck, dividing them when what they needed was mutual aid and protection to resist misfortune. In Europe, the Anglicans had persecuted the dissidents; the Catholics, the heretics; and the Inquisition and Calvin, popes and kings, Mohammedans and Christians, burned with such zeal that one did not know which way to turn to avoid being made into a beefsteak. In February 1631 a young minister arrived in America, filled with the spirit of God and endowed with great talents. His name was Roger Williams. At that time he was just a little over thirty years old, but in his mind an idea had been born which would give him immortality and would bring religious peace to America. He was a Puritan, and he came fleeing persecution in England. But oppression had not dimmed his intelligence. Depth of insight had revealed to him the nature of intolerance, and he, and only he, discovered an effective remedy. He described his idea as simply the sanctity of conscience.* "The civil magistrate should restrain crime, but never control opinion; should punish guilt, but never violate inward freedom. The principle contained within itself an entire reformation of theological jurisprudence: it would blot from the statute-book the felony of non-conformity; would quench the fires that persecution had so long kept burning; would repeal every law compelling attendance on public worship; would abolish tithes and all forced contributions to the maintenance of religion; would give an equal protection to every form of religious faith; and never suffer the force of the government to be employed against the dissenter's meeting-house, the Jewish synagogue, or the Roman cathedral."

Roger Williams' principles placed him in perpetual conflict with the clergy and government of Massachusetts. Williams would have nothing to do with intolerance, because, he said: " 'The doctrine of persecution for cause of conscience is most evidently and lamentably contrary to the doctrine of Jesus Christ.' "

The magistrates insisted on the presence of every man at religious services. Williams rejected this law, regarding it as an open violation of the rights of men by com-

* Sarmiento quotes directly from Bancroft from this point on. I supply the original English text rather than retranslating a translation: George Bancroft, *History of the United States of America* (New York, 1914), I, 242, 249, 251.

pelling them to worship with those of different faiths. "To drag to public worship the irreligious and the unwilling seemed only like requiring hypocrisy. 'An unbelieving soul,' he added, 'is dead in sin'; and to force the indifferent from one worship to another 'was like shifting a dead man into several changes of apparel.' 'No one should be bound to worship or to maintain a worship, against his own consent.' "

" 'What! Is not the laborer worthy of his hire?' " responded the Puritans. " 'Yes, from them that hire him,' " replied this heretical fighter for tolerance. "With corresponding distinctness, he foresaw the influence of his principles on society. 'The removal of the yoke of soul-oppression,' to use the words in which, at a later day, he confirmed his early view, 'as it will prove an act of mercy and righteousness to the enslaved nations, so it is of binding force to engage the whole and every interest and conscience to preserve the common liberty and peace.' "[3]

And this came to pass! From Williams down to today, some more rapidly, others less willingly and with grumbling, have had to put out their firebrands and abandon that worst kind of buffoonery which consists in burning men for the greater honor and glory of God.

I cannot stop once I get started on theology. As you see, I am becoming a Yankee to such an extent that I speak with a nasal twang while reviewing these ideas. But, though it may weigh heavily upon you for me to continue, I still have to list one of the forces of regeneration, of education, and of the struggle against inertia which American intelligence is using to force the indolent to move forward. Its origin and form is religious,

[3] George Bancroft, *History of the United States.*

though its effects are felt throughout society. I speak of the spirit of religious and philanthropic association which has put thousands of wills into motion for the attainment of laudable ends and caused giant fortunes to be pledged to the fulfillment of this work. Here the American has created spiritual necessities as costly and essential as those of the body, and this provision for the necessities of the spirit, this time, work, and money employed in satisfying a desire or a concern, shows how active is the moral life of this people. Who should be a more untiring propagandist than the strict Catholic, for whom there is no salvation outside of the church and who is in possession of a truth through which he sees so many thousands of his fellow men in error? But ask the most intolerant priest how much money he spends out of his own pocket for continuing to reduce the numbers of the unfaithful and for the moral betterment of the masses. Very little, unfortunately, and that little is not due to religious feeling but to the nature and extent of his devotion to the work of information and philanthropy. To whom has it occurred in Spanish America to attempt a crusade against drunkenness? In the United States there are already thousands of zealous propagandists for temperance, and men have signed up by the hundreds of thousands promising not to drink spirits. As a result, the human race may cure itself of this sickness which ruins all economy and destroys all morality.

The American satisfies obligations and fulfills desires of the heart and spirit with his money. If he were to list his annual budget it would be something like this: $100 for food and clothing; $20 for propagating good religious ideas; $10 for works of philanthropy; $50 for political ends; $30 for civilizing the barbarians. With the fruit of his work invested in this way, he has the right to be egotistic, stubborn, and self-seeking.

The American Temperance Society dates from 1826, and by 1835 there were already eight thousand societies with a million and a half members in the country. Charity for drunkards is not restricted to occasional good examples. Four thousand distillers of hard liquor have dismantled their stills, eight thousand merchants have abstained from selling liquors, and a thousand ships sail without whiskey provisions. The legislature of Massachusetts has prohibited the sale of alcoholic liquids in quantities of less than fifteen gallons. The Tract Society, whose purpose is bringing morality to people on the move, such as sailors and others, published in 1835 fifty-three million pages. The American Sunday School Union, formed in 1824, ten years later collected $136,-855 in one year. It produced 600 different publications and was in contact with 16,000 schools, 115,000 teachers, and close to 800,000 pupils.

The American Bible Society has collected from its founding up to today some two and a half million dollars and distributed nearly four million copies of the Bible. I have not mentioned the missions in the Occident*; in these lands one church maintains 308 missionaries, 478 schools, 17 printers, and 4 foundries for making type for printing books in languages unknown even by name in Europe. The results of the American missions in the Sandwich Islands are so well known that I need not pause to review them. My desire to record all these societies is only to bring to light one of the many civilizing forces which are continuously working

* Sarmiento surely means "Orient."

to better the condition of the people morally, religiously, and politically. A banker like Girard, who left a million and half dollars to found a college in which young men might be educated under certain conditions prescribed by him, and other philanthropists who, like Franklin, leave funds so that for two centuries the interest on the money may be used, are not exceptional cases. In all of this enormous and complicated national task you will see one great idea dominating: equality; one sentiment: the religious one, purified of its exterior forms; one means: association, which is the soul and basis of the individual and national identity of that people.

Elections

Two things made me want to inspect the United States personally: its colonization practices and the workings of its electoral system; the means used to populate the wilderness and the method of providing a government for society. With regard to the first, my desire has been satisfied, and I can clearly see and understand the whole mechanism. Though an event may seem so spontaneous and isolated, it encloses, nevertheless, a theory, a science, and an art. There is a system of principles, laws, and rules for colonizing prosperously, whose infraction or neglect has produced crumbling settlements in our countries. Rio de Janeiro, Montevideo, Buenos Aires, Valparaiso are cities created after those built during the Spanish colonial period. The settling of South America was accomplished with huge mistakes, and half the disasters of our Republics have been caused by the Spanish system of colonization. This handicap should have been overcome by the fires of independence. I intend to develop my ideas in a special work on the systems and means of populating and occupying territory. I believe I may fill a vacuum in our knowledge of America with such a study.*

As for elections, I did not have such good luck. General principles you can get from each state's constitution and the Constitution of the United States, but you need to see elections. During my quick trip through the country I was not lucky enough to witness elections except one in Baltimore, for Mayor, an office equivalent to the Lord Mayor of London, I believe. It would have been necessary to be present at many elections, in different places and for different offices, in order to penetrate into the workings of this American institution and into the role of political struggles and the arrangement of the parties. Can there be material for political study more important than that regarding the precise and exact means for assuring that the men most able to fill offices do indeed arrive there? We can be sure of having confided the execution of a picture, a palace, or a ship to the best artist or builder in the world, but can we even be reasonably precise in confiding to the right individual, to a representative, a president, or a mayor, the job of producing the most good for an entire society, perhaps for generations to come, or even for all of humanity? The electoral system is still a chaos which must be reduced to order, a seed which has just barely been fertilized; and only in the United States has it matured enough for there to have been a fair amount of experience with it.

The only election incident I experienced was the determination by the Democratic newspapers to excite the Irish immigrants against the candidate of the Whig Party

* Sarmiento's *Conflicto y Armonías de las Razas en America,* 2 vols. (Buenos Aires, 1883), is just such a work.

and their inviting them to join with the Democrats in the elections. This spectacle certainly was not very edifying. The Irish mob, just arrived from Europe, is in the States what the *rotos* are in Chile, and, according to the judgment of various people, is not of much account when measured on the scale of public values.*

. . . .

* At this point Sarmiento quotes at great length from George Combe, *Notes on the United States of North America during a Phrenological Visit in 1838-9-40*, 2 vols. (Philadelphia, 1841). Sarmiento writes: "Not being able through personal experience to give you a judgment on what I have not seen of elections, I will provide it by extracting from the travels of the phrenologist Combe as much on this subject as he has written. He is a good witness; being English, loving the Republic, and being an impartial and sincere critic, he is a competent judge and an authority. What follows is a translation of this author." It was not thought necessary to reproduce the many pages from Combe here. Though Combe is interesting, he is of no particular concern to American readers of Sarmiento. Sarmiento quotes him at length because he felt that it was important to make some description of American elections available in Spanish to Argentines. In *Obras*, XI, 23, Sarmiento mentions becoming familiar with Combe's work while in England, just before he came to the United States, and on p. 25 he makes a passing reference to Combe's trip through the United States. Also, Horace Mann and Combe were intimate friends (Mann's second son was named George Combe Mann), and Mann may have brought Combe to Sarmiento's attention during the latter's 1847 visit to his home in Massachusetts.

II. Travel Incidents

New York

My travel adventures in the United States should not
intrude into the reflections which the spectacle of that
country has set in motion, so I will only tell you of a
few which may interest you. Taking stock of my funds in
Paris those last days of July, I found that I had scarcely
six hundred dollars left. The trip home by way of the
Isthmus alone costs seven hundred, and I still had not
seen England. This bankruptcy, which would rob me of
some of my dreams, only (as is so often the case) increased my desire for them. Not to see England, or the
Thames, or the factories of Birmingham and Manchester! Not to wade into that ocean of houses that is London or to see those forests of masts that are the docks
of Liverpool! Could I as a schoolteacher on a world trip
of exploration to examine the state of primary education return to America* without having inspected the
schools of Massachusetts, the most advanced in the
world? In my search for data on immigration, which I
had wanted to study in Africa, how could I manage without visiting the United States, the country to which two
hundred thousand emigrants steer each year? As a republican, and having witnessed what form the republic
has taken in France, could I return without having seen
the only great and powerful republic that exists on the
earth today?

Well, where reality fades away, the imagination takes
over. If I could only get to Havana I would somehow

* Sarmiento means South America, of course.

manage to make it over to Venezuela, where through newspaper work, teaching, and other activities I could make enough money and the right connections to enable me to cross the continent to Bogota; from there I would go to Quito; and from there to Guayaquil, managing, by economies, the most eventful and exciting voyage that any American has made in our times. The Phoenicians, who sailed around Africa, stopped periodically, according to Herodotus, to plant and harvest enough wheat to continue their voyage. Why could I not stop in Caracas, for example, to demonstrate my method for teaching reading, to scribble things for the press, to inaugurate courses on pedagogy, harvesting enough money thereby to continue creeping little by little back toward the southern climes whence I had come?

Furthermore, to return to Chile by way of Cape Horn was so prosaic and uninteresting according to the nautical map which I had open in front of me that, screwing up my courage and weighing well the pros and cons, I decided to visit not only England but the United States, Canada, Mexico, and more if fantasy would help me carry out the idea which for a long time had excited my greed: to make a trip around the civilized world. What could come in the way of this plan? I would go with watch in one hand and pocketbook in the other, and wherever the torch went out on me I would continue groping in the dark and with luck find my way back to Chile.

Reassured by these thoughts, I passed in leisurely fashion through London and took my time traveling by train by way of Birmingham and Manchester to Liverpool, where I stopped eight days with a young Argentine emigrant, D. N. de la Riestra, who was well established in a commercial house. I embarked on the *Montezuma*, a large sailing packet which did eleven miles per hour with the slightest breeze and which was carrying 480 Irish immigrants to the States. My poor English led me to spend much time on board with a Jewish family that spoke French. One day as I was leaving the cabin and was having difficulty figuring out how to get the door open, a voice said in Spanish: "Pull. It's open." This was Mr. Ward of the House of Hutt Gruning of Valparaiso, and from that time on, believe me, he was, without the obligation to be so, of immense assistance in instructing me on the new world I was about to visit. A United States Senator who knew Horace Mann, the celebrated Secretary of the Board of Education of Massachusetts, was returning from Europe on this same boat. Mr. Ward being able to answer for my character and the nature of my mission, the Senator gave me a letter of introduction to this eminent teacher, which was manna from heaven. My path was bit by bit becoming clearer, and all of my fears, except those deriving from the thinness of my pocketbook, were by degrees disappearing.

There is little to tell about life at sea. In the afternoons I would go near the deck where the unhappy Irish came up from below like rats from caves. They were half-naked and emaciated, their spirits animated by the hope of seeing an end to their miseries in the promised land. There were old women in their sixties emigrating, and a blind beggar played the zampona in the afternoon so that the filthy, skinny, and disheveled ladies could dance. The little ragamuffins, naked or covered with rags, were not hindered from loitering near the dancers. These people looked like convalescents from a hospital or inmates in a house of correction. Some looked as though they were quite ready to die, and indeed six or eight were flung into the ocean on some days without this in any way affecting the attendance at the afternoon dance.

We finally reached the bay of New York, which because of its coves and depth as well as because of the beauty of the view recalls the harbor at Rio de Janeiro, though the colors are softer and the topography less dramatic. The peaceful scene involuntarily awakens in the spirit the memory of Washington and Franklin. They were prosaic and without glamor, but great in their simplicity. They were also GOOD-NATURED gentlemen with good sense, diligence, and honor. I was prepared for the spectacle, and neither the very beautiful hills covered by forests nor the creeks, canals, and coves which surround the city, filled as they were with barges and crossed by hundreds of steamboats, surprised me. New York is the center of American activity and the disembarkation point for European immigrants; it is, therefore, the least American in appearance and customs of the cities of the Union. Whole neighborhoods consist of narrow and dirty streets lined with houses of mean appearance. Pigs are at home in the streets and dark alleys, where no one disputes their rights of citizenship. Occupying the center of the most beautiful part of the city is Broadway, the wide street which begins at Castle Garden and passes in its course Trinity Church, a Gothic temple of beautiful architecture and a certain magnificence—a rare thing in the United States. It has been built by subscription, like all the great American works. On Broadway there are beautiful private homes, a white marble (FREESTONE) bazaar which has no rival in Europe, and a theater under construction in which Italian opera will be heard. In one hour 480 vehicles passed my boardinghouse window, including omnibuses, carts, and carriages. At night *Ernani* was being given in an improvised theater in Castle Garden, and there six of us South Americans gathered. There was Osma, of Peru; the young Argentine, Alvear; Señor Carvallo and his Secretary of Legation, my friend, Astaburuaga; and a newly arrived fellow who, after a little while, introduced himself into the conversation by asking: "Do any of you know Señor Sarmiento who should have just arrived from Europe?" This was Don Santiago Arcos, who, recognizing me, told me he had come from France in my pursuit, that from now on we would be inseparable until Chile, and that we were friends, very good friends of long standing, accompanying these words with that laugh of good will which has the power of disarming the most fastidious aloofness.

Because of the abundant applause, the *prima donna* sang the *jaleo* as an encore, directing words in Spanish up to our group from the boards, which were answered on our side by tomfooleries common to Madrid. We wanted to show her that she was among friends and in a country where Spanish is known. If I remember correctly, she and young Osma had met in Spain and had seen each other again in London. Even the ancient glories and the present miseries of our country were found represented in New York by General Alvear, with whom, after overcoming certain formalities imposed by conventional etiquette, I passed three days listening to tales of olden times. General Flores of Ecuador had also turned up in New York and seemed extremely fretful and annoyed at how Osma and I enjoyed recalling the trouble we had given him in Madrid.

New York is the capital of the richest of the American states. Its city hall alone would, because of its magnificence, be comparable to the Roman Senate, were it not composed of both a Senate and a House of Representatives that legislate the well-being of half a million citizens. Only Rome takes precedence over New York in the construction of gigantic public works, although from the remains of the famous aqueducts which brought water to the Eternal City we see that the Romans did not have to overcome such great difficulties, nor did they use such advanced techniques. The Croton Aqueduct has cost the City of New York $13,000,000. It produces an annual revenue of $600,000, and the inhabitants of the city get all the water they want, even those on the fourth floor of buildings, just by turning a faucet. The Croton Aqueduct begins in the Croton River, which flows five miles from the Hudson in a neighboring county. The DAM or reservoir which controls the flow of its waters is 250 feet long, 40 feet high, 70 feet wide at the base, and 7 feet wide on top, and it is of masonry construction. The lake formed inside these walls of granite covers 400 acres and contains 500 million gallons of water. From this great reservoir the water flows, the aqueduct piercing the mountains or held up by arcades over the valleys like the Roman aqueducts of Segovia and those of the Sabines, passing on high bridges over the rivers whose path it crosses. By the time the water reaches the Harlem River it has run for 33 miles. The aqueduct is made of stone, brick, and cement, vaulted above and below, 6 feet 3 inches wide below and 7 feet 8 inches wide at the high point of the side walls. It is 8 feet 5 inches high. It descends 13½ inches per mile and delivers 60 million gallons of water every 24 hours. It passes over the Harlem River on a magnificent stone bridge 1,450 feet long with 14 pillars, 8 sustaining arches 80 feet wide, the others supporting 50-foot-wide arches, with the superstructure 114 feet above the river. The canal passes here through iron filtering pipes which two men together could barely get their arms around. The receptacle which receives the waters is on 86th Street, 58 miles from the Croton Reservoir. It covers 35 acres and holds 150 million gallons. The distribution reservoir on Murray Hill, at 40th Street, covers 4 acres, is made of stone and cement, is 45 feet above the level of the street, and holds 20 million gallons. From there the water is distributed to the whole city in iron pipes placed in the earth at sufficient depth to insure that they will not freeze in winter. The pipes, which range from 6 to 36 inches in diameter, extend 170 miles. The water rises to the various floors of the buildings, and there are other pipes to return the dirty water to the earth. The amount that the city charges for the water is enough to pay the interest on the $13,000,000 which was invested and the salaries of the employees, with more than $500,000 annual profit left over. This system is saving the citizens millions of dollars which they were spending before in supplying themselves with water inferior to that they now get from Croton.

What made my examination of the great water works all the more pleasant were the intelligent commentaries and historical anecdotes which Don Manuel Carvallo, Envoy Extraordinary of Chile in Washington, recited while we looked over the beautiful surrounding areas of New York. The attentions of this friend (since then we use this word to describe our relationship) saved me from the feeling of helplessness I had thought would plague me among the people of the United States and from which I had suffered so much in northern Europe. I accompanied him on a visit to St. James College, a Jesuit school where several young Chileans were studying. We inspected the rubber factories where watertight military bridges and complete campaign units were being made, and we also visited everything in the way of monuments, construction, and institutions worthwhile for a traveler to see. With his *simpático* Secretary, Astaburuaga, I went on detailed wanderings which were seasoned by memories of Chile and made interesting by the natural affinity of two friends together again after some years of separation. He took me to visit Greenwood Cemetery, which is separated from New York by water.

The cemetery embraces an immense tract of ground maintained in a natural state. Covered with gentle hills, the land constantly changes in character as you explore it. Ancient trees shade the hollows, and rain water is deposited in little lakes and brooks. A wide carriage road snakes its way through the undulating landscape. At its sides grow native grasses, bushes, and shrubs, and atop small hills tower various characteristic American trees, singly and in clumps. There, in the bosom of nature, in tombs scattered according to the lay of the land, rest the ashes of those who wished to leave some trace on the earth of their ephemeral passage. Sheltered in the shade of an ancient oak is a Gothic-style tomb. A lantern of Diogenes crowns a grave, and at the bottom of a little valley, among lovely trees, there is a Greek temple containing a sarcophagus. Do not these rustic cemeteries, these camping grounds of the dead, inspire sentiments of quiet melancholy which are lightened by the contemplation of nature taking back to herself these organic remains which originally came from her, so that she can in her own way make new combinations and new existences? At least, this was my feeling as I leaned on a gravestone at a high point in the cemetery, looking out at New York crowned by smoke, at Brooklyn, her neighbor, at the beautiful bay with its groups of boats like a forest in winter, and at the straits agitated by waves thrown up by powerful steamboats. The ocean, the natural limit of terrestial things, the frontier of the infinite and the imperfect symbol of the vastness of the universe, framed the picture.

The Mecca of my pilgrimage was Boston, the queen city of primary school education, although when one heads for a place for reasons of study he is allowed to make detours in order to see some country on the way. To reach Boston, then, which lies east of the Hudson, I set my course due west for Buffalo. I would visit Niagara Falls and the Great Lakes too, without worrying about my larder, which had only enough provisions (I am referring to my pocketbook) for a few more days. I embarked at New York at seven o'clock in the morning, bound for Albany (144 miles for $1). Arriving in Albany in the afternoon, I just managed to board the train for Buffalo before it left (352 miles for $12). In all, traveling three days, with periodic stops of a quarter of an hour for dinner or lunch, I covered 469* miles by steamboat and rail.

The Hudson is the center of life in the United States poetically, historically, and commercially. It is the road to Boston, to Montreal, to Quebec, to Buffalo, to the Niagara, and to the Lakes, and it is the principal artery for the produce of Canada, Vermont, Massachusetts, Jersey, and New York State. Its waters are always so literally covered by boats that there are traffic jams, as in the streets of great cities. The steamboats cross each other's paths like shooting stars, and tugboats tow a veritable carnival of barges whose keels sent out a tide before them. Fourteen laden boats precede and follow

* 496 miles is intended.

the tugboat, covering much of the surface of the river. The passenger steamboats on American rivers are like two-story floating houses, with flat roofs and covered porches.

The spectacle of these colossal floating hotels is heightened by the cultured, well-groomed, and even ceremonious appearance of the passengers, for it is the common practice of American men and women to dress their best when embarking on water or rail expeditions. The generally cold reserve of the Yankee and his society, however, give these crowds an unsociable aspect which might be labeled aristocratic in Europe but which Europeans on the scene in America tend to find rather rustic. Actually, it is simply the way Americans are. The ladies occupy the forward parts of the great salons and are the object of every official attention. Adding to the excitement, the pilots and helmsman occupy an elegant little cabin at a conspicuous height in the bow of the boat, where they steer with a wheel which controls the ship's rudder by chains and discern the route ahead as though they were the brains and the heart of that machine. The bell tolls to announce the approach of a stopping place, so that those who intend to get off can get ready.

From the height of the upper deck, from which he dominates both shores, the traveler sees pleasant villas and knolls crowned by buildings and trees parade past him, while alongside him in the water there are hundreds of ships of all kinds and sizes traveling in the opposite direction along that great public street, which is as bright and polished as a mirror. In the same way, the ocean, the bay with its changing panorama of ships, and the picturesque islands, straits, and canals pass in review as one takes leave of New York. Opposite the Port of New York is Jersey City and Weehawken Rock, which rises abruptly from the waters and serves as the foundation for a villa built on top and as a picturesque gateway to the Palisades. These are a perpendicular wall of rock cliffs which rise four or five hundred feet above the surface of the water and border the river for some twenty miles. This accident of nature gives to the landscape on that side an indescribable grandeur, while the other shore boasts villages, cities, orchards, hills, and forests which also maintain the interest and excite the curiosity of the traveler. Occasional ruins crown the heights, and the names of Hamilton and Washington are brought to mind by the few stones remaining of forts captured and destroyed during the War of Independence. A living monument is West Point, the military academy where 230 cadets permanently maintain watch over the sacred fire of the traditions and science of war. The Greek forms of the Orphan Asylum, the Insane Asylum, and other public buildings decorate heights along the Hudson, which competes with the Rhine in beauty and has no rival, except in China, for the volume of its traffic.

At last Albany appears, the political capital of New York State, for it seems that Yankee legislatures flee the turmoil of big cities. The public buildings are more in keeping with the city's function as a capital than is the size of the city or the impressiveness of the private buildings. The railroad runs for 325 miles to the west from Albany, passing through Amsterdam, Fonda, Utica, Rome, Verona, Manlius, Syracuse, Camillus, Seneca, Ithaca, Waterloo, Geneva, Vienna, Victor, Byron, Batavia, Alexander, Attica, and many other cities whose names are connected with cities, countries, and men of other times and places.

Buffalo, the terminus of our journey, is at the eastern tip of Lake Erie, which in turn marks the eastern limit of the navigation of Lakes Huron, Michigan, and Superior. The German immigrants, especially, travel by way of the Lakes through Chicago, which is on the western side of Lake Michigan and in contact with the headwaters of the Mississippi, and through Buffalo, which is a center for traffic heading to the Ohio River by means of the Cleveland Canal and to the Hudson River by means of the Erie Canal. The sight of this city, which is small for the number of inhabitants it contains, had a singular effect on me. A throng of steamboats belched forth such a great mass of smoke that the fires which produced it must still be lit. The unloading of buffalo hides and other products of the trade with the savages counterpointed the activity of passengers moving toward the port. At the same time, if one looked toward town, he discovered hundreds of men earnestly occupied in putting up tall new buildings, enlarging the city to take care of the population, which increases by twenty thousand souls each year. Buffalo has at its disposal, as do all predestined centers of future commerce in the Union, a deposit of coal in the peninsula which is formed by Lakes Michigan and Huron.

From Buffalo go forth all sorts of human enterprises —railroads, newborn villages, new plantations—which compete with the sublime works of nature. To the north the most beautiful spot on earth begins. The Niagara River flows out of Lake Erie just as gentle and crystal-clear as can be, reflecting on its surface the mixture of rhododendrons and oak trees which makes up the bluish background of primitive forest in whose thickets one can still find the mysterious moccasin track of the indomitable Indian. The river opens to form Grand

Island, after which it comes back together again to prepare itself for the lovely play of waters which begins at the rapids and ends at the falls. The far-off rumor of the waters of the extraordinary cascade, the mist which rises to the sky, and the excitement which is caused by the closeness of sensations long anticipated and imagined make the traveler extremely anxious and irritated by the slowness of the train which is taking him there. At last he arrives at Niagara Falls, a village filled with sightseers. From here on the ears are numbed by the dreadful roar of the water, whose white violence can be glimpsed above the treetops. Through chinks between the tree-trunks, in contrast to the opacity of the shaded bower, a stretch of rapids shining like a fragment of polished silver can be seen as one draws near. These rapids, which give the water a marblelike whiteness, are subsurface cascades formed by the enormous mass of the Niagara hurling itself over a bed of unseen rugged rocks. A thousand tragic events have occurred here, beginning with the fate of the Indian hunter who, distracted by his ardor for the hunt, suddenly found his fragile canoe being carried away by the current; after making superhuman efforts to resist its pull, he drained his gourd of all its hard liquor and, standing, with his arms crossed, allowed himself to be carried to the precipice. Niagara does not even deliver up the bodies of its victims, as in the case of the prisoners who took command of a steamboat and, not knowing how to make it go, were seen to descend to the rapids and falls to be buried forever in the bottomless abyss which the falls have excavated. There is also the story of the recent end of a child who fell into the rapids; someone grabbed hold of his hand on Goat Island, which divides the two falls, only to have him slip away again and be lost.

To describe such a stupendous scene correctly would be an impossible task. The colossal dimensions actually lessen the terror, just as the distance of the stars makes them appear small to us. The following lines by a young woman describe them in a praiseworthy manner:

Flow on for ever, in the glorious robe
Of terror and beauty. God hath set
His rainbow on thy forehead; and the cloud
Mantled around thy feet. Awe he doth give
Thy voice of thunder, power to speak to him
Eternally—bidding the lip of man
Keep silence; and upon thine altar pour
Incense of awe-struck praise.

I considered myself a fairly learned traveler regarding waterfalls. I had seen the one at Tivoli that is beautiful, artistic, and poetically accompanied by historical memories; I had seen the falls of the Rhine, which are the biggest in Europe, and the hundred which brighten the landscape in the Swiss Alps. Nevertheless, no other falls on earth can be compared with Niagara. She alone offers such a terrific spectacle. Her colossal dimensions, the enormous volume of her waters, and the straight lines which they describe rob her, however, of all beauty, inspiring only feelings of terror, respect, and that sublime pleasure which comes from viewing great battles. Picture a crystalline river like the Bío-Bío descending in an instant from a high plane to one much lower, the water describing a right angle upon changing from the horizontal to the vertical, and, from there, after turning over and over on itself in silver whirlpools, following along the lower level with the same tameness it had before falling. The beauty of the falls is caused by the points of projecting rocks which force the water to turn back on itself, launch itself into the air, and divide itself up into atoms and impregnate itself with light.

The sight of the other falls had made me smile with pleasure. But at Niagara I felt my legs trembling and that feverish feeling which means the blood has left one's face. Arriving at the falls by way of Goat Island, which divides them in two, the mind, happily, can be prepared somewhat by the less tumultuous scene which is presented by the rapids, where the Niagara is descending fifty feet per mile. The primitive forest which covers the island, hiding the nearby city behind its foliage, and the upstream view of the winding river offer one of those startlingly lovely and unspoiled scenes so common to the United States. The English falls is in the form of a horseshoe and is four city blocks wide, with no obstacle to the smoothness of its flow. The American falls are 200 yards wide,* and for this reason are called the lesser falls. From both, the water falls 165 feet, and the canal carved in the rock which receives it is 100 yards deep and 130 wide. Upon seeing these figures, which have been checked by measurements, written down, one realizes how incapable the human eye is of grasping great size. Saint Peter's in Rome looks like a structure of normal dimensions and Niagara Falls becomes small to the naked eye in order to adjust them to our own smallness.

The mass of water coming down from the falls is 21 feet thick; so that, since light cannot penetrate it, it is green to its center; a fact which, suggesting as it does the vastness of the scene, increases the awe it inspires. One can observe the falls well from a lookout point on Goat Island. It is a good place, because it is approached from the English side where the eye can examine the

* They are actually some 1,400 feet wide.

225

vertical line of the falls and measure the abyss which rumbles like a thunderstorm or a shower of cannonshot at one's feet. One can see the falls in all of their splendor and magnificence aboard a steamboat which comes up the river from Lake Ontario every day loaded with passengers, stopping some hundred yards from the falls with her motor running to fight against the tug of the whirlpools, the hull shivering on water which is so tormented and covered with foam as to appear to be in a delirium. On the return trip, the passengers know that they have really seen something. But one doesn't really experience the falls except by descending to the cave at its base, wrapped in rubber gear and led by the hand by a guide under the falls itself, where a path has been carved in the rock with iron handrails to keep one from falling into the water. Hundreds of slimy, slippery eels cling to the irregular surface of the rock. Stunned and humbled by the noise and hit all over by a strong spray, one sees a wall at the end of this singular gallery which would be taken for crystal if it were not for the occasional drops which betray the presence of the liquid element. Coming out of that watery inferno and seeing the sun and sky once again, one can say that he has fully experienced the sublime. A battle of two hundred thousand warriors would not excite such profound emotions.

On the English side there is a magnificent hotel and a museum where live buffalos can be seen and where the sea sponges and petrified coral which are found in the ground around the falls are on sale. This region was all under the sea in other times!

These falls are different from others in the world in that they are situated in the center of a plateau. One quickly discovers the reason for this; when one descends the river toward Lake Ontario, the phenomenon is easi-

ly explained. Lake Erie is in the middle of a great uninterrupted plain. This plain is the upper part of a
tableland whose border is close to Lake Ontario, which
is situated on a lower tableland. The difference in level
between the two lakes is three hundred feet, and since
the Niagara River unites them, its falls should be at the
border of the tableland close to the shores of Lake Ontario. But the falls are found seven miles upstream, and
the rock is excavated in a deep ditch to the height of the
falls. The falls have thus been changing their position,
or, to put it perhaps more clearly, they are slowly moving toward Lake Erie, where they will someday arrive.
One can get an understanding of the history of this part
of the globe by carefully observing the distance the cataract advances each year as the rock which serves as its
bed crumbles or decays. According to the geologist Lyell,
who suggests that it has retreated only a foot per year,
it has taken thirty-nine thousand years to get where it
is from the edge of the tableland, which is near the city
of Queenstown. But this calculation must take into account differences in the altitude of the falls in each one
of the places where it has been and the resistance which
the varying consistencies of rock it has encountered have
been able to offer it. The first time a European described
the falls was in 1678, and these were French missionaries
who also did a sketch of them. There is another description of the falls in 1751, but geological investigations
did not begin until very recently. From 1815 on the two
falls have been altering their shape by eroding away
great chunks of rock, and since 1840 Goat Island has
also lost some acres of land.

Mr. Lyell discovered close to four miles below the
present position of the falls the ancient bed of the river,
which is at an even higher altitude than where Niagara

is today. The seashells which are found in banks of residue on Goat Island appear to be of the same species and from the same period as those found all the way to Ontario in a line indicating the direction the river once took. We have, says Lyell, in the walls of the gorge which the Niagara is making, a chronometer which roughly but significantly measures the many years which separate the present from the epoch when the Niagara flowed on the plateau many miles to the north. This timepiece shows us that two events which we had thought to have been contemporary, the extinction of the mastodon and man's first populating of the earth, may have occurred at times very remote from one another. The geologist adds that there is danger of considering these matters to such an extent that, obsessed by them, one may forget the presence of the cataract itself and neglect to experience the rush of its waters and hear the explosion they make as they fall into that deep abyss. But as one's thoughts return to the present, the state of the spirit and the feelings awakened in the heart will find themselves in perfect harmony with the grandeur and beauty of the glorious surrounding scene.

Canada

The railroad that runs along the side of the gorge made by the river as it flows to Queenstown, which is close to Lake Ontario, carries passengers heading for Quebec and Lake Champlain. After having savored that magnificent spectacle, I was riding along on the train, ruminating over my recent emotions, and allowing an exclamation of admiration for what I had seen to escape from time to time, when a Yankee, who had been listening to me with that placid indifference which distinguishes this type of man, revealed the falls to me from a new point of view. "BEAUTIFUL! BEAUTIFUL!" he said, and, to show me his idea of beauty, added: "These falls are worth millions. Already machines have been put into action along the rapids, where waterpower conveyed by cheaply constructed canals is used to turn them. When the population of the States has clustered around this region, the immense volume of water from the American falls can be subdivided and diverted by canals which will run along the upper level, conveying the water to the lower riverbed of the Niagara and discharging it at points where textile and other industrial machines have been placed. Can you imagine," he asked me, "that we will have at our disposition waterpower motors of forty thousand horsepower if necessary? Then the Niagara will be a street flanked for seven miles on both sides by turbines, each one with its own waterfall tailored to the needs of the motor. Ships will come to tie up at the port and carry merchandise to Europe and New York by way of the Saint Lawrence, Lake Champlain, or the Oswego canal. BEAUTIFUL! BEAUTIFUL!" he added, ecstatic over the useful application of that enormous mass of water which today serves only to demonstrate the power of nature. I believe the Yankees are jealous of the falls and will occupy them in the same way they occupy and populate the forests.

Passing from one railroad to another in the midst of still unpopulated forests, passing through hamlets still on the drawing boards, unable to see how trains can possibly move through these forsaken solitudes, one changes to a STAGE. These are diligences stitching together the intervals without rails. In Queenstown, one takes lodgings aboard the boat which awaits the train and then descends Lake Ontario, touching at Oswego at the mouth of the canal which links this lake with the canal that continues on to the Hudson. Ex-President Van Buren, in promoting the opening of this auxiliary canal, greatly increased the value of some lands he owned nearby without anyone criticizing his self-seeking measure because the canal really added to that wonderful system of water communications of which I have spoken in another place.

The country is still unpopulated here. The Lake Ontario steamboat puts in to the high banks where gentlemen in frock coats and girls wrapped in cashmere have come in order to board ship. Far off one can make out isolated cabins made of trunks of trees placed one upon another or of faded planks, which serve as a temporary dwelling place for the farmer who has just begun to clear the forest. The view has all of the fresh virginlike quality which Cooper captured in those inimitable pictures which make up *The Last of the Mohicans.* I have already said that from Buffalo on in this direction lies the most beautiful part of the world. Free of the aggressive luxuriance of the tropics or the cold severity of the forests of northern Europe, the scene includes rivers like lakes and lakes like seas which are surrounded by exquisite vegetation and placed in the most artistic manner. For two days I was enraptured by the contemplation of nature and at times discovered in the depths of my heart a strange feeling which I had never before experienced, not even in Paris. It was the secret desire to stay here to live forever, to become a Yankee, and to see if I might acquire a poor factory by Niagara Falls to earn my living. A factory for what? And here my delight in such a beautiful life turned to shame as I was reminded of those showy signs with their crooked letters which I had seen in Spain: *Match Factory.* And what matches! To teach or write *what* with this language that no one needs to know? To cure me of these illusions and to insure that I would not think of them again, and to recover my happiness, I needed to do nothing more than feel the thinness of my pocketbook and glance at my ledger.

Where Lake Ontario empties into the Saint Lawrence River are found the Thousand Islands, a relatively small area with no less than that quantity of islands. The most beautiful fluvial scene offered by Europe is on the Rhine below Mainz and Cologne. I had traveled the Rhine to Haarlem,* the frontier of Holland, from which a railroad runs to Amsterdam by way of Utrecht; from there, after visiting The Hague, one goes down to Rotterdam, and, by way of the Scheldt, on to Antwerp and Brussels. German traditions, feudal castles which still crown the heights, Rhenish cities which display the statue of Gutenberg, and the cathedral of Cologne beautify the Rhine. The river flows silently through dark and tortured gorges, coming out into more open country where one can see the steeples of churches and the vineyards spreading out, dwarfed by the foothills of the surrounding mountains. Further on, close to Holland, the land is lower. The river widens and windmills succeed castles, and the swamps of the lowlands demand canals which cut through the country in every direction and astonishing dikes which put their shoulder to the continuing struggle with the ocean, which is at a higher level.

On the Saint Lawrence, nature, free from any manmade ornament, is absolutely incomparable. Here the view expands as far as the eye can see without at any time becoming monotonous. The trip through Thousand Islands is a trip through a fairy land. It was

* Sarmiento probably means Arnhem.

autumn, and the American varieties of trees were already tinted iridescent shades of yellow and purple, colors which all painters desire for rustic scenes. The American oak and other trees turn such a vivid and pure red that they attract attention from leagues away. The islands, some large enough to hold a village, others so small that they look like baskets of flowers floating down the river, were dressed in this same apparel. From time to time the Saint Lawrence has rapids which give to its waters an enameled whiteness; though there is no foam, since the rocks which agitate the waters are far beneath the surface. The river thus appears as a wide silver band, interrupted by those lovely islands which excite the spectator and vary the scene, grouping themselves in capricious forms and combinations and making new horizons every moment, until the traveler is lost in their labyrinth. When the steamboat enters the rapids, the engineer shuts off the motor. The current of that restless waterway then snatches up the boat, and the pilot has to use a firm hand to guide it between the reefs and backwaters which occur along the way. I do not know if they were joking with me or not, but the pilot said, "We are making sixty miles an hour HERE," as he looked forward without blinking an eye at a difficult spot we had to pass up ahead. The EXPRESS-TRAIN between Manchester and Liverpool also makes sixty miles an hour. Arriving at Kingston, a city in upper Canada, I bought some apples to have something to do, and in the middle of the night we arrived at Montreal, a French city in this part of the British colonies.

The Hotel Donegan, which is as big as our cloisters and arranged in every way like the great American hotels, shelters the dislocated and beaten-about traveler who has been at the mercy of the trains, the linking stages, and the steamboats. The gong-gong does not fail to shatter the nerves of the unfortunate guest who insists on trying to sleep one hour more in the morning.

Montreal! What a jewel to encounter as part of one's trip! Dumas ignored the treasure which is hidden there, only ten or eleven days by steamboat from France. It is the most advanced city in the world in civil construction. The houses are of quarried stone or brick. The roofs are covered with a mantle of zinc, giving the city a sparkling look. All streets are paved with logs or boards in the manner planned for the street in front of the Opéra Comique in Paris, and the sidewalks are of crossed planks mounted on braces, a system which permits water to drain off below. In this respect, Montreal is the most highly civilized city on the planet; but because of an interesting moral aspect, it is also a fossil curiosity.

As you know, upper and lower Canada were ceded to England by Louis XIV* at the end of one of those disastrous wars which embittered his last days and which made France pay dearly for the pride of her kings and the arrogance of her armies; a sad but well-deserved end which fortune predestines from the first moments of the lives of tyrants. Old age has its wrinkles, conscience has its remorse, and weariness and exhaustion are the lot of nations who must indemnify those they have offended. With Napoleon this story was repeated, and with our imbecile** the same will occur, much to our expense.

I am always coming back to the good-for-nothings! The French population of Montreal bewails the day when, like Carthage condemned to destruction, they were exchanged like merchandise, sold like a herd of sheep to hated England. But crying and tearing their

* Sarmiento has the wrong Louis. Louis XIV died in 1715; Louis XV was King during the French and Indian War.
** Sarmiento is undoubtedly referring to Juan Manuel Rosas.

hair in no way changed the situation in which the mother country had left them, and they had to resign themselves to their unfortunate situation. From then on the connection with the mother country was broken and they no longer heard news of France. Her later revolutions, the Republic, the Empire, the Restoration, and the near-Restoration have all occurred without the man in the street learning of anything but the most superficial news—and this by hearsay only. There has been little awareness of the historical significance of these events.

French books stopped coming into the English colony, and all progressive ideas, all new things in literature and philosophy, from the ideas which began in Louis XIV's century on through Rousseau, Voltaire, and the eighteenth century, are unknown to these unfortunate people. Thus for the French of Montreal, the only France possible is the France of the grand king with his court at Versailles, his etiquette, and his Asiatic luxury; the only poets, Corneille and Racine; the only military glories those of Condé, Catinat, Villars, and Turenne. The Canadian is as ceremonious as an old courtier and so punctilious about nobility that the genealogy of families is as a looking glass which must not be clouded or soiled in any way. Living under English domination for one century already, mothers still refuse to teach their daughters English, so as to make it impossible for them to be influenced by the odious oppressors of their race. If you ask a question in English in the streets, you can walk all over the town without any person of French origin giving you the impression that he has understood you. Speak in French, and heads will turn from every direction, countenances will smile, and the good will and the desire *d'être agréable* will be painted on every face. "Ah!, Sir," a young man said to me in an emotional voice, "have you come from France? How happy you must be! Ah, France, our homeland! If she knew what she has done turning us over to the English! She has probably repented of that decision already, don't you think?" Not even in his reproaches does this type of person want to offend the mother country.

Opposition to their oppressors is organized around their religion, and Catholicism is a fortress behind which the distinguishing characteristics of this isolated people are protected. Catholicism, no matter how rigid its dogmas, has, over the centuries, progressed and reformed itself by accepting new institutions. But if you want to turn back the pages of history and see it as it was at the end of the Middle Ages, go to Montreal and there you will find it in all of its primitive simplicity, full of passion and force and concentrating in itself, as in Spain in the times of Queen Isabella, patriotism, power, and heroism. Toward the base of the mountain which provides the city's name, on a small rise, there is a very picturesque little brick house surrounded by trees. This house, which had attracted my attention, is completely boarded up and abandoned. I asked a Canadian the reason for this, and he responded: "What! Don't you know? It is the Jew's house. And, of course, because of his soul being in perdition, *le revenant*. A Jew (if naming the person such is not, as I suspect, an example of the superstition of these people) was the owner of that house. One evening, very late at night, a shot was heard. The following day the neighbors found him dead, a suicide. Some countrymen wanted to occupy the house afterwards, but the soul of the damned returned to his room every night, stirring up papers and making wailing sounds and rattling chains. No one has ever been able to inhabit the house again. Twenty years ago some poor neighboring people tried to live in it, but the soul of the condemned man returned: the lights went out by themselves, and the wailing and rattling of chains were heard. The authorities finally ordered that the doors be boarded up for fear that the house would become a hideout for thieves."

I listened with amazement to this tale, which brought to mind scenes of my childhood when I would listen horrified to stories of spirits and ghosts. I observed the storyteller carefully to see if he really believed what he was telling me and would not conclude the story in the manner of a few clerics in Rome who show tourists a table with three legs and tell them that Jesus Christ lunched on it with Saint Peter and Saint John, and then break into laughter at the serious expressions on the faces of their audience. But there was in the voice and eyes of the narrator such conviction that to have betrayed any doubts would certainly have demoralized him. He was so simple-minded, and this tale so widely sanctioned, even by the authorities, that it would never have occurred to him to doubt the possibility of such a thing.

Sunday came, and I visited the cathedral. I had never imagined a more imposing spectacle. Rome had chilled me, even during Holy Week. During those days Saint Peter's is, as always, deserted. Romans ask: "Have you been to Saint Peter's? Have you seen the Pope?" They themselves never go to the great basilica and rarely visit the other churches. If this is the case in Rome, you can imagine what goes on in France and Spain, and in the rest of Italy. I am trying to recall just where it was that I encountered, in three different churches, priests saying Mass without a single listener or at most some old beggar woman for their only audience.

In the Gothic cathedral of Montreal there were that Sunday from fifteen to twenty thousand souls following the main Mass. The Catholic population does not feel that it has wholly fulfilled its obligations unless it has listened to an episcopal Mass, presented with simple pomp and served by seventy-two acolytes, assistants, and priests (whom I could count because of their cut-off conical hats a third of a rod high). Since the floor of the cathedral does not offer enough space for so many people, galleries of seats have been put up along both sides of the naves, and all four galleries and the floor were packed. At that time the priest was preaching the doctrinal sermon. A profound silence reigned amongst that immense congregation, and a lady who saw me standing courteously signaled to me by eyes and hand to sit down at her side in one of the wooden pews which cover all of the available space in that vast building, which is broader than the cathedral in Santiago. What I noted that morning was to prove typical of Montreal; the church told me all too much.

The following day, in the street, I encountered a long procession of children in two rows, preceded by a cross with loincloth carried by a cleric. They sang hymns in chorus on their way to the church to hear daily Mass before class. They were followed by a priest and some assistant priests. The priest, as in olden days, is the parish's schoolteacher, and when the parish is large he has assistant priests as helpers. The children are indoctrinated with fervor in their beliefs and fortified against all dangerous innovations and against any lukewarmness which might open their souls to the Protestantism hated by their teachers. Thus Catholicism has solidified and concentrated itself here in order to combat the disintegration of the race and language. It has remained faithful to the most outdated practices and even the wildest superstitions so that no one can charge it with inconsistency. No doubt all of this is holy, beautiful, interesting, patriotic, and orthodox. But nothing under God's heaven is perfect! The Catholics of Montreal possess and cultivate a desperate ignorance. Isolated from the government, because they are afraid of contaminating themselves by taking jobs with it, they live outside of all public life. Next door to the Yankees, and governed by the English, they nevertheless have no industry, cultivate the land badly, and are diminished and narrowed in every way by poverty, darkness, incompetence, and misery. Today a patrician family sells its house, which is bought by an English merchant; tomorrow its sons are indigent; since they have no education or manual skills, the grandsons end up as good-for-nothings or servants. I estimate that in one century more this people will have disappeared, unsuited for living in today's world, obstinate in their patriotism and in perpetuating a mode of living which bit by bit is annihilating them.

The English inhabitants, meanwhile, are developing themselves by commerce, by the exercise of power, by immigration, and by following the English way of life, which is so flexible and active. The English agitate for separation from metropolitan England, and they curse the day when Montgomery, who was bringing them independence, was defeated.*

Montreal is the center of the fur trade in the north,

---

* Richard Montgomery, American Revolutionary War general, killed after capturing Montreal in the subsequent attack on Quebec of December 31, 1775.

and her warehouses are filled with an infinite variety of pelts. After having seen that lovely city which, for all its modern appearance, encloses within it the most outdated people, I wanted to go on to Quebec to examine a center which the English government has established for receiving Irish immigrants. They give them food and something to do there until they leave for the lands which have been set aside for them. Sometimes I think we should not invent new things all the time but should search for the place where a problem which is bothering us has already been solved. I had brought with me from Germany the idea of such lodging houses to shelter immigrants in our countries, and, when I spoke of this to Astaburuaga in New York, he told me about this one. Upon taking passage down the Saint Lawrence, I was struck with remorse by the prodigality with which I had been spending money on my travels, as though I were a Russian prince. My round-trip excursion to Quebec cost me some seven dollars. Quebec is very much like Montreal, although it is less beautiful and less primitive than Montreal. Seven dollars! I took a steamboat to cross the Saint Lawrence, and at La Prairie got a seat on the train to New York which takes one to the shore of Lake Champlain and then skirts the edge of that long lake. I watched the shores turn into bays or reach out into peninsulas. The panorama was infinitely varied. When we reached Whitehall, I got off and took passage on a canalboat for Troy, where there is a train for Boston, the object of my journey. Let us sum up the expenses of this journey: from Buffalo to the falls by railroad, $1 (22 miles); from Niagara Falls to Lewiston, railroad and STAGE, $6 (31 miles); Lake Ontario to Montreal, by steamboat, $10; from Montreal to La Prairie, steamboat and railroad, $1; from La

Prairie by way of Lake Champlain to Whitehall, $1; diligence to Troy, $3; railroad to Greenbush, $3.

Boston

This Puritan city, the Memphis of Yankee civilization, had 18,000 inhabitants in 1790, 33,000 in 1810, and 114,360 in 1845. It is built on a peninsula whose mile-wide isthmus serves as the principal means of communication with the mainland, although numerous bridges thrown over the interior bay are establishing new lines of communication. Gentle hills interrupt the terrain and provide lovely observation points. The oak beneath which the Pilgrims agreed upon their basic laws still lives. It was in Boston in 1676 that the famous law of general and obligatory public education was put into effect, a law which heralded the betterment of the human species. In Boston the colonists assembled in a MEETING and decided not to pay the tax on tea, to abstain from using this imported item, and to hurl the stored boxes of tea into the sea. In Boston the first shot in the War of Independence was fired. In Boston the public schools are, because of the magnificence of their architecture, like temples, and every person pays one dollar a year to educate the children of his fellow man and every child uses seven dollars of public money a year for his education. Boston is the site and center of Unitarianism, which seeks to unite all sects around what they have in common and to elevate religious faith to the level of moral and religious philosophy. From Boston, finally, depart those swarms of colonizers who carry to the FAR WEST the institutions, science, and practice of government, the Yankee spirit, and the manual skills necessary to possess the land. Four steamboat lines link her with Europe. A railroad runs along the coast to Portland, Maine. Another, which runs to Concord, puts her in contact with New Hampshire; still another, with Troy and its lines and many canals; three, supplemented by voyages by sea or through Long Island Sound, with New York. Her hotels are the best in the United States, and the Tremont Hotel is superior to any in elegance and comfort.

Night had fallen, and I had given myself over to that sleep of the dead which follows the sleepless nights and discomforts suffered on an arduous journey. At three o'clock in the morning repeated knocks on the door accompanied by tomfoolery and laughter which someone was unable to contain woke me up. No one on earth knew I was in Boston, but nevertheless the clown outside continued his joke: "Open up, Sarmiento. It's me." "Who's me?" And, sure that I'd given up: "It's me, Casaffoust."

One night in Naples I was eating ice cream in a cafe with a young Frenchman. As I saw an individual enter, I said to my companion in French: "That fellow is from the southern part of America. I'd say he's from Buenos Aires." Is there really a national Argentine type? Ruguendas knows how to reproduce him with a pencil, and this time I had looked at the face of a compatriot and guessed right. This fellow came closer reservedly, and at last he ventured to say to me: "I believe, Señor, I heard you call me an American." It turned out that he was a *Porteño,** one of those energetic characters who open up the world through their personal efforts. Leaving his country while still quite young, he had established himself in Rio de Janeiro, then passed on to Valparaiso, then to Bolivia, then to Lima, and had finally arrived in Cen-

* A Porteño is an Argentine from Buenos Aires, the port city.

241

tral America, where, having made his fortune, he began to think that the world simply would not be satisfied if he didn't go around it. We said good-bye in Naples, and we met again in Rome. There he headed for Trieste, and I left a little later for Florence. Entering a cafe in Venice, I found Casaffoust there, blocking the door; he had just arrived. We would not see each other again. The day I arrived in Paris I surprised him on the boulevard. He had come from London to have clothing made for his return to America. In the hotel in London where I took a room a month later I discovered Casaffoust, eating with great gusto. Was he some ghost that was haunting me? After crossing our arms and contemplating each other with astonishment, we threw ourselves upon each other laughing at these singular events. From London he left at last on the *Istmo* for Belize, from which he planned to head for Costa Rica. I had advised him to visit the United States, but he had not wanted to. The night I arrived in Boston he was scheduled to depart from the same hotel, and while he was paying his bill he spied the name "D. F. Sarmiento" among the latest arrivals in the open hotel register. He suspended his trip and accompanied me for two days, and we separated promising ourselves with great sincerity that we would not meet again, as these coincidences were really beginning to concern me. This time we have stuck to our word. We have not seen each other again.

The principal object of my trip was to see Mr. Horace Mann, Secretary of the BOARD of Education, the great reformer of primary education, who like myself had traveled through Europe in search of methods and systems, a man who combined an inexhaustible quantity of good will and philanthropy with a rare prudence and a profound wisdom in his acts and in his writings.[1] He lived outside of Boston, and I had to take the railroad to get to East Newton,* the small village where he resided. We spent many long hours talking on two consecutive days. He told me of his tribulations and of the difficulties which had beset his great work, such as popular prejudices on education, local and sectarian jealousies, and the vulgar pettiness which may bring the best of institutions to ruin. The legislature of the state had itself been at the point of canceling out his work, of dismissing him, and of dissolving the Commission On Education, yielding to the lowest motives—envy and conformity. His work was immense and the compensation tiny, but his pay was in the fruits already harvested and in the future which he was opening for his country. He was creating near his house a normal school, which I visited with his wife and where, not without surprise, I saw young women who paid to study mathematics, chemistry, botany, and anatomy as complementary branches of their education. They were poor girls who had to borrow money to pay for their education and would pay it back when they were placed in schools. Since they are well paid as teachers, the business was a sure and lucrative one for those who loaned the money. Thanks to his good work, the State of Massachusetts, of which Boston is the capital, had in 1846, in the 309 cities and towns which make it up, 3,475 public schools with 2,589 male teachers and 5,000 females, attended by 174,084 children. The number of teachers in that state is greater than the whole of the permanent army of Chile and a third the size of the United States Army.

[1] He is now a Representative in Congress.
* Horace Mann lived in West Newton.

The population of the state is 737,700, and 203,877 children attend school.

The revenues applied to public education are $650,-000, collected by contributions to the schools.[2] Besides the primary schools, there are 67 public secondary schools with 3,700 students and 1,091 private primary and secondary schools with 24,318 pupils who pay $277,-690 for the education they receive.

In addition to these magnificent sums, each community has funds whose interest is set aside for the support of the schools. These funds produce $15,000 annually, to which must be added more than $8,000 in surplus regular income which is applied by the administration to this holy objective.

To illustrate my point even better, I want you to know that this state contains only 7,500 square miles—that is, it is 30 leagues wide by 73 long. In this small space there are, as I have said, more than 70,000 inhabitants, and these have $300,000,000 between them.

So you see, my dear friend, these Yankees have a right to boast. One hundred inhabitants per square mile, $400 per person in capital, a school or academy for every 200 citizens, $5 set aside annually for the education of each child, and, besides, the academies. All of this for developing their souls. In raw materials for production Boston has a network of railroads, another of canals, another of rivers, and an ample coastline. For thought she has the Gospel and forty-five newspapers, journals, and magazines; and for the benefit of all there is the high level of education of her officials, the frequent MEETINGS whose object is society's improvement, and religious, philanthropic, and other groups which give direction and purpose to everything. Can you think of anything

2 By 1848, revenues had reached $800,000.

more beautiful than Mr. Mann's obligation as Secretary of the BOARD of Education to travel a part of the year, call an educational MEETING of the population of every village and city where he arrives, mount the platform and preach a sermon on primary education (demonstrating the practical advantages which accompany its wide diffusion), stimulate the parents, conquer selfishness, smooth out difficulties, counsel the teachers, make suggestions, and propose improvements in the schools which his science, his good will, and his experience suggest to him?

Near Boston, twelve miles away and united to the city by a railroad for people and a canal for raw materials, is Lowell, the Birmingham of American industry. Here, as in everything, shines the sovereign intelligence of this people. How is competition possible with English manufacturing, which is the product of huge quantities of capital employed in the factories and the lowest possible salaries paid to miserable and ragged people? It is said that factories increase capital in ratio to the popular misery they produce. Lowell gives the lie to this theory. It has very little or no advantage over the English in the cost of raw materials, since it costs about the same amount to take bales of cotton from Florida to Boston as to London. But the differences in the salaries paid are enormous, and the textiles of Lowell, nevertheless, compete with the English one in price and are ordinarily better in quality. How is this possible? By exhausting all the intelligent means in which the country is so rich. The workers and machinists are educated men. Their work is so perfectly done, their methods so ingenious, that time and the finished product can be so accurately predicted that both quantity and quality are improved.

The spinners and workers are educated girls, conscientious and devoted to their work. They come from eighty leagues around seeking to make a small fortune by their own means. Daughters of more or less comfortable farmers, their decent habits keep them from a loose life. They are looking for money to establish themselves, and in the men around them they see nothing but candidates for husbands. They dress well, going through the streets on Sunday in silk stockings and with a shawl and parasol. They save $150 or $200 some years and return to the bosom of their families ready to help defray the cost of establishing a new family. They are aided by the presence of spacious and comfortable hotels in Lowell which provide economical board and lodging for the workers, libraries, newspapers, and even pianos for those girls who know a little music. Europeans say a lot of bad things about the United States, and Americans, in turn, brag about advantages which the Europeans then dispute or balance with various defects. But Lowell is above this debate and remains a model and an example of what capital combined with the moral elevation of the worker can produce in industry. There high salaries produce a better product at the same price as the factories of London, which assassinate generations.

These textiles from Lowell, like those from Pittsburgh and from the two hundred factories which are going up at different points in the Union, still are not having much effect upon the mass of manufactured products which flood the world market. The great bulk of them are consumed within the country. Even here the United States demonstrates in bold statistics how much of the good life the mass of the population enjoys. Statistical data from France shows that its population consumes only 1 meter of cotton fabrics per capita each year, and in Ireland 1½ yards per capita, while in the United States 21½ yards are consumed per capita, which leads one to the conclusion that there is not a man there who does not have sheets on his bed and several changes of shirts. From this fact American publicists have come to a valuable conclusion. In place, they say, of looking for foreign markets for our products, let us bring people here to populate our forests. If we had to provide cotton textiles for Ireland, which has 4 million inhabitants, we would take care of their needs with 6 million yards of goods. To consume those same 6 million yards of fabric here, 285,714 immigrants would be enough, which is more or less the annual immigration figure. Twenty years of immigration will give us a market for 120 million yards of cotton textiles.

The other manufactured articles are consumed in like proportions. In the year 1842* 11 million dollars worth of wool fabrics was imported into the States; in 1836 the amount was 21 million; but it was down to 8 or 9 million in 1840-1842. In 1839 21 million dollars worth of silk fabrics was imported, while in 1841 the amount was 15 million and in 1842 only 9 million. There was 9 million dollars worth of linen imported in 1836, nearly 7 million in 1841, and it was down to 3½ million by 1842. To this enormous consumption of products from Europe must be added figures no less bulky on national production. It is calculated that for the year 1843 agricultural products reached $654,387,597, manufactured goods, $239,836,224, and commerce, $79,721,086.

Until the year 1825 not one yard of calico (chintz) had been printed in the United States. In 1836, 150 million yards were imported from England, which means that, according to the census of 1840, which states that there

* Sarmiento must mean 1832.

were 17 million inhabitants, each woman (figuring that they make up one third of the population) had two dresses using some ten rods each. In 1842 American printed fabrics rose to the enormous sum of 158 million yards, importation of English printed fabrics having fallen to 15 million. The factories in the New England states made use of one third of the cotton which was harvested in the Southern states in 1845, and the workers consumed more wheat and grains than the quantity exported by the Port of New York.

Mr. Mann favored me with many letters of introduction to learned men, pedagogues, and prominent people. His name alone was, wherever I went, a passport for me. I had a long discussion with one of the high officials in the state government, who provided me with an order requesting that various editions of books and public documents which would bring me up to date on education in Massachusetts be turned over to me. After looking around Boston and seeing how beautiful it was, I set out for New York. By a series of combinations of railroads and steamboats which went night and day, I was brought, I do not know how, to the pier at New York.

Baltimore and Philadelphia

Still full of the emotions of this trip (the most *impressive* one you can make in fifteen days), and with the sights of Niagara Falls still etched on my brain, I attended a performance of the delightful Tom Thumb, the dwarf who is only twenty-five inches tall.

Don Santiago Arcos was waiting for me impatiently, ready to set out on the return trip to Chile. Each time he spoke to me of the matter I showed him a face like that of a government official who has not decided whether he will agree to do what you want or not. We would open up the map, trace the route, and were almost underway without my having given the slightest sign that I was in favor of it. Finally, we had to speak plainly. I had in my pocket twenty-two guineas and thirty paper pesos, no more and no less. I screwed up my courage and laid out my financial situation with all the dignity of one who is not asking for and who will not accept help, suggesting that I would separate from Arcos in Havana, traveling on from there by way of Caracas. Arcos had listened to me with interest and even was tempted with the thought of crossing the tropical solitudes of South America, facing unknown adventures, enduring hardships, and not being able to count on anyone but oneself to overcome them. But the idealistic and masculine side of his character is no less developed than the frank and jovial side. While I was awaiting offers and protests he began a pantomime dance and side-splitting laugh which made me rear up with all my dignity once again. "Splendid!" he said, jumping up and down and laughing. "Because I have only four hundred dollars! Let's travel together, and when our combined funds run out we'll figure out what to do at that point."

We decided that I would continue my journey to Washington by way of Philadelphia and Baltimore, and that we would meet in Philadelphia to set out by way of Harrisburg and Pittsburgh on the descent of the Ohio and Mississippi to New Orleans, 22,234 miles* from the point where we were at this time. The departure time of the morning train drawing near, I hurriedly packed my bag and gave the bills and guineas to Arcos for him to change. He gave me thirty or forty dollars for the expenses of my side trip. This little incident was, as we

* Sarmiento means 2,234 miles.

shall see, the beginning of the most terrible drama of which I have been victim during my travels. I would tire you if I continued by describing important cities. But Philadelphia and Baltimore are examples of civil construction in the United States which, unlike New York, are original. The Americans have the knack of reducing everything to a science and applying common sense and functionalism to all things. You know our South American cities, how they are all cut on the same pattern, with streets one hundred and fifty rods long, twelve wide, and laid out on straight lines. To us this seems ideal. But what if one wanted to go out from downtown in an oblique direction? In other words, if all the streets run north-south and east-west, how much ground will you have to cover to get to the extreme southeast or northeast? Surely double the distance you would cover following a straight line, because it is necessary to zigzag from street to street at each corner, looking for the diagonal. Each property on the hundred-and-fifty-rod-long streets is seventy-five rods deep, more than sufficient space for a vineyard, vegetable garden, and some trees in the inner yards. But with an increase in population a relatively vacant center of the block is no longer possible, though each house is given more frontage, thereby spreading out the houses somewhat. Afterwards there are the pipes for distributing drinking water and those for gas, etc., and one finds that the costs for such large areas are beyond the means of the townspeople. The Americans have invented a city plan which takes into account all of these factors. The block is or can be some hundred and forty rods long, but it is only thirty or fifty in depth, so that the houses can face on both streets and the city can be populated advantageously.

As the street is for public convenience and for recreation, it is ordinarily thirty rods wide, flanked at a distance of five or six rods from the buildings by copious trees which offer shade in all directions. The sidewalks are themselves streets separate from the central one, leaving a thoroughfare twenty rods wide which is taken over by carts, horsemen, omnibuses, and even railroads, with everything and everyone having room to get about. The streets cross at right angles, with alternating wide ones and narrow ones. Occasionally they are intercepted by a wide transversal street which runs out to the extreme corners of the city. The streets change in form and direction from time to time, especially those near ports. All over the city the crowded streets have forests of trees which close off the perspective at a short distance. Above the treetops one can see the cupolas of banks and hotels, the steeples of temples, and the facades of government buildings. There is nothing more spacious, airy, and countrylike than these streets of trees and houses in which the activity of others is a thing which does not need to concern or interest us.

In Baltimore I took the train for Washington, but just after we got started there was an incredible event: another train was bearing down on us on the same rails from the opposite direction. Great uproar within! There was much thrusting of heads out of the window, wide-eyed staring, waving of handkerchiefs in both trains— in short, fear that we were about to have a headon collision and be made into omelets! What had happened was that a bridge had been washed out, and the approaching train was the one that had left for Baltimore the previous day. We had to get off the train and, with the combined strength of all the passengers, while mired in the mud, we all but carried the locomotive and tender to the rear of the train for the return to Baltimore.

One could not go on to Washington, because, in the United States, if there is not railroad, canal, or river it is considered impossible to go anywhere. A steamboat was found which would carry the passengers by river to a certain point. From there they could take a stretch of railroad, walk a distance, take another railroad, and embark on another steamboat to enter Washington by way of Chesapeake Bay and the Potomac River. The bay steamboat was an old hulk with an abominable form and bad disposition, filled with bunks placed one upon another for six or seven levels like drawers in an immense wardrobe. The STEWARD showed me mine on the fifth level. The day passed in looking at the landscape. Night fell and sleep called me, but, like those chickens which carefully appraise the branch where they will roost, I walked about a bit until I resolved to set out on the journey of arriving at my bunk by climbing up the others like a lizard. I was halfway up when there began below the sound of voices and laughter which in a moment reached great proportions. Calmly I continued my ascent and was putting a leg into my nesting place when someone got hold of my other one and began to curse me roundly in the Yankee way. I looked down and—oh horrors!—saw that I was the object of the laughter of three hundred rascals. The one up here was disputing the bunk with me. He claimed he had placed a handkerchief on it as proof of his possession that he had been signaling to me as I ascended without that having slowed me down the least bit. My friend, imagine my position in that absurd situation, exposed to public shame, the object of the ridicule of that mob.

There was nothing else to do but come down, hide my face with both hands, pass through the crowd, and throw myself into the water. But I did something better. I did get down, I headed for a light which was nearby, and, putting myself in such a position that the rays illuminated my face perfectly, I said, with a full and obstreperous voice and putting on a calm but severe face, directing myself to the multitude which was hoping for some new incident over which they might laugh: "Gentlemen! If there is someone among you who understands Spanish or French do me the justice of letting me know, because I wish to explain myself, both to give and to ask for satisfaction." A profound silence came over the chamber. Those who did not know French (in which I was speaking in order not to provide material for further ridicule with my poor English) looked at one another, while there at the back I heard my words being repeated, in English. The atmosphere changed at once. The Yankee is a good soul, and all were sorry that their joke had struck me in the heart, since they had not meant to be malicious. Several came forward now giving me cordial excuses. My empty-headed opponent came down and told me in soft tones what had happened. I abandoned my position of a treed cat and went to sleep in a spacious bunk which the STEWARD, who announced publicly that he had assigned the disputed bunk to me, now gave me in exchange. The following day was passed calmly looking at the coasts of Virginia and at prairies which were in part cultivated and in part covered with little groves, until, traveling up the Potomac, we arrived at a rugged spot which had the distinction of being the main docking place of Washington, capital of the United States.

Washington

On a hill which dominates the surrounding panorama rises the American Capitol, whose cornerstone was laid by George Washington in 1793. This monument is the seat of power in the United States, recognizing no other mother institution than the Congress. To assemble in order to deliberate all questions which affect the interests of more than one person is the national instinct of the American people. The infant colony of Virginia, founded by a company from London to whom the king had given a great concession of lands had, after many vicissitudes, fallen under the provisional government of one Argall, a violent and rapacious man who, to assure the obedience of the colonists, proclaimed martial law. The fruit of the colonists' work was confiscated by the governor, and in punishment for the smallest crimes he imposed months of forced labor on his plantations. The violence of the government, which signified the transplanting of tyranny to America, retarded European immigration, while the colonists, discouraged by their sufferings under oppression, began to abandon the task of clearing the land. Then the colonists lifted their voices to ask vindication of the London company and accused Argall of defrauding the company itself while tyrannizing them. After heated discussions, their pleas were answered. Argall was deposed and censured and in his place Yeardley, an earlier Washington, was sent to take charge of laying the foundation of the future organization of the United States.

Thus the arbitrariness of rulers, which had been introduced into America like moth larvae in the baggage of the first colonists, was extirpated before the eggs were able to hatch in this country. The constant concern of the colonists in every part of the infant plantations from that time on was to combat the pretensions of the governors sent by the crown; to refuse to recognize an exequatur in regard to decrees and laws of the kings of England themselves, when their liberties were invaded; and to oppose the encroachments of the English Parliament, whose authority regarding taxes they never recognized because the colonies were not directly and duly represented in the Parliament. The revolution for independence was the last act of the drama begun in 1618 in Virginia, a drama which reached its conclusion in 1774* with the last battle of the War of Independence.

These events took place in 1618, at the beginning of the seventeenth century, when Europe, not excepting England, lay under royal domination, and the bonfire and axe of the executioner, sacking and pillage, were punishment not so much for the victims' crimes as for their weakness! Yeardley put everything in order, liberating the fledgling plantations of the colonists from all of those obligations previously exacted which were not strictly necessary for the conservation and progress of the colony. The authority of the governor was limited by a council which had the power to revoke those decisions which it deemed unjust or prejudicial, and the colonists themselves were allowed to participate in legislation. In June 1619, in Jamestown, the first American congress, the first example of popular representation, composed of the governor and his council and of two representatives from each of the eleven humble hamlets which at that time made up the colony of Virginia, met to discuss all means by which improvement and progress might be made in the infant colony. The London Company, and not the king, would ratify the laws here ap-

---

* Sarmiento never was a stickler for details.

proved. That nation, with a congress and a council of state, was in 1619 made up of only six hundred men, women, and children. In 1851, on another part of the soil of the Americas, there are millions of men who do not have sufficient dignity and power to put rational limits on the inquisitorial and destructive power that dominates them. That was, thus, the dawn of North American liberty. The colonists, filled with enthusiasm and with their spirits open to every hope, "began to put up houses and sow wheat," already sure of having a homeland they would never have to leave.

Legislatures date from the beginning of all the colonies, and in several of them congresses were called to resist the incursions of the savages or to organize expeditions of community militia to punish them. Thus George Washington at an earlier time exhibited in several states those military talents which he would later apply to securing the liberty of his country. At a time when the idea of separating from England had not occurred to anyone, the different colonies sent representatives to general congresses to fix the policy they would follow in resisting the pretensions of the English Parliament, just as, in the tradition of the land, they had resisted the Long Parliament. Although Congress moved from place to place during the War of Independence, it was to this body that the mutinous soldiers directed their complaints and threats and from it that they collected their salaries. Even after independence was assured, Congress was attacked at Annapolis, which then served as its seat. Then Washington, without partisan motivation but only because of the need to fix the capital's location, pointed to the site of the city of Washington as the place to shelter the tabernacle of the Union, as Solomon constructed a temple in Jerusalem for the Ark containing the books of law of the Hebrew people.

In the United States there is no capital strictly speaking, or rather, according to the Latin meaning of the word. You see this on contemplating the relative isolation of that monument, thrown up as if by chance in the center of a town which is in the center of nothing, neither of the country's geography, nor of its intelligence, nor of its wealth, nor of its culture, nor of its communication system. Placed on the left bank of the Potomac, one hundred and twenty miles above its outlet into Chesapeake Bay, its deserted wharf where a few ships tie up does not even deserve to be called a port. The District of Columbia is an area of sixty square miles remaining of the hundred which originally were ceded by the neighboring states of Maryland and Virginia. The latter reclaimed, this past year, forty square miles on the opposite side of the river which the infant capital could not utilize. Thirty-five thousand inhabitants is the entire population of the area, of whom more than twenty-five thousand live in the capital itself. The Congress is considered sovereign over this territory.

The city is surrounded by pretty hills, covered with greenery and cultivated on some of their slopes. The terrain of the city itself is elevated, with the Capitol occupying the center. From it streets go out in the direction of the four cardinal points, dividing the city into square blocks like our towns. The streets carry the names of the different states of the Union, and the most important ones among them are forty-five and fifty rods across. The greater number of them have not even been laid out, but Pennsylvania Avenue, which connects the Capitol with the President's house, has flagstone sidewalks nine rods wide and lines of trees on both sides. Around the Capitol there is a garden of twenty-two acres, adorned with a great variety of trees and animated by the sound of crystalline fountains, so that this place is also, in addition to its more important uses, a park which attracts inhabitants and visitors by its beauty.

The building belongs to the Corinthian order and is constructed with the beautiful American stone called FREESTONE. It is situated on a rise 78 feet above sea level, and is made up of a central building, two wings, and a projection on the west side, with a total length of 352 feet including the wings. The east facade is 65 feet wide, and from it projects a portico of twenty-two columns, each 38 feet high. The great central cupola is 120 feet high, and the rotunda which is formed in the interior is 90 feet in diameter and adorned with sculpture and high relief. In the south wing is the chamber in which the House of Representatives meets. It is circular, 96 feet in diameter and 60 feet high, and is covered by a cupola supported by twenty-four columns of American jasper with capitals of white Italian marble. On the opposite side, in a somewhat similar but smaller chamber, the Senate meets, and on a lower and less ornamented floor the Supreme Court of the United States holds its sessions. There are, besides, seventy rooms for committee meetings and for the offices of congressional employees. A stone wall surrounds the building. A reservoir of gas provides fuel for the six thousand jets which illuminate the spacious monument. At the time I was there they were close to completing the electric light apparatus which will be placed above the cupola on a mast sixteen rods high and should illuminate the city and almost the whole District of Columbia. A perfect symbol, certainly, of the mission of that building, from whose halls goes out the light of intelligence which illuminates the whole nation! Astaburuaga (who was serving as cicerone in the examination of the building) and I remembered that little Chamber of Deputies we had left behind in Chile, into which Representatives are crammed like sardines; or, if we really want to be disrespectful, like excrement in lamb intestines—which reminds one of the old proverb: "Let him be wretched who thinks himself so." The madmen in London, Genoa, and other places in Europe reside in palaces more noble than those that shelter our congresses in South America.

Well, since I have started describing buildings, I will conclude with the few which attract the traveler's attention in the so-called capital of the United States. The *Casa Blanca* ("White House," as the people call it) is the presidential palace and is situated in the still-deserted part of the city at the point where Pennsylvania, Virginia, Connecticut, New York, and Vermont Avenues cross. It is surrounded by a park of twenty acres and is elevated forty-four feet above the river. The facade which serves as an entrance faces north toward Lafayette Park and the one which faces south on the garden dominates the beautiful panorama of the city, the Potomac River, and the Maryland and Virginia shores. On the north facade there is a beautiful portico which rests on four Ionic columns. An exterior row of columns provides cover for the carriages of visitors. The intermediate space is intended for those walking, and an elevated platform leads from both sides to the entrance gate. The interior of the palace is passably decorated, although not as it should be for the President of the United States. The appointments of the palace are modest and even mean in outward appearance. You can see the President walking alone along the beautiful paths of the adjacent garden. There are one or two porters in uniform, the only servants the state puts at his service; the President is not permitted to have a bodyguard. The President receives without ceremony those who wish to see him, and there is one day in the week and two or three special days in the year on which anyone has the right to enter the rooms of the President. On July 4, that day of rejoicing, Lafayette Park is filled with visitors' carriages. These folk get down from their carriages followed by their coachmen, who give a few cents to some helpful lad for watching the horses. On those days the President is truly on exhibit. The coachmen open a passage through the multitude, their hobnailed boots resounding on the marble pavement. Arriving before the President, they extend a calloused hand and squeeze and shake his hand forcefully, looking him in the face, and smiling good-naturedly and with satisfaction. Returning to their horses, they turn every few steps to get a last pleasurable and self-congratulatory peep at the President. Poor President of a democracy!

On the eastern side of the WHITE HOUSE there are some large buildings, and on the western side two more for the offices of the Departments of Treasury, War, and Navy. The General Post Office is a palace in the Corinthian order, and the Treasury boasts a colonnade 457 feet long. The Patent Office, the storehouse of models of inventions, has a portico imitative in its form and extension of the Parthenon in Athens, and will be, when the wings are finished, 400 feet long. The part already finished contains a salon 275 feet long and 65 wide.

In Washington there are, in addition, thirty temples of the various faiths, twelve academies, a university, three banks, two orphan asylums, a municipal building, a hospital, a penitentiary, a theater, and some private buildings which give the infant city some importance. My residence in Washington was one of those oases of happy domestic intimacy—in which the heart plays the great part—so important for him who roams in far-off lands. Señor Carvallo, Envoy Extraordinary of Chile, insisted upon my accepting the hospitality of his Embassy's residence. His wife lavished such attentions on me as to make me feel a member of the family; and if anything was lacking to make me feel at ease, my friend Astaburuaga, the Chilean representative's Secretary, accompanied me about, putting his experience and knowledge of Washington entirely at my disposal. Thus he was able to point out for me on Pennsylvania Avenue, among the young girls passing by that attracted our attention, which was the daughter of a senator, which of a banker, and which a simple dressmaker or other less important person. The simplicity of their dress, their unaccompanied walks and ambles through the streets, and their right to stop and look at anything that strikes their fancy give an idea of American customs and of that liberty which the single woman enjoys here.

My friend Astaburuaga wanted to put me in contact with the editor of the *Washington Intelligencer*, an important newspaper of the capital and very much of the opposition then, since at that moment the Democrats, with Mr. Taylor, dominated the government.* We found him in the country, on land destined for the foundation of a school for whose support a citizen had bequeathed a million and a half dollars. He was surrounded by seven or eight young men who were occupied in discussing the bases, as I later learned, of a grand

* James K. Polk was President at this time. Taylor, a Whig, was elected in 1848.

261

project. Mr. Johnson, the newspaperman, had been chosen to rule over the proceedings as president. We approached to a prudent distance and awaited the end of the session, fearful of being an annoyance, as when our people are praying and you wait until they have crossed themselves before greeting them. The president spoke. Someone answered. A third replied in a severe and cold voice. Having heard all points of view, the president submitted the subject to a vote, counting the twangy voices—YES, YES, NAY, YES, NAY—and declaring which idea had come out supreme. The procedure was repeated several times, and the sharp retorts of YES, NAY, NAY, YES, YES put an end to the matter. Then they came over to Astaburuaga, and, following the customary introductions, as the conversation went on, I learned that they had gathered together there to organize an association whose grand object would be . . . bowling! Oh Yankees!

They had thus proposed, discussed, and resolved by a large majority of two or three votes: first, their president, who would be Mr. Johnson; then the locale, which would be where they were presently gathered; game time, four o'clock in the afternoon; length of the game, rules, arbitration in disputed cases, fines for infractions, etc. Mr. Johnson was and is[3] a citizen of forty years, son of a general in the War of Independence of the same name, well-mannered, and learned, as befits the director of a highly important newspaper.* We passed entire days in heated arguments on one point, over which I had not expected to find differences of opinion in the United States, namely, democracy and republicanism.

[3] Astaburuaga writes me that he is now a government official, and, since the Whig party dominates, at the height of power.

* Johnson may have been Reverdy Johnson, later Postmaster General.

Mr. Johnson was under the thumb of the Democratic Party, which had dominated since the presidency of Polk. He was angry and demoralized by the tyranny of his oppressors, because in the United States the prevailing majority in the government is implacable and intolerant, the curse of the Republic, of democracy, and of that ignorant and brutal license which is adorned with the name liberty. Merit is ignored, that is certain; the public interest is neglected, and that too is certain in many cases; services are forgotten or miserably remunerated, something which is the rule in the United States. In short, the party's interest serves as the criterion and as the scales and measure for judging everyone and everything, charlatanism is preferred over science, and the least justifiable passions serve as the force behind public opinion. All of these defects and many others which deform democracies he passed in review in order to get me to detest that liberty which I showed myself so passionately in favor of. When I persisted in disagreeing with him he said to me with sincerity: "What I want is for you not to delude yourself with this appearance of order, prosperity, and progress and attribute it to the form of government. Under this outward appearance you will find nothing but misery, angry passions, ignorance, and caprice. What I am asking is that you do not go to South America to propose us as the model for a government." Other times, when he was more pacific, he confessed to me that the exasperation which the tyranny of the opposition party caused him, he who was the son of an illustrious general and was by education prepared to occupy a better position in society, at times blinded his reason and made him exaggerate the very real inconveniences of popular government. Despite these quieter moments, we did differ on essential points. He asserted, for example, that liberty in the various nations is an aspect which needs to be reconsidered. Liberty, he felt, engenders license; license brings anarchy; anarchy, despotism. Here there is a difficult moment. While despotism is in the process of consolidating itself, while it is still uncertain, it is cruel, bloodthirsty, and mistrustful. When it is accepted by all it enters into a time of indulgence and tolerance which gives birth to well-being and provides for the development of all the physical and moral faculties of man. With civilization and security liberty develops, the people win their rights one by one, the principle of authority under which they are governed is immediately under debate, and from extreme liberty society passes to license, from there to anarchy, returning to run through that fatal cycle in which the life of nations is eternally enclosed.

The first time this doctrine was expressed its author gave it the pompous title of *scienza nuova*, and it can be supported, using a bit of skill and sagacity, by the history of all peoples, from Greece and Rome down to modern times. This one and that one can be invoked in its support. Polemicizing mightily and disputing the terrain foot by foot, it is possible to interpret each fact to fit this point of view without putting its historical authenticity in doubt.

My argument went by another road. Humanity, I said, is the total of all societies, which have in history their high points, their times of affluence, and their intimate organization. The moral world resembles the physical world. The history of the world is found in the geological layers which reveal the monstrous world that preceded ours. The earth, considered from the poles to the equator, has different gradations of temperature and vegetation. And if we consider it from the valleys to the tops of the mountains, it offers us the same phenomenon of levels of climates and produce.

History, then, is moral geology. Let us see if its different layers indicate improvement and progress. Let us imagine a day long ago when the world was first populated. What do we see? Almost the entire globe immersed in barbarism; powerful empires whose different parts cannot be distinguished one from the other except by the extent of their conquest and violence. At last Greece, a tiny portion of the earth shining with liberty, democracy, the fine arts, and science. Let us not go into details: Rome assimilates Greece, destroys Carthage, and subjects the world. But Rome develops the notion of law and extends its practice over all the civilized world, which is, nevertheless, a small fraction of the globe. As they did with the Greeks and the Egyptians, the Romans absorb or assimilate the barbarians at the extremes of the empire, making them a part of the civilized mass. The Middle Ages is a time of fusion. At the end of the fifteenth century all of Europe is in possession of the conquests made by human thought in four or six thousand years. With the Renaissance come Luther, Galileo, Columbus, Bacon, and others. America is added to the mass of civilized lands, and here the idea of the natural rights of man is put into practice, an idea whose development impregnates even the slag heaps left by the Middle Ages in Europe. All of a sudden we are in the nineteenth century, and we open the world map. Where are the barbarians? They have taken refuge in the islands, are discovered exhausted in Russia and on the steppes of Northern Asia, or are buried in the inaccessible interior of Africa. The civilized world, that which is in possession of liberty or on the road to achieving it, is the major part of humanity, the majority numerically, the majority in terms of moral force, intelligence, and possessions. It has in its possession the richest, most temperate, most productive part of the globe. It has the cannon, the steamboat, and the printing press with which to subjugate, assimilate, or annihilate the remaining savage part of the world. In view of this, why should we subject the social movement of nations to some cycle, comparing them with the truncated, isolated examples which the ancient nations have left us? If there is a cycle, then one must agree that, just as nations passing through it together have immensely improved their condition, so the length of the various phases must be longer. I do not worry too much about the kind of tyranny which will come to weigh on the world from India, the far lands of Russia, and the Rocky Mountains of America within one thousand years.

Now let us look at the nations closely, at their internal organization, although it may not be possible to consider them without relation to historical periods. Let us suppose a town in Italy which has been there since history began: the town of Fiesole, for example, which is Florentine and Tuscan and which has been Roman, Etruscan, Pelasgian, aboriginal, and indigenous—if I am not leaving something out. What were these peoples like, and how are they today? What transformations have they experienced? First they were cannibals; immediately after that they began having human sacrifices in the temples; later they made slaves of their prisoners of war and engaged in pillage and devastation as an industry and occupation; the conquerors divided the conquered soil and people among themselves; aristocracies were born as were slave peoples, an ignorant rabble subject to torture in the tribunals of justice, to misery, and to degradation. Christianity found the world organized thus. Let us now take a look at the world from the vantage point of the nineteenth century and the United States, from the bosom of this democracy which you damn as the prototype of moral and political disorder. There is no war. There are no nobles or aristocracy. There are no common people in the Roman sense. There is only the nation, with equality of rights, with personal industry the only talent necessary for life, with labor-saving machines, railroads, telegraphs, the press, primary schools, academies, asylums, hospitals, penitentiaries, etc. Observe the internal organization of this part of humanity, of this modern Attica which occupies half a continent. And however backward we may think the other nations to be, it does not take much imagination to see that individuals in those societies will also arrive at the same grade of civilization because they will be exposed to the same ideas and the same institutions. When there is a school in a town, a press in the city, a ship on the sea, and an asylum for the sick, democracy and equality begin to exist. The result of all this is that the power of the mass is immense, there are no nations or races properly speaking, and individual liberty in every point of the globe is aided by all of civilized humanity. And when a nation is tending toward the fatal cycle of despotism which you allot to them, the spectacle, the influence, of a hundred other nations which are in a period of liberty will keep them from that course. The first period of the cycle was cannibalism. What people has run through it again once having left it? The last period is democracy. What people has been democratic in the modern sense, and with today's means at its disposal—the press, industry, and the favorable atmosphere of a civilized world around it—and has abandoned this position to found monarchies and aristocracies? The Italian republics?

On this topic Mr. Johnson and I battled without ceasing. At times he said to me: "The American masses would be nothing if every year three hundred thousand savages from Europe were not endlessly poured in like water from the pitcher of the Danaïdes to improve the situation."

"Ah, if you like ourselves in South America had to fight with a mass in which the European, backward as you find him, is the precious and scarce element of civilization and liberty!"

American Art

Fifteen miles from Washington is Mount Vernon, the home and tomb of that great man all of humanity has accepted as a saint. He was great in virtue and the grandest of men for having laid the cornerstone of his nation, the only one in the world which sees its future clearly and which is the ideal of modern nations. I take a description I find at hand of the Yankee sanctuary, that Holy Kaaba I so happily remember:

> After having traveled on horseback for a little while through the forest, which from time to time opened into isolated oases of civilization, my friend showed me a stone buried in the earth alongside the path which, according to him, marked the beginning of the Mount Vernon lands. We went two miles more before we saw the door of the gateman's house. After entering, we covered a distance of almost half a mile, the carriage path continually crossing a varied terrain which was shaded by great trees in full leaf. We crossed a brook and passed through a gully, feeling

ourselves so much in the middle of primitive nature that the sight of the house and the surrounding garden had an effect on my spirit like that of a surprise meeting. The path leads to the west facade of the house. The main door opens on a large room, into which we entered. It was not habit but a more profound feeling that made me take off my hat and walk carefully as though I were on sacred ground. . . . The rooms of the house are spacious and have a certain elegance, though the decor is simple. Everything the eye embraces among those public relics seems to breathe sanctity, and everything is preserved almost as Washington left it. Every American, especially young people who visit this place, experiences a strong feeling which will last all his life. . . . At some distance from the house, in an out-of-the-way place, is the new tomb of the family, a simple structure of brick with an iron gate through whose bars two white marble sarcophagi can be made out standing side by side, which contain the remains of Washington and his wife. The old family tomb was in a more picturesque place, on a hill overlooking the Potomac, but the present location is quieter and conforms more closely to the desires of that modest man.

How much subtle artistry is in the placement of this tomb, how much grandeur in its being so hidden, and how American and national is that accompaniment of primitive forests, wild brooks, and gullies! This is the art of the home of Washington, the American planter, that genius of a democracy which had just begun to take possession of nature. Hadrian was appropriately laid to rest in what is today the Castel Sant' Angelo; Raphael equally well in the Rotunda of Agrippa, which he himself had erected on pillars in Saint Peter's; Napoleon, also, under the dome of the Invalides. But the spirit of Washington could never have rested had it been denied the sight and shade of the ancient trees of the forest which surround his home and the combination of the land in its natural state with the fruits of his own labor.

Washington, the hero of American independence, the founder of this positive-minded nation of workers, was destined also to inspire a love of the fine arts in the sons of the Puritans and return this group, led astray by religious concerns, to the path humanity has always walked, from the strange fetishes which man worshiped in his infancy to the pyramids of Egypt, the Roman Colosseum, the Parthenon, and the more modern Saint Peter's. The ruins of Palenque and the sculptures found by Stephens in Central America are just like the statues of Michelangelo or the paintings of Raphael. They are pages from that book which describes the day when each nation became conscious of itself and desirous of perpetuating some memory of its past in stone or bronze; when it began to see its place in history and decided to leave to coming generations monuments, statues, and public works which required centuries to complete. Sometimes it seems to me that the Egyptians made the captive Hebrews work so hard in the construction of pyramids and other monuments that when the slaves rose up and took to the desert they remembered the beatings their oppressors had given them, and swore that in the promised land the construction of monuments and the erection of statues would be prohibited. How else can we explain the horror of temples and images shown by Moses, that disciple of Egyptian priests? Art is the fulfillment of man, is man himself. Although as with the other animals it is not necessary to his existence, it is, nevertheless, his most constant preoccupation—just as much among the savages as at the heights of civilization. It seems to me that Rome died suffocated by monuments; that they are the goal of the great cities of history; and that Paris will surely completely cover its terrain with public monuments, so that by the end of time the people will go underground, there not being space for them on the surface of the earth. When the first Christians, fleeing persecution, hid themselves in the catacombs of Rome, it seems to me that the exchanged environments were not dissimilar. The exploration of those immense caverns and caves shows the archaeologist today the remains of three centuries of primitive Christian art, testimony that for three centuries, and until the destruction of the monumental city by Attila, the Roman masses lived hidden in these catacombs, where they had their temples, subterranean plazas, markets, and cemeteries. It is ridiculous to think that in a city there should live hidden for three hundred years hundreds of thousands of inhabitants, who were constantly in contact with the outside for their necessities.

Mohammed and the Protestants will probably not distinguish themselves through originality in the fine arts. These two protesting groups reminds us in their works of Moses' reaction against pyramids because of the bad treatment received by the Hebrews, who developed a permanent antipathy to piling up stones.

The Americans believe they have no vocation for art and affect a disdain for art as the fruit of old and corrupt societies. Nevertheless, I have surprised a profound and exquisite feeling for the beautiful and the great in this people who are leaving all their works half-done or incomplete behind them in their race for material wel-

271

fare. Is there anything of value disqualified from inclusion in the lovely ideal of moral beauty? What people in this world has felt so profoundly the need for comfort, for decency, for leisure, for welfare, for cultivating intelligence? What people has been more horrified at the spectacle of the ugliness, poverty, ignorance, drunkenness, and physical and moral degradation which covers European societies and is the first thing one notes there? In Rome, from behind monuments and basilicas, well-cared-for hands extend begging for alms.

I will not speak of the hotels, banks, churches, wharves, and aqueducts which assume monumental forms all over the Union. Nor will I speak of the columns and obelisks of great grandeur and height which are being raised up in Boston, Philadelphia, and New York in honor of Washington and Franklin. All of these are artistic examples or, rather, products, but they do not demonstrate the American idea of art. The European immigrants who came two centuries ago, and those coming now, by necessity and as a means of earning a living communicate the artistic skills which they possess. But this is not American art. I assign that name only to the manifestation of that constant and continuous aspiration of a people for a national ideal which exists and is revealed in each man in successive generations. I call art not the levels of civilization of the nations but the ways in which the genius or national character takes tangible forms and affects history. What was Roman art? Without doubt this name should not be given to the different orders of architecture or to the statuary and other decorations whose forms were adopted from the Greeks; the Romans imitated, assimilated, and conformed to the Greek ideas in their public works. I call Roman art that grandiose vision which led to the creation of the Baths, the Colosseum, the tomb of Hadrian, the aqueducts of Segovia, and the amphitheater of Nîmes; that monumental spirit which dominated nature and overcame the obstacles she put in the way of continuous and smooth expansion as well as the permanence of the grand and persevering Roman artistic ideal—which was the incorporation of all the known world under the dominion of her laws and the adoption of the religions, civilizations, and customs of all these peoples. An internal revolution—the rise of the masses—and an external one—the incorporation of the barbarians—destroyed the works of the Romans; trying to digest all of the world at once, Rome was destroyed by a superabundance which its body could not tolerate.

Perhaps the Yankees are in danger of succumbing to the crisis of an internal change just as dangerous as the rising of the Roman masses. Everyone today is afraid that this colossus of a civilization, so complete and so vast, may die in the convulsions which will attend the emancipation of the Negro race, a menacing possibility and yet as foreign to American civilization in its essence as it would be foreign to the laws of the universe if one of those thousands of comets that wander through space should crash against our planet some day and make it explode.

Where, then, is the American artistic genius? In a modest little house not far from the Capitol in Washington, my friend Astaburuaga, who had brought me to that sanctum, and I were shown, on a buffet made of unvarnished pine, a model of a monument to be erected to the memory of the hero of America. The construction will consist of a large Ionic building from whose center will rise an obelisk. According to the scale model, its total height will be two meters more than the pyramid of Cheops in Egypt. The architecture is a more or less happy combination of known forms and styles inherited from all the civilized peoples. That in the monument which is illustrative of Yankee genius is the height, that is, the national desire to boldly surpass the entire human species, all civilizations of all centuries. Two meters higher than the highest monument built by man! Here is the characteristic quality of these people, their feeling for the grand and their understanding that they are without rival, sentiments which have preceded or accompanied the greatest epochs the human species has known. The people who constructed the pyramids obeyed this same impulse. It was behind the idea of making Mount Athos into a statue of Alexander, whose hand would hold the sources of a river. It was the inspiration for Nero's colossal palace and the neighboring Colosseum, and directed the construction of Saint Peter's in Rome, the road through Simplon Pass, etc., etc.

The idea of erecting a monument to Washington has been embraced in the Union with feverish enthusiasm, for the simple reason that it appeals to the national desire to surpass the other nations.[4] You see this spirit in naval architecture. A ship of under 2,500 tons does not deserve the name, nor will it be eligible as an example of national pride. What would Columbus, who crossed the ocean in brigs of 80 tons, have said if he had seen floating over the waters these monsters that can hide in their bosoms fifty thousand quintals of ice or granite? (Quarried granite and ice are two export items in which the Americans carry on a commerce in the millions.)

---

[4] The construction of the monument is already underway and amazingly advanced, according to the newspapers. In 1847 not even the foundations were laid out yet, which gives some indication of the Yankee's speed in execution, another of his skills.

About ten years ago the Yankees were obsessed with the idea of crossing the American continent with a railroad from New York to Oregon, uniting the Atlantic with the Pacific and interposing themselves between Europe and Asia so that they could pass to the English with the right hand that which they obtained on the coasts of China and Japan with the left.[5] Certainly the Americans have invented neither the railroad, the ship, nor the Ionic order, but theirs are the colossal applications and perfections which are every day being put into use. If they have not been able to invent new architectural orders, something of the national character has been added to the known ones, as in the installation of the previously mentioned statues of Franklin holding the lightning bolt atop cupolas and in the use of the ear of corn as a crown and finial, instead of the traditional pine cone. The train station, the viaduct, the bridge, the hotel, and other constructions which our times require are being given in the United States architectural forms unknown in past centuries and a distinctive character is being stamped on every class of monument.

The economic aspect of the Washington Monument is another sign of the artistic genius of the Yankees. That colossal work is going up by means of a popular subscription of only a few copper coins per individual. Thus, year after year, the nation en masse lays at the foot of the monument to that great man, that representative of the national ideal, a spontaneous tribute of gratitude and praise. On this score the other nations of the world cannot compete. All the world's monuments

[5] This idea was present long before the acquisition of California (though it was one of the underlying factors behind the War with Mexico by which that conquest was made) and before the expectation of putting themselves in direct contact with China and India.

have been built of tears and inequities. Even Saint Peter's in Rome speaks not of *gloriam Dei* but of the perversity and the extortions of His ministers. For two thousand years, Rome's monuments have represented the blood and the spoils of the earth. Versailles, the Escorial, the Arc de Triomphe, all the monuments in the world protest against the despotism whose whim and vain ostentation produced them. But the Washington Monument is as pure as the immortal idea it represents. Generations will go on embellishing it year after year for centuries without a sad memory to grieve the spirit of the spectator, who will be pleased rather than awed. Today twenty million happy citizens, tomorrow one hundred, dedicate a small part of their labor to the task of consecrating the most important of historical mementos. This is the highest personification of moral dignity which has been offered to the human species. What is Napoleon seen from this point of view? He is the last and the most sublime of those bandits who have razed the earth and covered it with dead, and he did this in order to pit his pride against that work of social perfection which he destroyed along with the Republic. What is Washington, buried alongside his wife in an obscure and solitary corner of his home? He is the genius of modern humanity, the symbol of an era which is dawning and which is already marking for the world the path to justice, equality, and hard work which it shall follow.

Decorating the interior of the Washington Monument will be stones and inscriptions sent by all of the states of the Union, by its cities, and by scientific, philanthropic, and even industrial companies and societies.[6] The practice of popular and spontaneous contribution

---

[6] California has already sent her quartzes intermingled with gold.

for the realization of a national ideal constitutes, in my opinion, the clearest example of a national artistic sentiment. I do not know if there have ever been people in Europe who have become passionate en masse about the realization of an ideal, unless it be the French of a certain class or the Catholic artisans' guilds of the Middle Ages. But in the United States, if this feeling is not yet developed throughout all of the nation, it is (far from disappearing, as did the Christian interest in beauty of the Middle Ages) just beginning to grow, and every day it takes more obvious forms. There is no city of any importance in the United States which does not have a rudimentary museum in which works of art, curiosities brought by explorers, objects of natural history, and even grotesque presentations of scenes which took place at sea or at other points and which have interested the public are barbarously mixed together. These collections are shown to the curious for an admission fee, and that fee forms the capital which is incessantly employed in enriching, beautifying, and completing the collections in order to attract more and more interest. During my stay in New York a beautiful statue of carrara marble, executed in Rome by Poper,* a young American artist of rare ability, was on exhibition. The statue represents a captive Georgian, a Venus in chains. For the Puritans this may have been the first time they had seen displayed one of these nude female forms which are so common to the museums of Italy and France and which ennoble modesty. The first few days there was a great scandal, but finally the prigs lifted their eyes and accustomed themselves to contemplating the artistic

---

* Sarmiento must be referring to *The Greek Slave*, by Hiram Powers. Powers went to Italy in 1837 to spend the rest of his life, and his *Greek Slave*, which was modeled in 1843, caused a sensation in the United States.

277

beauty in that looking glass of marble. The result was that the exhibition of the statue produced thousands of dollars for the artist in a few months. When the curiosity of New York was sated, the statue took to the railroad and went from city to city exhibiting itself to the coarse eyes of the people, collecting hard cash in exchange for shocks, whispers, and appreciations. The artist obtained in compensation for his talent more than Canova or Horace Vernet ever obtained for their most famous *capi d'opera*. This state of affairs offers to American art the most powerful stimulus and a more resounding glory than the kings of the earth, who supported the fine arts with sums that were not theirs to spend and who made the sweat of peoples flow to satisfy their own pleasures, have ever been able to concede. This is no paradox. It is a fact that the money collected by citizens, women included, in voluntary subscriptions in the United States to pay for the projects of the Cincinnati astronomers far exceeds the funds given by the English government for the same purpose. The day is not far off, then, when great European artists will come to exhibit their masterpieces for profit throughout the United States, gathering thousands of dollars while the national taste is educated, as well as enjoying the ovation which the people, already competent judges of art, give to talent. Singers and dancers are beginning to indicate the road which painters and sculptors will later follow. So congenial is the atmosphere for the arts in America that many years ago there was a magnificent theater constructed on a ship which went about giving shows on the riverbanks and visiting towns and cities of importance.

Americans have public and private customs which should help the development of the arts. The active lives they lead and their business activities force them to travel continuously; they display a certain need for excitement, to go and to do, which sends them off on a pilgrimage to Niagara Falls, or to the Lakes, or to the cities on the coast. The old part of the Union exerts a great moral influence over the population of the interior, since it is the center of intellectual and commercial activity, the point of contact with other nations, and the site of the government; and since all the families of the interior are originally from the old states, eyes are always turned toward former homes, the lack of certain pleasures to which elders were accustomed embellishing these memories.

Washington, the nominal capital of the Union, will in the near future, without doubt, take advantage of these tendencies of the national character, if the Capitol, the Museum of Inventions, and the monument put up for Washington are accompanied by other attractions which at last make of the capital a center of spectacles which will excite the curiosity of travelers and awaken nationalism. As the residence of senators, of departmental secretaries and other high functionaries, and of representatives of other nations, Washington should be able to beautify its night life with the opera, the drama, and the ballet, assuming religious ideas do not put strong obstacles in the way.

Add to all this the fact that the sentiment of unity, centralization, and organization struggles at a disadvantage against local and individual energy, which is the basis of the political organization of that country and the product of the Protestant spirit. I know of no institution, unless it is the BOARD of Education of Massachusetts, that has finally succeeded in overcoming local resistance and parochial ideas with regard to education, stamping a scientific and systematic influence on the general education of the state. Could this influence be extended over all of the Union and come from one official center? If that should happen, which would take time, you would have to say that a radical revolution had taken place in the lives of these people. The movement for reform and systematization in primary education began in Boston; New York, Maine, and the other states, including the Western ones, later took up the struggle, but each one applied the ideas in their own way and adopted measures in accord with the consensus of feeling. It is impossible that those states will finally end up with identical legislation, without having their institutions in common or being linked to a common center. The civilization and power of the United States are equal to the sum of the civilization and power of the individuals who make it up, but that sum, represented by the national government, is not as our Latin ideas of government dictate. Statistics, monuments—all is done by independent groups, and such is the idea of the negation of the personality of the nation that after a war the ships, guns, and cannons which served to make the national power effective are sold at public auction.

Despite this, Americans claim a national art, defining it as those artistic products produced by ingenious Americans, a puny idea for a nation so cosmopolitan and made up of the old European peoples. The Americans ought, as a nation, to undertake the conquest of the artistic treasures of Europe. Every day sales of private collections are announced in Venice, in Genoa, and in Florence which include Titians, Riberas, Carraccis, and even Raphaels. The French have sacked Spain of the works of Zurbarán, Murillo, and Velázquez, and even Ireland has been enriched by artistic treasures, while barbaric United States consuls do not even feel Marcellus' temptation on seeing the statues of Corinth. One hundred thousand dollars annually, designated for the acquisition of works of the old and modern masters, would take care of laying the foundation for a future American art. In France, so advanced is that nation in the fine arts (more so than is Italy), it is felt necessary to have copies at least of the great examples of foreign art. Washington should have perfect imitations to teach with; like a school, it should have a Rotunda of Agrippa, a Parthenon of Athens, a Cathedral of Rouen as the model of the Gothic, and a half dozen more celebrated buildings. In this way this useless village which rebels against time and the progress that is aggrandizing and beautifying all the other American cities, from what you can see of them, will be converted into an artistic capital. For Washington, not being a commercial center, nor having political activity indigenous and natural to it, but only that which comes from outside, is condemned to insignificance if she does not take advantage of the only area in which she can organically be the leader: that of art and monuments which will attract the nation to a common center for vanity, glory, and veneration.

There is already in Washington an establishment which attracts the attention of all the nation, a place which is visited daily like a national school. The Patent Office contains in its museum of models the history of progress in the industrial arts. Up to 1844, 13,523 patents for inventions or improvements have been granted, 531 in the year 1843 alone. In this branch of the intelligent activity of the country the Yankees have behaved exactly as they should act in everything having to do with culture, namely: first, importing; then pillaging the other nations to enrich their knowledge with data; and then going to work. The results have not been long in coming. In an extract from "Reports on Exportation of Machinery" made in 1841 to the House of Commons in England,* where it was asked whether England relied to any important extent on foreign inventions in machinery, this question was answered thus: "One could say that the greater part of the new inventions lately introduced in the factories of this country come from abroad; but it should be understood that these are not improvements in machines, but entirely new inventions. Certainly there are many perfected processes emanating from this country, but I am afraid that the majority of the really new inventions, that is, ideas entirely new in the application of certain processes, by new machines, or by new means, have their origin abroad and principally *in America*."

This confession by England of her sterility with regard to machinery and of the fruitful invasion by her young rival is like the mournful wail of the shipwrecked, who know that there is no possibility of aid forthcoming. The United States today is invading the world, not yet with products and inventions, but with engineers, craftsmen, and machinists who are going to demonstrate the art of producing much for little cost, daring all and realizing marvels.

I have gone on about this strange artistic backwardness, the consequence of inherited preoccupations, because not only in the practical arts but also in intellectual works the Americans are beginning to take their place in the world. You are familiar with Cooper, Washington Irving, Prescott, Bancroft, and Sparks as histori-

* *Sessional Papers of the House of Commons* (Great Britain, 1841), VII.

ans of the first rank on American subjects, some of them venturing to undertake the explanation of events in European history. But the number of writers of renown who have dealt with more speculative subjects such as philosophy, economics, politics, and theology is even greater. It is enough to say that, in the twelve years from 1830 to 1842, 106 original works of biography were published; 118 books on American history and geography; 91 in the same fields on other countries; 10 on philosophy; 103 books of poetry; and 115 novels. In almost the same period of time 382 original American works have been reprinted in England and accepted by that same public which twenty years before asked through the medium of a magazine: "Who reads American books?" Orators and statesmen of the caliber of Everett, Webster, Calhoun, and Clay can be matched only in England and France, it being worthwhile to note that brilliance in historical works and in elocution is beginning to be, as in France, the ladder which leads to power and influence over public opinion. Travelers, naturalists, archaeologists interested in American phenomena, geologists, and astronomers, who undertake the enrichment and even the making over of science, are relatively abundant, showing by the results they obtain in their projects that they are very much more advanced than Europe, not being able to observe them closely, would have believed.

You will tell me that this account of the intellectual progress of the Americans has nothing to do with Washington, the desert capital. But where can the nation's history be stored, and how can it be given body and unity if a center for this is not developed?

My stay in Washington was prolonged a day longer

than the time agreed upon with Arcos, as we had arranged to meet finally on a certain date in a place I had suggested, the Hotel United States in Harrisburg.

I returned to Baltimore and there got on the train to Harrisburg. Arriving in that city, I inquired the whereabouts of the Hotel United States. I was shocked to learn that there was no hotel by that name in Harrisburg! As there is a Hotel United States in every American city, I had made an appointment with my future traveling companion to meet him in a place I had supposed to exist in Harrisburg. With much trouble I was able to find out Arcos' whereabouts, as he had left written in the register of the hotel near the station these laconic words addressed to me: "I'll be waiting for you in Chambersburg." Very disgruntled and mournful at this turn of events, I traveled to Chambersburg, where, after going through all the inns with growing anxiety, I was able to find no one who could give me information on the person I was looking for. What made it worse was that Arcos spoke English with a rare perfection, putting on a twang just for the mischief of it when addressing Americans. So not even those who may have spoken to him were able to give me news of the young Spaniard for whom I inquired in an English which shivered the timbers of the poor Yankees. I clung to the hope that perhaps he was nearby, hunting, a camping trip in the Allegheny mountains being included in our program for the trip. At last I learned of a note he had left me at the station in which he repeated the same sort of message as in Harrisburg: "I'll be waiting for you in Pittsburgh." "*Malheureux!*" I exclaimed in distress. Fifty leagues from Chambersburg to Pittsburgh, the Alleghenies in between, ten dollars for the stagecoach, and I did not have more than three or four in my pocket, barely enough to pay for the hotel in which I was lodged! I learned, upon asking the details of the indiscreet departure of my elusive precursor, that, not having a seat on the inside of the stagecoach, he had been put on the bag of hay which is carried on top for the horses' food, and that he had traveled in this way two days and two nights, driven to such a sacrifice by the restlessness of youth, which made him incapable of staying in one place for eight hours, the time between trains. Here I was, then, in the heart of the United States, "inland" as they say, without means, making myself understood with great difficulty, and surrounded by those impassive and frozen American faces. What a fright and what afflictions I experienced in Chambersburg! Every other minute I called the owner of the hotel and explained my situation to him by mouth and pen. "A young man who has gone on ahead has my money without knowing that I do not have enough for travel costs. They are asking ten dollars for the trip at the station, and I have no more than four and I need that to pay for the hotel. But I have some objects of intrinsic value in my bag and I would like the station to retain them as collateral until I get to Pittsburgh." The innkeeper, on hearing this sad story, shrugged his shoulders as all the answer he meant to offer. I told the master of the station of my misfortune and he remained looking at me as though I had not said anything. Two days of continual supplication and desperation had already passed, and to make things worse there were no seats on the stagecoach. They were all reserved by people who used this service to complement the railroad terminating at Philadelphia. Finally, they suggested that I write to Arcos by the electric telegraph, which I did in forty words for four reales and in the most feeling way.

Regardless of the laconic nature of such messages, I began mine in this way: "Don't be an animal!"—and I told him of everything that had befallen me because of his indiscretion. "Where is the person you are addressing?" "In the Hotel United States," I answered, suddenly full of doubts that there would be a hotel of that name in Pittsburgh, and, in order to not let myself in for more misery, I asked that they look for him in all of the prominent hotels of the city.

My impatience and fear of not catching up with the rat probably made the reply take longer. I did not take my eyes off the little machine which with repeated raps continually indicated the passage of messages to other points, which were not received here, not being preceded by the word Chambersburg and the normal warning sound calling the attention of the operator. "I am going to inquire," he told me, and when he touched his instrument the little raps of long and short duration began again, the magnetic key tracing fifty leagues away the question being put in Chambersburg. "What news is there of the youth Arcos we asked about?" A moment later—the Chambersburg attention signal! "They're answering," the operator said, drawing up to the machine. The Chambersburg key began putting marks on the strip of paper which the cylinder feeds out little by little. What I would have given to be able to read those characters which consist of dots and dashes, stamped on the white surface of the paper by pressure! When the operation had concluded, he took the strip of paper and read: "He cannot be located anywhere. He is being searched for again." Two hours later a new interrogation, a new martyrdom of waiting for a yes or no on which depended my salvation or my end, and again, and more definite this time: "There is no such individual!"

I felt as though I had been hit by a bolt of lightning. Interested in my fate and making various conjectures, the hotel man happened to mention the word Philadelphia. "What do you mean, Philadelphia?" I interrupted. "Pittsburgh is where Arcos is and where they should have been looking for him." "We'll take care of it," he answered. "Since it is in Philadelphia that the stagecoach is paid for, the telegraph operator thought it was there that you wanted them to look for him. BUT NO MATTER, I am going to correct the error." Heading for the office, he suddenly stopped and, pointing to the door, said: "They're closed already—until eight in the morning." The great passions of the spirit cannot properly express themselves except in one's native tongue, and, although English has a passable GODDAM for special occasions, I preferred to use Spanish, which is so round and sonorous as to be just the thing for launching a proper howl of rage. The Yankees are little accustomed to manifestations of southern passion, and the hotelkeeper, hearing me curse with terrific excitement in a foreign language, looked at me astonished. Making a sign with his hand, as if he were trying to stop me before I bit them all or committed suicide, he ran out into the street, looking, no doubt, for some constable to take me into custody. That was all I needed! And the thought suddenly brought back the composure which, in the grip of my affliction, I had lost for a moment. Minutes later he entered again, accompanied by a person who wore a pen behind his ear and who coldly asked me, first in English, then in French, and finally with a few words of Spanish, the cause of my excitement,

287

of which the innkeeper had given him an idea. I told him briefly what had happened to me, indicating my origins and my destination, and pleading for his intercession with the station so that they would take my watch and other objects as collateral until I had repaid my fare in Pittsburgh. That individual listened to me without one muscle of his impassive face moving, and, when I had finished speaking, said to me in French: "Sir, the only thing I can do (what an introduction, I said to myself, swallowing hard)—the only thing I can do is to pay for the hotel and your trip to Pittsburgh on the condition that, when you arrive in that city, you pay at the Merchants-Manufacturers Bank to the account of Lesley and Co. of Chambersburg the amount which you feel you need here." I found it necessary to take in a lot of air before answering him: "My dear sir, thank you, but you don't know me, and if I can give you some guarantee. . . ." "That's not necessary. Persons in your situation never cheat," and with these words he took leave of me until later. At once I went and ate a real's worth of apples, my hunger awakened by the series of incidents through which I had passed during the past three days. I took advantage of the afternoon to examine the city and suburbs. I needed to walk, to use my limbs in order to believe in and feel master of myself. In the early evening my guardian angel reappeared, loaded with books. He brought me a work by Quevedo, another by Tasso, in Italian, and one or two miscellanies in French to distract me. He stayed with me for a few moments speaking alternately in Spanish and in French. He told me he was familiar with Latin and Greek, inquired about certain details of my trip, and wished me good night upon leaving.

The following day he returned and gave me four

five-dollar bills, despite my insistence on returning one to him as being unnecessary. Then, as he was leaving, he returned, saying almost embarrassedly: "Pardon me, sir, but I find another bill in my pocket which I would like you to add to the others." This man had exceeded the sum I needed, because, figuring everything, only ten dollars was necessary. I understood the delicate feeling which motivated him and I resisted the bill only weakly, finally accepting it cordially. The stagecoach left at last, and my usually calm spirits returned; I was pleased at having had the opportunity, though so painful for me, of inspiring an example of such nobility and decency as that of that gentleman, Lesley. The night came on, the placid moon appeared on the horizon, and the stagecoach slowly began to climb the Allegheny Mountains. When we had arrived at the highest point some passengers got out and a feminine voice inside the coach said in French: "They are getting out to see the view, which is beautiful." Taking advantage of this opportunity, I got out behind the others and was able to enjoy one of the most beautiful and peaceful spectacles in nature. The Allegheny Mountains are covered to their peaks with thick, leafy vegetation. The tops of the trees on the lower hills, illuminated from above by the rays of the moon, seemed to be a nebulous blue sea, which, as the spectator changed his position, undulated in silent, dark waves. One felt the excitement there of seeing familiar objects which cannot be distinctly discerned because the eyes are not powerful enough or the light uncertain or flickering.

When we arrived at an inn, after continuing the journey, the same voice, again in French, said: "Here you can get down and eat something. We will be going all night without stopping." I got down, therefore, and, a woman presenting herself at the door, I offered her a hand in support. In a little while we took our seats again to continue the trip. I began to feel sleepy when the same voice as before, that of the woman, said to me timidly: "I believe, sir, that you have been in some difficulty." "Me? No, madame," I answered peremptorily, the conversation ending there. But while I was thinking about this question, the lady added with obvious embarrassment: "Excuse me, sir, if I have put an indiscreet question to you, but this morning in Chambersburg I found myself by chance in a room from which I could not help hearing what you were saying to a gentleman." "That is true, madame, but you must know, then, that everything was straightened out." "And what are you thinking of doing, sir, if you do not find your friend in Pittsburgh?" "You frighten me, madame, with your question. I have not thought of this, and I tremble to think that such a thing is possible. I would return to New York or Washington where I have some acquaintances." "And why not continue your voyage?" "How can I move further on into an unknown country without funds?" "I say this to you because my house is five leagues this side of New Orleans, and I can make it available to you. From there you can try to find your friend, and if you cannot locate him you can write to your country and wait until they send you what you need." The noble action of Mr. Lesley had apparently been contagious. That lady had heard all, and she wished to do her part too. This reflection came to me first, touched as I was by such kindness, before another came to me which would have attributed her behavior to her sex. The lady told me at once, perhaps reading my mind, that six weeks ago she had lost her husband and that she was going to New Orleans to settle the business of their house there. She was accompanied by her little nine-year-old daughter, and both of them were dressed in deep mourning. It was the mother, then, and not the woman, who offered her domestic asylum to an unknown person, who probably had a mother of his own. Obedient to this idea, which sanctified the offer and its acceptance, I treated this lady with less reserve from then on, sure, nevertheless, that the difficulty she had foreseen would not occur.

When we arrived in Pittsburgh, the lady let me know that she would be leaving by steamboat and that, if I were to accept her offer, I would have to take passage on the same boat. I went out looking for Arcos in the Hotel United States, for where else was I to find him if not there? Fortunately for me there was indeed a Hotel United States in Pittsburgh, where I found my Arcos at that moment engaged in writing an announcement for the newspapers advising me of his whereabouts to clear himself of what he was beginning to regard as his foolishness in causing my delay. I approached him, disposed to reprimand him in a friendly but serious manner, but he put on a face so comically anguished upon seeing me that I just burst out laughing and we shook hands. We left together immediately, and I told him of my adventures as we walked along. We headed for the steamboat *Martha Washington*, on which the lady had taken passage, in order to thank her and make sure she knew I had come out all right and did not leave anxiously concerned that I had been left stranded. We had no more than set foot in the spacious salon of the boat when the lady got up from the opposite side of the room. She had been waiting for me, and coming toward me with the pretense of shaking hands, she tried to slip me a little purse full of gold. Without accepting it, I presented her to the fine friend who was accompanying me and who was the cause of all my tragedies, and both of us thanked her a million times for her kindness. We separated in Cincinnati never to see each other again, and, as if ingratitude were the compensation for such disinterested behavior, I have forgotten her name.

Cincinnati

From Pittsburgh, which I had no time to examine, the steamboat takes the traveler for $5 to Cincinnati, 458 miles down the Ohio. This magnificent river provides the state with a name, even though it begins to be navigable in Pennsylvania. In another place I have spoken of the richness of that privileged land, where, over immeasurable beds of bituminous coal, great stretches of forest and cultivated lands extend, interrupted by mountains which guard iron in their flanks and from whose sides flow waterways like the Ohio which are linked to the Mississippi and her tributaries, bringing the world within reach of her factories.

To give you some idea of the astonishing growth of the State of Ohio, I should begin with the *sicut erat in principio*, that is, the aspect of the country up to just yesterday. This state has 40,000 square miles and extends from the Ohio River to Lake Erie on the north. The southern and eastern portion of the land is flat and very fertile. The rest, more hilly, has beautiful valleys, savannahs, swamps, and rough ground. It is estimated that there are 35,000 square miles of arable land; the rest is marshy, rocky, and sterile. Until 1840 there were less than 12,000 miles under cultivation. The first settlement was made in 1788 in Marietta. The Christian population of the state in 1802 was 50,000. In 1810 it had increased to 230,760; in 1820 to 937,679; and in 1840 to more than 1,500,000. Today it has more than 2,000,000 inhabitants. The following comparison is not mine; I have copied it from a little book: "It is said that the territory of the United States is one-ninth or, at most, one-eighth of the part of the continent colonized by the Spaniards. Nevertheless, in all of those vast regions conquered by Cortés and Pizarro there are no more than two million inhabitants of pure Spanish blood, so that they do not surpass by very much the population which Ohio has accumulated in half a century and are much behind in wealth and civilization." If the observation is not correct in every way, the increase in population of Spanish America from that time is still without doubt infinitely less. The populations of Mexico and the Argentine Republic have decreased. It is clear that it is an unwritten article of the political constitutions of the new South American states always to ignore how many bipeds inhabit the country. Someday our government will know officially how many stars there are in the sky, just as restless children strip a rose to know how many petals it has, but ascertain the number of inhabitants in the country, fi donc! A government descend to such mean details! In the United States everything depends upon the decennial census and the registry of property, and their results have administrative certainty. It is calculated that the census will yield twenty-two million in 1850;[7] twenty-nine million in 1860; thirty-eight million in 1870; fifty million in 1880; seventy million in 1890; and eighty million in 1900. There may be an error of some ten or twenty million in all.

[7] On carrying it out, they have found there are more than twenty-three million inhabitants.

The value of the products of Ohio rose in 1840 to something like twenty million dollars, including five million in meats and domestic animals and five million in manufactured articles. As the population of that state is approximately the same as they say Chile has (the actual figure in Chile is a secret known only to God), Chile should have been producing twenty million dollars every year, assuming it has a million and a half inhabitants. Not content with the facilities that their river offers them, the Ohioans have opened seven navigable canals which are spread out over the country. In 1834 these took in $88,000 and in 1844 $172,659—that is, twice the previous year's amount, evidence that the quantity of products doubled from one year to the next.

The state is for the most part populated with new immigrants, especially Germans and Irish, as well as many from other nations. These farmers are increasing in number every day and form a majority over the Yankees *pur sang*, which means that they always win the elections, all people of foreign origin supporting the Democratic Party. This makes the Puritans despair, for the Europeans are generally very ignorant and, many of them being Catholics from Ireland (who do not have a monopoly on brains), they oppose useful improvements and neglect to contribute for schools, canals, and roads. They show the greatest indifference to the arrival of letters and periodicals, "at the same time," says an author, "as they are always disposed to give their votes to the demagogues who would be quick to submerge the country in the most violent course of political change." The same thing goes on in our countries and makes me believe that the more ignorant people are and the less disposed to advance improvements useful to the nation, the more they aspire to political change. They are like those lame animals that leave the beaten path to find something better and head for rocky and broken ground.

To arouse these undisciplined democrats there is *Stump oratory*, called this because of the custom of popular candidates mounting the stump of a tree to speak to a rough audience. An English traveler refers in these terms to the speech which one of these personages read him:

A farmer who came on board the train at Worcester spoke with vehemence against the new tariff, saying that the agriculturalists of the West were being sacrificed to the manufacturers of New England, who wanted to compel them to buy their ready-made goods, while the primary materials of Ohio and the West are excluded from the market of England. He praised the advantages he enjoys in the United States, sympathizing with the masses of the English people, deprived of their political rights and exposed to the oppression and tyranny of the rich. With the design of distracting him, I told him that the day before I had seen in the city of Columbus a minister preaching in the Welsh dialect before a congregation of three hundred persons, that these and other poor Irish and German farmers were ignorant of American laws and institutions and were persons without any education, and I asked why they had been permitted to have their way and dominate the elections as I knew they had just done in Ohio? On this topic a speech sprang from him whose theme was the equality of rights of all men, the division which some were trying to establish between the old and the new farmers, the good policy of receiving immigrants when the population was scarce, the advantage of common schools, and, finally, the evil in endowing universities which, he said, are *nests of aristocrats.*

This popular hatred for universities does not change the fact that there are very well-endowed universities in Athens, Oxford, and Willoughby, 7 colleges in various other cities, various theological institutions, 75 academies, and 5,200 schools.

The principal city of the state is Cincinnati, whose population numbers approximately fifty thousand. It is situated in the opening of a lovely valley formed by hills which ascend gradually to a height of three hundred feet, adorned by groups of trees and even spots of forest on their flanks. The city is situated on two embankments, one of which is fifteen or twenty rods higher than the other. At the port the beach is covered with flagstones down to the river, and there are wharves which rise and fall with the tide. The streets are shaded by trees and well filled with buildings. The city's communications with the interior are aided by canals which link it with Lake Erie and the Wabash Canal. There are in addition railways, macadam roads, and local roads. The Whitewater Canal extends for seventy miles into the interior. It is interesting to realize what can be accomplished in just thirty years, so I will tell you that this city was recognized as such in 1819, having been founded as a village in 1789. From its port steamboats depart daily for Pittsburgh and downriver for St. Louis and New Orleans. In all directions, stagecoaches bridge the distance between neighboring cities. There are forty churches, a theater, a museum, an office for the sale of public lands, four markets, and a town hall. The city obtains its water, which is raised by powerful steam engines, from the river.

But what most distinguishes Cincinnati is the growing number of literary, scientific, and philanthropic societies of which I will make brief mention, especially since, from now on, I will be abstaining from going into these details. I am pleased to enumerate the elements which enter into the composition of American life and society, even in these brand new states, because the comparison can be a useful lesson for our compatriots. An English traveler, Robertson,[8] speaking of Corrientes and Entre Rios in the Argentine Republic, says: "I am astonished on contemplating these beautiful lands to consider what the Spaniards have not done in three centuries."* The idea is sublime and profound. What they have *not* done in three centuries! Astonishing, indeed. Cincinnati College, founded in 1819, has excellent lands and a beautiful building in the center of the city. Woodward College, San Xavier (which was founded by the Catholics), and the Presbyterian Seminary have fifteen thousand volumes in their libraries, endowments, and professors corresponding to the different branches of learning. The Ohio School of Medicine, founded in 1825, possesses beautiful buildings and is under the supervision of a council of directors. It has two thousand volumes and complete equipment for anatomy, comparative anatomy, surgery, chemistry, and materia medica. The College of the Science of Jurisprudence is connected with Cincinnati College. The Institute of Me-

---

[8] *Letters on the Paraguay.*

* *Letters on Paraguay* is a three-volume work written by John Parish Robertson (1792-1843), an English merchant, adventurer, and author, with his brother William. Its full title is *Letters on Paraguay: Comprising An Account of a Four Year's Residence In That Republic Under the Government of the Dictator Francia* (London, 1839). The passage in the work closest to what Sarmiento has "extracted" reads: "but notwithstanding all these advantages [the beauty and natural resources of Corrientes province]; notwithstanding that the country has been for three hundred years in the possession of a civilized European nation; after I had galloped two hundred and eighty leagues, I did not see above four or five small towns . . . while at every fifteen miles' distance a miserable hut, with its half-dozen inhabitants, was alone interposed to relieve the monotony of the scene" (I, 250, 251).

chanics was created in 1828 for the instruction of mechanics and gives courses in the arts and sciences. It has important apparatus for physics and chemistry, a library, and a reading room. In one of its halls the Western Academy of Natural Sciences meets. In another hall an annual fair is held to encourage the arts and manufacturing. A normal school for the instruction of teachers was established in 1821.*

The mercantile library for young workers has a reading room and two thousand volumes. The apprentices' library has an even greater number of volumes. There are two Catholic asylums, the orphan asylum and a poorhouse. Establishments not supported by spontaneously formed associations are paid for by the state with special taxes which are collected for this purpose. With regard to taxes for schools, the law obliges even settlers living in the forest to contribute to the sustenance of those which exist. In addition, holders of vast stretches of uninhabited land are obliged to contribute to the state's expenses, and if they are absent and behind in their payments the SHERIFF takes a portion of the land and sells it at public auction. In this way the law assures that rich proprietors cannot monopolize the land, waiting without cultivating it until they can take advantage of the progressively higher value which time gives it. The occupation of this country proceeded from the Ohio River northward. When the Erie Canal was finished, which put Ohio in communication with the Lakes, the Hudson, New York, and the Atlantic, another wave of population began to invade from Lake Erie southward, an immense forest remaining in the center providing a

---

* This date is incorrect, since the first normal school in the United States was founded by Horace Mann at Lexington, Massachusetts in 1839.

place for successive future generations. The provision of the law which requires landholders to pay their share of the taxes assures that few will want to acquire land without plans for working it immediately.

Cincinnati is the center of the pork industry, and there is a group in society who have been given the title "Pork Aristocracy" for having enriched themselves in this industry. Two hundred thousand porkers are salted in the packing plants annually, and when the harvest season arrives the wooden barns around the city are filled with buyers of lard, hams, etc. It is impossible to comprehend the tremendous sums involved in this industry. The most notable thing about Cincinnati is that ownerless pigs live by the thousands in the streets. Neighbors take one to fatten in their houses, children mount them when they can succeed in catching them, and the police round them up to be exterminated when they propagate too much. Cincinnati is the place where they tie up dogs with choice pork sausage, which the dogs do not even eat.

I passed four or five days with Arcos in Cincinnati, carried away by the pleasure of walking the streets and suburbs, visiting the museum, and enjoying the *dolce far niente* of the tourist. It was in Cincinnati that Arcos, seeing a peaceful Yankee seated at the door of his rickety shop reading his Bible, stopped in front of him, took the cigar he was smoking from his mouth, lit his own, returned it to its place, and went on his way without that good man having raised his eyes nor made any movement except to open his mouth so that the cigar could be reinserted. Patience, brother, in exchange for any impertinence of yours.

We embarked on a steamboat of great size, the third to descend the Mississippi since the announcement that

299

the ravages of yellow fever, endemic to New Orleans during the summer, had ceased. From Cincinnati to that city is a distance of 1,548 miles, which are covered by steamboat in eleven days, traveling day and night and stopping only to load firewood or change passengers in the cities or at landings along the shore. Four abundant and sumptuous meals are served counting the LUNCH; and the trip, food, and service for eleven days costs fifteen dollars, somewhat less than one would pay to live for the same length of time in a hotel.

I will say very little to you about the cities whose ports and wharves the boat successively visited on the trip, for in none did we remain sufficient time to retain even a distinct memory of it. Marietta, Louisville, Rome, Cairo followed each other day after day until the barbaric country, the FAR WEST, began and the scene recovered its rural and semisavage character.

The trip on the Mississippi is one of the most beautiful, lasting, and peaceful experiences I have ever had. The majestic river descends, undulating smoothly through the center of the greatest valley on earth. The scene changes at every bend; the moderate breadth of this largest of rivers permits the eye to examine both banks, to penetrate the shady bowers of the forests, and to enter the savannahs and openings which appear in the thick vegetation from time to time. The encounter with another steamboat is a wonderful experience because of the closeness and rapidity of the passing. One's gaze wanders from the high galleries of that floating palace down to a squadron of barges descending at the mercy of the current, loaded with coal. Further off one can see a hawker or peddler who goes about in his little sailboat selling his notions and trinkets retail in the neighboring villages. We got off at the cities and towns where the steamboat touched, went through the streets, entered a mine, curious about everything, bought apples and biscuits, the ear attentive to the sound of the bell which would announce departure—all this a delightful and coveted change which we did not fail to add to our experiences, just as we never failed to jump over a fence, get to the forest, and run a little while the steamboat was loading firewood to burn in its furnaces.

Arcos, who had begun our association with a childish prank, attempted during those days to conquer my affection, making a show of all the grace and joviality there is in his character, which is fed by an inexhaustible repertory of absurd, ridiculous, and erotic stories, the kind which only the madcap youth of Paris and Madrid collect. We proceeded with this merrymaking and permanent fiesta to the point where we became notorious with as many as three hundred passengers on the steamboat.

On board they laid the table three times for each meal to be able to cope with the overwhelming number of diners. Since everyone knocked each other down to get a seat on the first shift, the second day we decided on the second shift, later settling on the third to be able to relax, until, finally, we arranged to eat with the servants on the fourth shift, which was just right, since just the two of us were capable of prolonging the table conversation for hours as we had done at the Hotel Astor. We liked molasses, which they gave us for dessert the first few days, and when it did not appear on the fifth day we demanded it, raising a great clamor. This was why a waiter was observed to get off the ship and run along the wharves seeking molasses in the nearby ale houses. "It's for the Spanish gentlemen," he said, "who get sick if they don't eat molasses." We would speak so loud in

301

Spanish at the table and laugh with such abandon that we attracted around us a circle of already stuffed fellows to see us eat and to enjoy our inextinguishable good humor. One morning Arcos tried it out on a good-natured Protestant minister. "Sir," he asked, "of what profession are you?" "Presbyterian, sir." "Tell me, what are the special dogmas of this creed?" The minister proceeded kindly to answer him. "But you, sir," said Arcos, with a convincing air and as if both were in on the secret, "you don't believe any of that, of course. You are too sensible to put faith in these jokes." The features of the unhappy man took on the anguished look of one whose corns have just been trod on. The good clergyman turned all colors and, half-indignant, half-beseeching, made a solemn profession of devotion to his religion. But being relentless, and a joker who takes his occupation seriously, Arcos replied with an imperturbable serenity: "I understand! I understand! You preach and sustain these doctrines before the people, you live by them, and the dignity of your position requires it. But here, just between you and me, come now, I know perfectly well what the truth is."

Another time he was surrounded by a group of horrified Yankees, among whom he raised his voice more and more to make a bigger scandal out of it and said: "Government? It is what the Emperor of Russia has! Yes, that is a government! When a general is delinquent or displeases his sovereign, they take down his breeches and give him five hundred lashes! But these Republics! These are nothing but corruption and disorder. What do your elections signify, and what do you or you"—directing himself to this or that astonished listener—"know about what is good for the state, when it ought to go to war, and when it ought to make peace? The only function of the people is to pay the expenses of the sovereign's court, he who rules by divine right. . . ."

And this said with a seriousness and an air of being so completely convinced of his rightness that those men crossed themselves to hear it. And when the storm had passed they signaled to each other that he was a strange animal, a Russian, or a dangerous madman. All of this to laugh over later as more food for our banquet. Can you imagine that it struck his fancy one time to persuade a forty-year-old lady covered with tatters and heavily rouged that I was the nephew of Abd-el-Kader traveling incognito? Favoring this joke was the circumstance of my being the only one there who wore a full beard and a Greek cap. Having them half-persuaded, he spoke to me in Spanish so that they would believe I was an Arab, exaggerating the sound of the "j" and insisting that I put on a Moorish cloak to complete the joke.

Later, this young man showed me the serious part of his character, which, because of his good sense, is no less significant. He also has good manners and the rare ability to clothe common matters in style and nobility, qualities which, with his learning in economic matters, would make him a notable young man if he knew how to control the impatience of his impressionable spirit. He has no fixed ideas or moral ideology, though his conduct is normal. I am glad to add these rectifications for fear that, without them, I will in my narrative be giving the impression that a companion who accompanied me for four months and lent me the most friendly services is a great rascal.

The nearness of New Orleans can be anticipated by visible alterations in society and in the form of the buildings. You can make out plantations, and in them, lines of wooden shacks, all of the same form and size,

303

showing that freedom played no part in the building of them. The land is divided into larger-sized plots. The country people disappear; from time to time strange buildings come into view which assume forms and a size which denote the presence of a rural aristocracy.

The shacks are, of course, the homes of the slaves, and the large buildings around which they are gathered are the mansions of the masters. This is the aristocracy of bales of cotton and bags of sugar, fruit of the slaves' sweat. Ah, slavery, the deep ulcer and the incurable fistula which threatens to corrupt the robust body of the Union! What a fatal error Washington and the great philosophers of the Declaration of the Rights of Man made when they allowed the Southern planters to keep their slaves! And why should the United States, which in practice has realized the most progress in regard to equality and humanity, be condemned to the strange fate of being the site of the last battles against the ancient injustice of man to man, conquered already in the rest of the world?

Slavery in the United States is today a question without solution. There are four million Negroes, and within twenty years there will be eight. Redeem them? Who will pay the thousand million dollars they are worth? Free them? What can be done with this black race which is hated by the white race? In the time of Washington and for thirty years afterwards cynicism had not yet been elevated to theory to justify in the minds of the masters the greed they practiced. But today, slavery is supported by doctrine because it has been made the soul of the society which exploits it. In those days the number of slaves was small and, so, thus there was a better chance of eliminating slavery from an economic and social point of view. At the same time, slavery has relentless and fanatical antagonists in the most genuinely Yankee states, which are the richest, the most highly populated, and the most numerous. The Puritan spirit of equality and justice is elevated in the North to the height of religious feeling. They regard slavery as a leprous abomination and a stain on the honor of the Union. In their ardor they preach a crusade against the reprobates who exploit the abjection of an unfortunate race. Should we throw the perpetuation of slavery in the face of the Yankees? My God! It would be the same as afflicting and humiliating the white hair of the virtuous father by throwing in his face the misbehavior of his prodigal son. Slavery is a parasitical vegetation which English colonization has left glued to the leafy tree of American liberty. They did not care to pull it out by the roots when they pruned the tree, hoping that time would kill it, and the parasite has grown and threatens to kill the tree.

The free states are superior in number and wealth to the slave states. In the Congress, in the law, slavery will not conquer one more foot of ground north of the present line which circumstances have traced. If war comes, are the Negroes going to battle alongside the whites to keep their chains from being removed? Will the masters form armies to guard their slaves? The division of the Union into free and slave states, so crowed about by the Southern states, would bring about the disappearance of slavery. But where would the four million freedmen go? Here is the Gordian knot which the sword cannot cut and which fills with dismal shadows the otherwise clear and radiant future of the American Union. It cannot advance or retreat. And, meanwhile, the Negro race swarms, gains assurance, becomes civilized, and grows. There will be racial war within a century, a war of extermination, or a black, backward, and vile nation alongside a white one, the most powerful and cultivated one on the earth.

From Pittsburgh to New Orleans we had passed through ten states which were not members of the original federation. The city of New Orleans is the capital of Louisiana, which was originally French and whose varied population is made of American, Spanish, and French Creoles. The appearance of the city from the port is magnificent, and the steamboats, of which there are always hundreds at anchor, are enough to suggest the commercial activity of the inhabitants. You might say that the steamboat was invented for the Mississippi. Before its use in water travel it took months and months for boats to go up the rivers, as is the case today on the Paraná and Uruguay Rivers. Ocean-going ships cruised for many days in the Gulf of Mexico awaiting a favorable moment for entering the mouth of the great waterway, whose bed for many leagues from the coast is still flanked by dangerous banks. With the invention of the steamboat, however, flocks of tugboats appeared in the mouth of the river, ready to launch themselves into the Gulf at the first sign of a sail on the horizon. Thousands of steamboats travel up the river, dispersing themselves in every direction by following the hundreds of waterways into which the principal channel subdivides at the point where the tributary rivers flow into it. And when the Mississippi Valley is occupied by man, the volume of products which will come to the wharves of New Orleans will no doubt be astonishing. Then the broad channel between the city and the Gulf will be too narrow for the uninterrupted procession of ships which will scatter themselves like handfuls of grain in the immensity of the ocean; the Mississippi is the only exit for an entire world.

Unfortunately, New Orleans is incurably sick. Yellow fever appears there every year, starting on a set day and remaining until another set day. It kills those who do not flee from the center of the city. The city then recovers and reestablishes its health until the same time the following year. At one league from the city conditions are perfectly healthful, and not even by contagion can the periodic scourge reach there. The city had 102,000 inhabitants in 1840, a figure which is not increasing to any appreciable extent, even though New Orleans is the port of disembarkation for French immigration.

We stayed in New Orleans for ten days, until we booked passage for Havana on a wretched and pestilent sailing vessel which, like the Mediterranean tender which took me from Majorca to Algiers, carried its cargo of pigs plus three or four moribund consumptives who embarked with us and bunked in extremely narrow, hot cabins filled with cobwebs. The North American world was ending, and we began to sense through anticipation the Spanish colonies toward which we were heading.

Diary of Expenses

During the Trip to Europe and America
Undertaken from
Valparaiso the 28th Day of October, 1845*
By Domingo F. Sarmiento

* That part of the diary concerning Sarmiento's days in the United States is reproduced here. Sarmiento's *Diario de gastos*, a notebook, was discovered among his papers in the Sarmiento Museum in Buenos Aires in 1947. It appears that Sarmiento may have planned to have it published, since he carefully wrote out the above title page and the foreword that follows. The museum has published the notebook in facsimile: *Diario de gastos*, ed. Antonio P. Castro, Series IV, No. 2 (Buenos Aires, 1950).

Foreword

The present book of expenses incurred during my trip will be one of my best souvenirs. Being by nature disorderly, I have decided to register my expenses, and if I get nothing else out of it but to know how my money has been employed, I shall be satisfied. It is, besides, a register in which are found recorded, in this or that incident, the places in which I have found myself and the dates of all my movements. In South America it will be useful for its information on the cost of stage-coaches, railroads, steamboats, inns, etc., in each country. Lastly, going over the items, one will even be able to find out the sum total of the funds necessary for undertaking voyages, separating out objects purchased and other special expenses. The exchange rates and relative value of currencies may also be compared.

United States

New York

			Dollars	
Sept. 15	English teacher	$	2	50
	Extra expenses aboard ship		1	50
	Tips for the servants		1	76
17	Peaches in New York			33
	Boots repaired		3	50
19	Cigars			50
20	Peaches			50
	Hotel bill		12	75
	Tip for the waiter		1	50
21	GEOLOGY			25
	A map of the U.S.		1	
	Change money		2	30
	Baggage			50
	Steamboat to Albany		1	
	Lunch on board			50
	Peaches and coffee			50
22	Railroad to Buffalo		12	
	Fruit on the way			50
23	Hotel in Buffalo			75
	Railroad to the Falls		1	
	Passage to the English Falls			50
	Museum and cicerone			75

Montreal, Canada

25	Pair of moccasins	$	1	
	Steamboat to Montreal		10	
	Boots cleaned, peaches, etc.			60
27	Hotel Donegana		3	
	Steamboat and railroad to La Prairie		1	
	Steamboat on Lake Champlain		1	
	Food, boots, lunch		1	
28	Stagecoach to Troy		3	
	Lunch and cigars			75
	Hotel in Troy			75
29	Railroad to Greenbush			20
	To Boston		5	
30	Baggage			25
	THE PRAIRIE BIRD			25
	Cigars and fruit			60
	A handkerchief		1	
Oct. 1	Round trip to Mr. Mann's house,			
	Newton			75
	2nd. of Oct. cigars			12
3	Moses in Egypt,			
	Señorita Fedesco			50

Boston

Oct.	3	Various books on education	1	
		AMERICAN FACTS	1	50
	4	Hotel BILL	7	50
		Baggage		12
		Railroad and steamboat to New York	4	
		Supper and boots		75
	5	Baggage in N. York		25
		Tom Thumb Show		25
	6	Fair		25
		Hotel and coach	4	
		Cigars and fruit		50
		Railroad to Philadelphia	4	
	7	Academy in [illegible]		25
		Hotel	1	50
		Coach and baggage		75
		Steamboat and railroad to Baltimore	3	
	8	Baggage and boots		37
		Hotel in Baltimore	3	
		Cigars, baggage		52
	10	Steamboat to Washington via		
		Chesapeake Bay	2	50

Washington

14	Coach		50
	Hotel one night!	1	80
	Laundry	1	
	Cigars and tips		50
	Stage to Baltimore	5	
	Baggage		25
15	Hotel	1	50
	Baggage		50
	Stagecoach to Harrisburg	3	
16	Hotel	1	
	Railroad to Chambersburg	2	12
	Baggage		25
18	Telegraph message to Arcos		44
	Fruit and cigars		32
	Hotel bill	2	50
	Lent by Mr. Lesley to continue my trip	8	
	Little expenses		50
20	Food and lunch en route	1	
21	Hotel in Pittsburgh		75
	For errands!		25
	Steamboat to Cincinnati	5	
	Baggage and cigars		75

New Orleans

22	Visit to the coal mines			25
	Newspapers and apples			55
	Baggage in Cincinnati			75
	Museum			25
	Cigars		1	75
	Books (wicked ones)		1	50
	Boots, apples			37
Nov. 4	Unloading at New Orleans			50
	Summer frock coat		4	50
	6 shirts		7	
	1/2 dozen socks		1	50
	Shoes		2	50
	Bath			50
	Passport for Havana		2	
	Baggage to the port		1	
	The *P. Soule*, sailing boat for Havana		30	
	A coach to look for the Diary of Expenses (which I had not lost)		1	50
	Tips on board			75

Index